IN
DEFENSE
OF
LIVELIHOOD

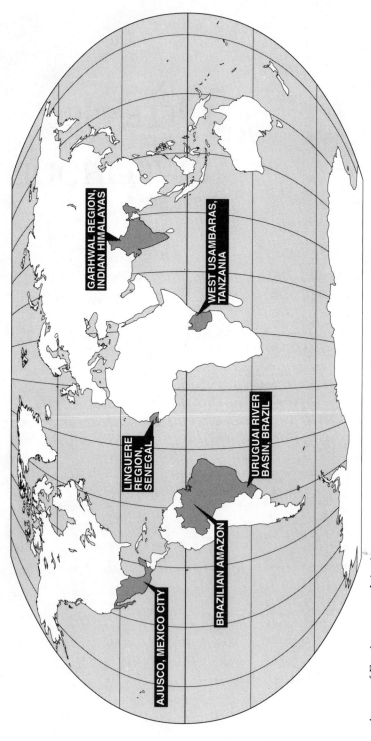

GARHWAL REGION, INDIAN HIMALAYAS

WEST USAMBARAS, TANZANIA

LINGUERE REGION, SENEGAL

URUGUAI RIVER BASIN, BRAZIL

AJUSCO, MEXICO CITY

BRAZILIAN AMAZON

Areas of Environmental Action

IN
DEFENSE
OF
LIVELIHOOD

*Comparative Studies on
Environmental Action*

edited by
John Friedmann
Haripriya Rangan

KUMARIAN PRESS

In Defense of Livelihood: Comparative Studies on Environmental Action

Published 1993 by Kumarian Press, Inc., 630 Oakwood Avenue, Suite 119, West Hartford, Connecticut 06110-1529 USA.

Copyright © 1993 United Nations Research Institute for Social Development. All rights reserved.

No part of this book may be reproduced or transmitted in any form or by any means, electronic or mechanical, including photocopy, recording, or information storage and retrieval system, without prior written permission of the publisher. Direct all inquiries to the publisher.

Cover design by Emily Sassano

Book production supervised by Jenna Dixon
Copyedited by Linda Lotz
Text design by Jenna Dixon
Typeset by ProProduction
Proofread by Jolene Robinson
Maps by Chase Langford
Index prepared by Alan M. Greenberg

Printed in the United States of America on recycled acid-free paper by McNaughton & Gunn. Text printed with soy-based ink.

Library of Congress Cataloging-in-Publication Data

In defense of livelihood : comparative studies on environmental action
    / editors, John Friedmann, Haripriya Rangan.
        p.   cm. — (Kumarian Press library of management for
    development.)
        Includes bibliographical references and index.
        ISBN 1-56549-020-7 (alk. paper)
        1. Sustainable development—Developing countries—Case studies.
    2. Environmental policy—Developing countries—Case studies.
    I. Friedmann, John. II. Rangan, Haripriya, 1960–   . III. Series.
    HC59.72.E5I5   1993
    363.7'056'091724—dc20   92-44208

---

97 96   95   5   4   3   2

CONTENTS

FIGURES AND TABLES

FOREWORD

IN 1989, THE UNITED NATIONS Research Institute for Social
Development (UNRISD) initiated a new research program on sustainable development through people's participation in resource management. This program has examined the dynamics of local-level initiatives concerned with environmental degradation, the strengths and
limitations of traditional resources management practices, and the factors that facilitate or constrain community participation in projects
and programs concerned with resource management. A specific sub-
theme is the potential for collective environmental action to protect or
rehabilitate the natural resource base.

This book, edited by John Friedmann and Haripriya Rangan, presents a series of case studies of struggles and innovative practices of
local groups in seven regions of the developing world: the Shambaa
people in northeastern Tanzania involved in a large agroforestry soil
erosion project; gum collectors in northern Senegal, who attempted to
protect the acacia forests, which were crucial for their livelihood;
small farmers in two southern Brazilian states threatened by flooding
resulting from dam construction; the rubber tappers of northern
Brazil, whose access to the forest was restricted by outsiders and the
state; squatters on the edge of Mexico City threatened with expulsion;
groups from the Garhwal Himalayas, whose access to forest resources
has been affected by the Chipko conservation movement; and groups
in Karnataka State, India, involved in social forestry programs.

At a time when the dominant development paradigms associated
with both free-market capitalism and state control are being seriously
questioned, these studies reveal how progress along a sustainable development path requires transferring resources, responsibility, and
power to local communities directly affected by process of environ-

mental change. As the editors point out in the introduction, self-organization is the first important step in this process of "empowerment."
Not only can it lead to material betterment but it obliges state agencies
to acknowledge the claims of hitherto "invisible" groups.

By highlighting the constraints and limitations of certain experiences, several of the studies also warn against romantic visions of collective action. Actions or environmental movements may, for example, prove to be short-lived and fizzle out once partial gains have been
made, or internal divisions or rifts between local groups and external
supporters may develop. Several contributors to this volume suggest
ways in which local environmental action can be sustained.

In order to actively engage in sustainable development, people
need access to information and resources, and they must have the options and the ability to make decisions concerning resource use. In
some situations, the introduction of market forces and the priorities of
national policy agendas have contributed to a breakdown in systems
of collective local decisionmaking. In such cases, there is a need to
recreate local social responsibility through local government, judicial
systems, and local civic institutions. In other cases, new forms of organization, both sociopolitical and socioeconomic, must be established,
transforming traditional power structures into more representative
and accountable institutions.

But creating local responsibility and ensuring local empowerment
is not simply a matter of local-level changes and organizational efforts. Local action is constrained by economic, political, and social cir-
cumstances at the local, national, and international levels. The
progress made in the local arena can be easily overwhelmed by the effects of interest groups, policies, and social and economic structures.
These obstacles to empowerment can be addressed, in part, by local
people's efforts to form themselves into a constituency that is able to
demand accountability from leaders at different levels. Engaging the
support of outsiders and forming alliances are also vitally important.

DHARAM GHAI
Director, United Nations Research
Institute for Social Development

PREFACE

THIS COLLECTION IS THE RESULT of several years of research by graduate students in the Urban Planning Program of the Graduate School of Architecture and Urban Planning at University of California at Los Angeles. Despite its name, this program has maintained a lively interest in rural and environmental issues in both advanced industrial and poorer countries of the world. Under the guidance of professors Susanna Hecht and Margaret FitzSimmons, as well as the senior editor of this book, a large number of students have undertaken serious research into what we have called environmental action: activities carried out by people defending the immediate sources of their livelihood in land and natural resources.

On a visit to Geneva in 1990, the senior editor proposed a research project to Dr. Dharam Ghai, director of the United Nations Research Institute for Social Development. The proposal was received enthusiastically, and led to the work contributed in this volume. We would like to thank Dr. Ghai and his Institute for their moral and financial support throughout this project. Without it, there would have been no book.

We trust that this volume will be of interest to many people, among them students, practitioners, activists, public officials, and development professionals. We have written it with a wide readership in mind and avoided unduly technical language.

The environment and social practices must be viewed as inextricably connected, with outcomes the result of struggles involving many actors. Local people are our predominant focus here; nevertheless, the role of the state and of external actors such as nongovernmental organizations and activist groups and individuals must not be lost from sight. None of the outcomes described in these essays was necessarily predetermined by structures alone. Agency brought with it scope for innovative action and opened up unexpected opportunities for change. In this period of intense social and economic transformations across the globe, this offers a ray of hope for those of us who believe in the possibilities of a more humane and just society than what we presently have.

CONTRIBUTORS

JOHN FRIEDMANN IS PROFESSOR and head of the Urban Planning Program at the Graduate School of Architecture and Urban Planning, University of California, Los Angeles (UCLA). He has worked for several decades as a planning consultant in Latin America and East and Southeast Asia and has written extensively on regional development, urbanization, planning theory, and alternative approaches to development. His latest book is *Empowerment: The Politics of Alternative Development* (1992).

MARK SCHOONMAKER FREUDENBERGER is currently with the Land Tenure Center, University of Wisconsin, Madison. He has worked for over a decade on rural development and resource management issues in West Africa and has been a visiting fellow at the Botanical Institute, University of Arhus, Denmark. He obtained his doctoral degree in planning at UCLA in 1992.

RICHARD J. MASSARO began his career in development planning with the Catholic church in Tanzania. After working in Tanzania from 1975 to 1980, he returned to Washington, D.C., to research U.S. policy on African development and served as project director of the Africa Faith and Justice Network. He was a program associate at the UCLA African Studies Center while working toward his doctoral degree in planning. He is now completing his dissertation, *Seeds of Hope: The Experience of Regional Planning in Tanzania.*

MARK D. MCDONALD is a doctoral candidate in the planning program at UCLA. His experience with agencies such as the Environmental Defense Fund has given him strong impetus to focus on environmental law and on providing legal support to communities

threatened by environmental and economic devastation. He has worked with planning and research agencies in southern Brazil and the Brazilian Amazon.

MICHELLE A. MELONE is in the doctoral program in planning at UCLA and has worked with researchers and activists in the Brazilian Amazon over the past five years. Her interest in tropical rain forest conservation began with the rubber tappers' struggle and now encompasses an international and comparative perspective regarding the use of community and business coalitions to manage local environments and natural resources. She is actively involved with citizens' groups, local planning agencies, and the Coastal Commission in Monterey, California.

KEITH PEZZOLI teaches at the Urban Studies and Planning Program at the University of California, San Diego (UCSD), and also serves as its director for field research. A graduate of UCLA's planning program, he is associated with the U.S.-Mexican Studies Research Center at UCSD and has worked on urbanization and barrio movements in Mexico for nearly a decade.

HARIPRIYA RANGAN is a doctoral candidate in the planning program at UCLA, completing her dissertation on regional development and natural resource management in the Indian Himalayas. Trained initially as an architect, she is now interested in urban and regional development and agroforestry. She has researched and worked for nearly a decade on urbanization, decentralized district planning, agrarian and rural development in western India, and natural resource management in Himalayan regions.

SHIVSHARAN SOMESHWAR is a doctoral candidate in planning at UCLA, currently doing field research on the politics of forestry and rural development in India. Trained initially in architecture and urban design, he has worked on natural resource management, social forestry, and integrated rural development in southern India.

INTRODUCTION

In Defense of Livelihood

JOHN FRIEDMANN AND HARIPRIYA RANGAN

Environment and Sustainability

Terms such as *environment* and *sustainable growth* have gained currency
in our vocabulary, similar in many ways to the catchwords *development* and *balanced growth* of the past four decades. At the 1992 Earth
Summit, however, the debate reached a remarkable degree of confusion regarding the meanings of *sustainability* or *sustainable development.*
On the journey toward the Earth Summit in Rio de Janeiro, environmental groups and activists brought along every possible issue—
global warming, endangered dolphins and elephants, Atlantic bluefin
tuna fishing, deforestation of tropical rain forests—and gathered them
under the broad umbrella of "the environment." As the event
unfolded in June 1992, the summit resembled a teetering Noah's ark,
with a motley collection of environmental issues jostling for attention
aboard a crowded agenda.

Having been subjected to a barrage of emotional appeals and pseu-
doscientific statements regarding the impending global ecological
crisis, many lay observers may dismiss what they hear as routine
prophecies of doom. Yet they may also feel decidedly uncomfortable
with the pronouncements of multilateral agencies such as the World
Bank and with the General Agreement on Tariffs and Trade (GATT),
which maintain a Pollyanna-like faith in the benevolence of free trade
and the ability of multilateral negotiations between countries to solve
the world's environmental problems. The GATT document on trade
and the environment warns the world against "environmental imperialism"—a curious turn of phrase by an organization that is, in
essence, committed to preserving the economic interests of rich,
industrialized nations. It points to the threat of trade protectionism

1

parading in environmentalist clothing and the dangers of self-appointed vigilantes using trade weapons against countries arbitrarily identified as environmental violators (Dodwell 1992). The odd sight of GATT fighting on the side of poorer, export-oriented economies against environmental lobbies and groups gives a new political twist to both the Earth Summit and debates on the environment. The duel, in the overheated atmosphere of the summit, resulted in an impasse between those who want to sustain the world environment through vigorous economy and trade and those who want to slow down economic growth for the sake of the environment. Given these entrenched positions between the economy and the environment, it seems unlikely that any sustainable policies will emerge as outcomes of the summit in the foreseeable future.

Sustainability has been a much-debated topic in international development conferences over the past few years. In a useful survey of literature on this topic, Diana Mitlin points to two major concerns around which these debates have been centered: conceptual definitions and theoretical approaches to sustainable development, and issues of how sustainable development can be achieved through policy interventions and programs (Mitlin 1992). Although concerns regarding the global environment go back to the early 1970s, in documents such as *Limits to Growth* and the well-known writings of E. F. Schumacher and Paul Ehrlich, conceptual debates about sustainability can be traced back to the arguments set forth by the World Commission on Environment and Development (WCED) in 1987. In its document, *Our Common Future*, WCED defined sustainable development as that which would "ensure that it [development] meets the needs of the present without compromising the ability of future generations to meet their own needs" (World Commission on Environment and Development 1987, 8). Mitlin observes that many researchers and activists have engaged themselves with the issues raised by this definition, despite the substantial criticism it received.

However ambiguous, contradictory, and even oxymoronic the term, *sustainable development* has gained a foothold in international parlance (see Daly 1991; Redclift 1987). The growing acceptance of this term among policymakers and planners in multilateral aid agencies has led people who are critical of economic development priorities or processes to jump on the sustainable development bandwagon and cast their concerns in ecological terms. This acceptance is primarily a result of innovative scholarship on relationships, interactions, and processes between environment and society. Buttel and Sunderlin (1988) provide an excellent assessment of this literature, pointing to two broad perspectives emerging from this research and scholarship. The first approach is that of political economy, in the sense that there is a critique of neoclassical development of environmental economics; development processes are shaped by a complex interaction of social institutions, of which the economic and political are the most important; and the prevailing development patterns have been largely adverse or of limited benefit for the majority of Third World peoples and nations. The second approach is that of political ecology, which is broadly characterized by the beliefs that environmental factors are major constraints on development, prevailing development patterns have undesirable effects on the biophysical environment, and environmental degradation threatens future development and progress.

Buttel and Sunderlin go further in classifying the research on sustainable development under four categories: (1) studies that adopt an ecocentric analysis focusing on the natural resource constraints that define extractive economies; (2) those that provide environmentally deterministic explanations of human activities within a clearly bounded ecosystem; (3) those that incorporate the environment into an analysis of political economy; and (4) those that can be categorized as critical political ecology, which works from an ecocentric view of the biophysical environment but stresses social forces as the major causal factors.

These studies have made important advances in the integration of development theory and environmental processes and go far beyond existing thinking regarding sustainable development. Yet there is far more work required to develop a richer, nuanced view of the complexities of social actions amidst diverse environmental resources and phenomena. We believe that one of the major weaknesses in most of these studies is that they rarely go beyond describing why certain places are the way they are, or how these places are affected by larger economic and political processes. In short, most of the studies describe localities in terms of their biophysical, economic, and social structures. The people in these places do not act, but are acted upon. Another problem with such studies is that their focus is often microstructural; the analysis is caught up in a web of fine details and provides explanations of change in terms of simple additions to the locality's ecological, economic, and social features.

Protests and struggles over control, access, and management of natural resources have only recently gained attention, following the growing recognition of environmental movements around the world. These movements have brought human agency—the much-neglected dimension of theoretical debates regarding structure and agency—to the forefront by highlighting the concerted actions of people in relation to their particular locales. Can localities act? asks Richard Meegan. His answer is that localities can be proactive precisely because social structures are localized:

> If people interpret localized social structures in explicitly territorial terms, come to view their interests and identities as "local," then act upon that view by mobilizing locally defined organizations to further their interests in a manner that would not be possible were they to act separately, then it would seem eminently reasonable to talk about "locality as actor." (Meegan 1992)

The essays in this volume focus on social actions and economic processes that unfold within the particularities of locality, environment, and culture and how they interact with political and economic institutions and actors at regional, national, and global levels. Some important work has been done in this area of research (see Hecht and Cockburn 1989; Guha 1989) and our volume of essays on popular environmental action should be seen as a contribution toward expanding this effort. The essays are written by a younger generation of planners, their research sharpened by an awareness of critical studies of earlier efforts in rural development and planning in different parts of the world. In an attempt to present alternative approaches to development that ensure social justice and environmental and economic sustainability, the case studies in this volume seek to integrate both macro- and microlevel analysis by focusing on actions of localities and regions.

Environmental action, in this book, refers to the efforts and struggles by rural and urban communities to gain access to and control over the natural resources upon which their lives and livelihoods depend. For a majority of people living in rural regions and squatter settlements in poor countries, their natural and physical surroundings are not abstract entities defined in contrast to the urban environment. They are social artifacts produced by their labor, history, technology, and culture. As David Cleary points out, "To those close to . . . the ground . . . reality is a seamless mesh of social and environmental constraints which it makes little sense to atomize into mutually exclusive categories" (Cleary 1991, 119). This is the perspective adopted by the authors of the essays in this volume. Environmental action in each case study is intricately woven with the lives and livelihoods of the people involved on the ground. They may not seem heroic or revolutionary to us, but they reflect the complexities and diversities of human actions in defense of livelihood.

Case Study Synopses

In this section, we present a synopsis of each case study included in this volume. They focus on environmental actions in seven regions of of world—two in Africa, three in the Americas, and two in the South Asian subcontinent.

The first case study describes an agroforestry soil erosion control project among the Shambaa people in northeastern Tanzania. Richard Massaro describes this densely settled, mountainous region of small peasant farms where the land has lost much of its former fertility as a result of overuse. Population has more than doubled over the past thirty years, and erosion threatens the very existence of this once prosperous area.

Beginning in 1981, the West German technical assistance agency Gesellschaft für Technische Zusammenarbeit (GTZ) initiated a largely successful program aimed at the recovery of eroded hillsides and the improvement of material life in Shambaa villages. Guided by a philosophy of self-determination, agency personnel assisted by Tanzanian counterparts worked patiently with local communities to restore their will to take positive action to reverse long-standing environmental abuses. According to Massaro, key to the relative success of this program was a realistic assessment of local opportunities and constraints, the realization of the need for a long-term approach to a complex issue with deep historical roots, a belief in the efficacy of social learning, and an awareness that the program would succeed only if local village communities came to regard it as their own.

Next is Mark Freudenberger's fascinating history of the gum arabic economy in northern Senegal. His essay explores the numerous constraints one resource user group has confronted in trying to protect, conserve, and regenerate the *Acacia senegal,* a forest resource central to its livelihood strategy. Gum arabic, an exudation of the acacia, is the economic mainstay of an ethnic minority group known as the black Maures. They have evolved sophisticated techniques in the collection of this precious substance, which has found widespread acceptance in modern manufacturing processes (paint, soft drinks, and so on). Over the course of 400 years, the Maures succeeded in creating for themselves a niche in the intricate social ecology of the region, between sedentary Wolofs and Fulbe pastoralists, selling the gum they collected to Arab-Berber merchants in southern Mauritania.

This traditional activity of gum collection was severely disrupted by the divining of a deep and ancient aquifer. Beginning in the 1950s, a state-sponsored project was implemented to tap the aquifer by a network of mechanized boreholes and bring water to this arid region. For the Maure gum collectors, the new water technology heralded the end of their seasonal separation from Fulbe herders and the start of severe competition over the region's acacia forests. Further devastation followed with the great Sahelian drought from 1968 to 1974, when roughly 70 percent of the *Acacia senegal* perished. At the same time, world markets for gum arabic were declining as synthetic substitutes gained in popularity. The Maures' answer to these disasters was to retreat to more peripheral, inhospitable regions where they would free themselves from Fulbe competition. In this new, harsh landscape, the Maures continued to eke their livelihood from their traditional collecting economy.

Freudenberger concludes by calling for the comanagement of the acacia forests in northern Senegal, involving both the communities of Maure collectors and the state. He believes that the solution lies in restoring the seasonal separation between Fulbe pastoralists and the Maure. According to Freudenberger, future policy interventions should center around two objectives: the reconstruction of an arrangement that allows temporary exclusion of livestock and herders from gum-collecting areas at key times during the early dry season, and the creation of suitable resource management institutions.

Mark McDonald's account of small farmers in southern Brazil resisting being flooded out by the construction of hydroelectric dams on the Uruguai River tells a very different story. It is a story of escalating conflict between some 200,000 agriculturalists and the government-owned electric utility ELETROSUL, which planned their displacement with ruthless efficiency. Initially, the concern of those likely to be affected by the flooding—*os atingidos*—was simply to receive fair and timely indemnification for the loss of their lands. A regional commission known as CRAB was organized to represent the farmers in negotiations with the utility. Formed in 1979, CRAB grew out of a meeting that included 350 small farmers as well as representatives from Catholic and Lutheran churches, rural unions, and universities. The next decade saw the mobilization of local communities in the continuing struggle with ELETROSUL, whose normal mode of communication was either not to respond at all or to treat the concerns of citizens as peripheral to what it regarded as the all-important progress on the dams, leaving behind a trail of blatant deceptions and broken promises. In 1983, a petition drive against the first of the region's dams, Machadinho, gathered over a million signatures. What had begun as a fight for just and timely compensation had broadened into a regional movement opposing the construction of hydroelectric dams, which many people believed were superfluous.

By 1985, CRAB had grown into a consolidated organization with an executive committee and a secretariat headed by a full-time director. A regular publication, *A Enchente do Uruguai* (The Flooding of the Uruguai), kept the region informed. Neither the executive committee nor the secretariat, however, was given decisionmaking powers, which were retained by local communities. Four years later, construction of Machadinho had still not begun, although a second dam, Ita, is currently under construction. That dam is governed by an accord reached between CRAB and ELETROSUL in 1987. Farmers subject to flooding are being resettled, and even *sem-terras*—landless peasants—are being assigned viable plots of land in the region.

The years of the struggle established an important point: Project companies would have to include resettlement programs in their feasibility studies. As McDonald observes, social movements in Brazil are establishing new relations between civil society and the state, creating new historical subjects in the process and redefining the meaning of citizenship.

Michelle A. Melone reports on the rubber tappers' movement in the Brazilian Amazon. Like the Maures of Senegal, rubber tappers are principally collectors of natural sap drawn from the trees. They are the first, almost invisible link in a chain that transforms the precious raw material into a series of final consumer products for urban use. Unlike the peasant farmers of southern Brazil who have settled in villages, rubber tappers live in dispersed homesteads on small clearings in the forest surrounded by rubber trails called *colocações*, each household collecting sap from trees spread over 200 to 500 hectares. Their legal claims to this land were rendered insecure when the region was opened up through state incentives for large-scale investors. Wealthy investors from the south hired *pistoleiros* (gunmen) to intimidate those they deemed illegal occupants of their newly acquired lands. Despite repeated provocations and threats to their lives, however, the rubber tappers refrained from violence. Instead they used *empates*, or stand-offs, which often involved hundreds of families, to confront ranchers. Violence escalated in the face of these challenges, and an alliance between ranchers, urban elites, and government officials strengthened the ranchers' position. When violence occurred, it often went without legal repercussions. Bitter struggles continue to this day over both the right to the land and its use.

Melone narrates the remarkable story of how the rubber tappers gradually gained international support for their organized movement to fight dispossession and, at the same time, help save the rain forest by proposing the creation of "extractive reserves," which could be managed on a sustained-yield basis. Eventually, the rubber tappers found allies among North American environmental groups, which provided them the recognition and legitimacy to challenge the lending policies of the World Bank. The movement built steadily throughout the 1980s and, in 1989, joined with Indian tribes and rural workers to form the Forest Peoples' Alliance. According to Melone, rubber tappers are now at least formally recognized within the political system in the Amazon. Some leaders of the National Rubber Tappers' Council even ran for state office in the 1990 elections and have formed a close alliance with the Brazilian Workers' Party.

Keith Pezzoli's essay is an example of environmental action within an urban context. He recounts the struggles of squatter communities to gain security for their settlements in the hills on the southern edge of Mexico City. The heights of Ajusco form part of Mexico City's greenbelt, and over the years they have become contested terrain. With spectacular views of the city, especially at night, and a location well above the smog ceiling that usually blankets the city during the day, Ajusco is perhaps the only area of this giant metropolis that is still relatively natural and undeveloped. Not surprisingly, the communities of working-class squatters living in Ajusco have had to struggle against both the government of the Federal District and private developers eyeing the hills as a site for luxury villas.

Pezzoli focuses on an unusual strategy adopted by the squatter settlements of Los Belvederes during the 1980s in their fight to secure tenure for their households. Los Belvederes would point the way to new development for Mexico City: Far from being a blight on nature—which was the general view—the settlements would be transformed into a *colonia ecológica productiva* (CEP), suggesting a productive, sustainable future. The objectives were ambitious:

- To promote an integral, barrio-based model of urban development to generate jobs and resources and to foster the production of goods in a way that was socially necessary, ecologically valid, and economically viable.
- To intervene positively in the transformation of daily life, generating new relations between humankind and the surrounding natural environment.
- To employ alternative technologies as part of a collective strategy.
- Over the medium and long term, to implement a conceptual transformation of residential space from a place of consumption to a place of production.
- To put into operation an urban buffer zone (a greenbelt for production) to mediate the contradictions between the city and the outlying rural land, recovering or reincorporating intrinsic rural values into urban life styles.

The proposal contained specific programs for afforestation, the protection of biotica against insect plagues, the installation of appropriate technology for the recycling of organic wastes, and pilot projects involving horticulture, rabbits, mushrooms, and pisciculture. Initial efforts were directed toward recycling organic waste.

Late in 1989, when the intensity of grassroots ecopolitics was reaching a peak, the government announced that it would desist from its efforts to relocate families from the area and would legally incorporate Los Belvederes into the designated built-up area of the city, thereby making it eligible for public services. This policy shift dramatically changed the terms of the struggle. Having attained their primary objective—to secure tenure to land in the heights of Ajusco—popular enthusiasm for the CEP plummeted. Winning the right to have their settlement incorporated into the legally designated urban area highlighted problems outside the ecological realm. New battles had to be waged to secure the best terms for regularization and to resolve litigation regarding fraudulent land transactions and boundary disputes. As the inhabitants pulled away from the CEP vision, university activists, who had been among its most enthusiastic advocates, withdrew from the area. Only a waste-recycling pilot project is actually functioning, and the hope of converting Los Belvederes into an exemplar of sustainable development has all but died. What the squatter communities wanted primarily was a permanent foothold in the city. They were only marginally interested, it seems, in sustainable development.

What happens in the wake of a well-recognized and successful environmental movement? Haripriya Rangan focuses on a scenario in the Garhwal region of the Indian Himalayas, where local populations are angry and resentful of being held hostage by Chipko, a movement of their own making. Rangan attempts to explain the current antagonism of diverse communities in Garhwal by recounting the tale of Chipko's emergence nearly two decades ago, the initial vigor and enthusiasm of the villagers as they challenged state claims to local forest resources, and how the struggle came to be adopted by environmental activists and intellectuals. Chipko's growing international and national recognition as a transregional environmental movement within India overwhelmed the local struggles over access to forest resources. The environmental rhetoric of saving "nature" in the Himalayas took over, and Chipko today has been reduced to a "green" symbol that conjures up images of bucolic mountain folk hugging trees.

Rangan sets forth a critique of the different perspectives adopted by the state and the environmental activists in defining the problems faced by local populations in Garhwal. In the process, she attempts a revisionist history of institutional intervention and conflict over access to forest resources in Garhwal through colonial and postcolonial rule in India. The popular antagonism against Chipko today, Rangan notes, is ironically against the movement's attempts to change state forest policies. Successful lobbying by Chipko's leaders and spokespeople has led to amendments of forest laws that, in effect, tighten the central government's control over forest areas in the region and further reduce access to forest resources for local communities. As local communities battle these new laws and policies, they have taken a stance against Chipko's proclaimed leaders and activists. The roles are now reversed, with the state being represented as protector of the environment, holding back local communities from ravaging Himalayan nature and forest resources.

ShivSharan Someshwar's critical essay focuses on the weaknesses of the populist perspective on environmental action. In India, community forestry programs promoted by the state have faced substantial criticism, especially by intellectuals inspired by a Gandhian vision of local control over resources for village use. Someshwar's essay is intended as an answer to these critics. He points out that the concept of a classless and undifferentiated village community functioning as a unit of mutual cooperation to reach common goals of environmental sustainability does not reflect the reality of unequal access to and control over natural resources for different classes and castes. Rather than describe the actions of disempowered sectors among the rural population, Someshwar attempts to reveal the state's role as arbiter of the competing claims made on forest resources and focuses on new modes of action that would more adequately represent the claims of poor peasants.

Someshwar investigates the outcome of the government's social forestry program in the Kolar District, a densely populated forest region in the southwestern state of Karnataka in India. The program consists of two major components: a farm forestry component, with tree planting on private lands through the development of nurseries, the distribution of planting material, and the provision of advisory services; and a community forestry program, with tree and fodder planting on government-owned pasturelands and agriculturally unproductive state wastelands and village commons.

The farm forestry component has, by all accounts, been a success. Biomass markets for urban and industrial consumers are being met through normal market channels from privately grown trees. But the needs of the rural poor for biomass are not being met, and the community forestry program is to a large extent considered a failure. In response to the critics of the state-sponsored community forestry programs, Someshwar argues against the idea of rural self-sufficiency. Such a concept implies socioeconomic stability or stagnation and is possible only in a society with stable cultural demands and a stable population. If biomass markets are constrained, the economic dualism between city and country will be perpetuated by the maintenance of technically modern, energy-intensive, commercialized enclaves oriented toward economic exchange on the one hand and ecologically stable regions isolated by traditional, labor-intensive, and depressed economies on the other.

Someshwar concludes by sketching the outlines of a program of community empowerment through mediating institutions such as cooperatives, not unlike Mark Freudenberger's proposals for the co-management of acacia forests in northern Senegal. He argues that only the state can intervene to help bring these institutions into existence and points to the necessity of building social institutions such as resource-based cooperatives, which would have the capacity to articulate the needs of poor peasants.

The Lineaments of Environmental Action:
A Comparative Analysis

Earlier in this introduction, we highlighted the need to focus on human agency—environmental actions that emerge in relation to particular localities and conditions. Yet these case studies can be seen as discrete examples of local actions, with little relevance to planners and policymakers who might view this volume as an interesting anthology of ecostories from around the world. What we need at this critical juncture is an effort to transcend the impasse created by debates around abstracted and ambiguous categories such as environment, development, and sustainability and the romanticized notions of popular environmental action. In order to move beyond the totalizing tendencies of grand structural theories, we need to develop middle-range explanatory frameworks that integrate global processes with local environmental action and reveal the particular outcomes experienced by peoples and communities living within localities and regions.

In an unpublished paper on ecological movements, Lisa Peattie describes the problems encountered while attempting to compare environmental movements that emerged in different parts of the world. She identifies the need for "a mode of analysis which makes it possible to focus on the connections between each movement and its social setting" (Peattie 1990). One way of doing this kind of comparative analysis, Peattie suggests, is to think of each movement as having a base and a superstructure. The base, in her view, comprises communities and groups organizing around a local ecological cause or issue, and the superstructure consists of persons or formal organizations that incorporate local causes as examples of a more general concern about the environment.

In this section we touch on some lineaments of the case studies that not only reveal the connections between base and superstructure but also go well beyond to identify the critical planning and theoretical issues that emerge from comparative analysis of environmental action.

Table I.1 provides a framework for identifying some of the important features of environmental action. Although all the case studies focus on the regional and local particularities of social action, two distinct perspectives emerge from the ways in which the authors have narrated their stories.

The first perspective adopts a clearly sympathetic position toward particular communities or classes of people—peasants, petty extractors of forest products, semiproletarianized agricultural communities, urban squatter groups—and sees them responding in their localities to pressures exercised by larger economic and political forces. Six of our case studies are written at least partly from this perspective. Freudenberger, McDonald, and Rangan describe, in essence, defensive maneuvers by local communities; Melone and Pezzoli emphasize proactive resistance strategies. The essay by Massaro is devoted to an account of a proactive form of environmental action.

The second perspective, adopted explicitly by Someshwar, recognizes a multiplicity of claims on environmental resources. Although acknowledging the historical claims of local communities, Someshwar considers that nonlocal actors have equally legitimate claims to the natural resources available in particular regions. For example, an industrializing nation may need to utilize its own forest resources to produce pulp and paper rather than importing it from abroad; it may need timber for railroad or construction projects, and its growing cities may need charcoal. From this perspective, therefore, the state is a legitimate agent for resolving conflicting claims over resources within its territory. Despite the possibility of the state being swayed by powerful interests, this position promotes the idea of an effectively neutral, beneficent state. Overall, this approach tends to be less critical of powerful economic and political interests than the first perspective and is more likely to acknowledge the priority of national development and markets.

The case studies in this volume do not attempt to fit their analysis into any typology of social movements, or engage in the futile exercise of ranking certain kinds of actions over others by developing a hierarchy of environmental movements; instead they focus on the complex outcomes of human agency and locality. Although we have, in this introduction, broadly categorized the case studies as showing either a defensive or proactive character of environmental action, the authors focus their attention on the dynamic nature of each locality, describing how communities and groups seek to change the course of events affecting their lives. The outcomes of environmental actions, and whether change occurs for better or worse, depend on several conditions and factors. We identify five major themes that emerge from the case studies as issues that need to be addressed by planners and policymakers who concern themselves with sustainable development.

The History of Localities

The pronounced historical emphasis in five of the seven case studies may at first glance seem surprising. Planning studies are typically oriented to the future more than to the past, and the normal mode of bureaucratic discourse—in this case, possible interventions—is present oriented. Also, most of the sustainable development literature lacks a sense of the history of localities in relation to the broader historical processes within which they are set. Yet as we can clearly see from the case studies, communities and groups of people cannot be separated from the history of their localities; their environmental actions are the product of local history, just as their actions transform the history of their environments. Through the process of recounting the histories of regions and localities, the case studies synthesize political-economy and political-ecology approaches in innovative ways to reveal the particularities of environmental action and point to the areas where interventions are needed. Both Massaro and Freudenberger go to exceptional lengths to narrate the history of regions and communities in a part of the world that is seen as having no history of its own. The two Brazilian studies use a historical mode of narration to make the environmental actions that emerge as social movements both dramatic and intelligible. Rangan recovers the distinct history of natural resource management in a Himalayan region that is persistently relegated into the peripheries of Indian history. In the process, she reveals the region's geopolitical importance in defining the identity of the Indian state.

Subsidies from Nature and Locality

In a study of the effects of enclosures in late eighteenth- and nineteenth-century England, Jane Humphries tells how peasant families and cottagers were denied access to natural resources such as bulrushes, peat, game, and timber, thereby forcing them off the land and intensifying the process of proletarianization (Humphries 1990). This reexamination of agrarian transformations in Europe has come about due to an awareness of a growing Third World literature on the environmental effects of socioeconomic change. A seminal study by Hecht, Anderson, and May (1988) titled "The Subsidy from Nature" describes the importance of resource extraction from babassu forests in Maranhão in Brazil. They note that most interventions in rural areas through agricultural extension programs or rural development projects focus primarily on providing access to land, inputs, or markets but fail to recognize that most rural households depend on natural resources available in their localities. For example, the babassu palm is crucial

Table I.1. Case Study Profiles

Author	Country/Region	Environmental Resource at Risk	Historical Perspective	Class Position in Region
Massaro	Tanazania/ West Usambara Mountains	soil	yes	small farmers
Freudenberger	northern Senegal	*Acacia senegal* (gum arabic)	yes	simple commodity extractors
McDonald	Brazil/Uruguai River Basin	land	yes	small farmers
Melone	Brazil/Amazon	rubber trees	yes	semipro-letarianized simple commodity extractors
Pezzoli	Mexico/Mexico City (Ajusco)	land	no	urban proletarian households
Rangan	India/Garhwal Himalayas	forests	yes	small farmers with simple commodity production
Someshwar	India/Karnataka	forests	no	large, medium, and marginal farmers

Environmental Action	State Action	External Actor	Outcome
soil conservation; afforestation	sympathy toward and promotion of soil conservation activities	technical and planning assistance from international NGOs	ongoing project
struggle over returning access	indifference to gum arabic collectors	none	further marginalization
struggle over dispossession of land and compensation	firm commitment to dam building	Catholic and Lutheran church activists, labor unions, university researchers	effective standoff on dam project
struggle over rights and access to forest resources	support to powerful classes	university researchers, agricultural labor unions, North American envir-onmental groups and organizations	plans for extractive reserves
strategies for securing tenure for housing	defense to maintain control over its territory	university students, volunteer groups, and labor unions	security of tenure
protests over rights and access to forest resources	intensive regulation of forest resource extraction	intellectuals, volunteer groups, environmentalists	tighter forest laws, further marginalization
social forestry	mediation of use of forest resources by different classes	environmentalist critiques of program benefits	ongoing debate

for large numbers of rural households, since their earnings from extracting palm products make up more than half their total household income.

With the exception of McDonald and Pezzoli, all the authors in this volume highlight the need to view the locality or region as more than a sum of the factors of production. Freudenberger and Melone describe the actions of groups struggling to maintain access or gain usufruct rights to the acacia trees in Senegal and the *hevea* stands in Amazon forests. Rangan focuses on the gradual decline in access to various forest resources in Garhwal due to increased regulation of extractive activities, which led to a decline of economic opportunities for communities within the region. Someshwar points to the varied dependence on and use of forest resources by different classes and groups of people in the Kolar region of India. Massaro's study describes the efforts of Tanzanian peasants, secure in their ownership of land, to conserve and restore the quality of the soil upon which productivity depends. Even Pezzoli's case study of squatter communities of Ajusco struggling to secure access to their housing—though not, technically speaking, a factor of production—is about their attempts to continue their livelihoods in Mexico City.

Status and Visibility of Communities

The case studies reveal that environmental actions are as much about people standing up to be acknowledged as about defending their livelihoods. History reveals time and again that powerful groups can empty landscapes by rendering entire communities invisible. Quoting from Salman Rushdie, Haripriya Rangan dramatically calls attention to it:

> The idea of environmental action implies several things simultaneously—that people living within any given physical environment assert the need to enhance its quality, to ensure the availability and continuity of the resources they depend upon for their livelihood; and equally important, to cry out a version of their lives to a larger world that is either indifferent or threatens to undermine their attempts at self-definition. Their voices cry out partly for the semblance of safety they have lost; but they also seem to say, we "cry to affirm ourselves, to say, here I am, I matter too, you're going to have to reckon with me."

A more matter-of-fact observation is made by McDonald in his essay on the potential victims of the flooding of the Uruguai River Valley. The public power utility estimated the number of potential displacements at 35,900, but the citizens' organization estimated the number of potential victims at around 200,000. By these counts,

164,000 people would appear to have fallen into the black hole of bureaucratic amnesia. But because the peasants in the Uruguai Valley have recognition and status both in their locality and in the eyes of the state, they were able to organize and demand resettlement and just compensation. And recall that the number of people who signed the petition to stop further construction of hydroelectric dams exceeded one million.

Melone is similarly explicit about the fact of invisibility, and about how the invisible forest dwellers of the Amazon gained a collective voice. She writes:

> The rubber tapper movement demonstrates how a population that is traditionally disempowered through economic relations, physical isolation, illiteracy, and little or no social recognition can come to have a voice in national planning bureaucracies. Both locally and regionally, the rubber tappers have stepped out of the forest into the political process. Their collective actions have first and foremost provided them with a collective voice. This "voice" can speak for the interests of the rubber tappers and represent them in political forums.

The case of the Senegalese Maures illustrates a different reaction to invisibility. As an ethnic minority subsisting primarily from the collection of gum arabic, and stigmatized as the descendants of former captives and slaves, the Maures have been unable to gain any visibility or legitimate status within their society, and therefore they have no voice. So they did what disempowered peoples have usually done when their lifeways were being threatened: They retreated into inhospitable regions where their enemies would not intrude, so as to eke out a livelihood.

Gaining voice through organization is the first step in a long process of self-empowerment. Organized, people begin to matter politically. Two forms of empowerment are discussed: collective resistance to external aggression and proactive action. Both can lead to material betterment, and both ultimately affect state planning agencies that must acknowledge the newly empowered groups and their claims.

The Critical Role of External Agents

In nearly all of the environmental actions described in this volume, outside groups have played key roles. In southern Brazil, it was the Catholic and Lutheran churches, labor unions, and universities. In Mexico City's Ajusco zone, support for self-organization came from university students and from a labor union at the national university, where some of the grassroots activists of Los Belvederes had gained their early training. In the Amazon, it was a labor union, the Confederation of Agricultural Workers, that provided the impetus for what would grow into the National Council of Rubber Tappers and the Coalition of Forest Peoples. There were individual university researchers as well, who began as anthropologists studying the rubber tappers and ended up as their champions. In Tanzania, the external agent was the West German technical assistance agency GTZ. In Garhwal, the Chipko movement gained its recognition through the involvement of environmental activists and intellectuals.

So-called external agents engage in a variety of activities in their support of local groups: assistance with self-organization, advice on tactics, leadership training, provision of technical information, access to media and national and international bureaucracies, help with coalition building, and financial assistance. But the danger in depending on external agents is that grassroots struggles for livelihood may become mere exemplars of larger societal processes that have become ideologized. For instance, when Marxism was still in its ascendancy, the labor movement was frequently portrayed as part of a class struggle that would terminate in the inevitable victory of the proletariat. In the case of the Chipko movement, local villagers' claims over access to forest resources were transformed into a variety of ecological ideologies for which Chipko became merely a symbol unrelated to the continuing struggles of those villagers.

Sometimes the efforts of external agents are rejected by local groups. For example, the concept of extractive reserves was accepted by the rank and file of the rubber tappers, but the parallel concept of a *colonia ecológica productiva* (CEP) was rejected by the settlers in Los Belvederes in Mexico City. Both embraced the vision of an alternative development based on ecological principles, and both saw the disempowered groups as their champion. The idea for CEP originated with university students who envisioned a noncapitalist scenario consistent with their ideological beliefs. But the squatter communities wanted only the rights to their land. They used the CEP concept to serve that end, but they were not interested in a noncapitalist ecological utopia and declined to become its vanguard.

On the other hand, the concept of extractive reserves was accepted by the Amazonian rubber tappers. Based on the idea of Indian reservations, it appealed to them because what the tappers ultimately wanted was to be allowed to continue in their accustomed way of life. The legal designation of their life space as an extractive reserve made sense to them: It would keep cattle barons and logging interests out of their territories. Some activists may have intended more than merely a "reserve," envisioning an ecologically sustainable development of which the rubber tappers, like the squatter communities of Ajusco, would be the vanguard. It is still too early to judge whether this idea will continue to appeal. Rubber tappers are undoubtedly interested in finding a larger market for the forest products they collect and in getting better financial returns. It is questionable, however, whether pursuing these interests will lead to the development that university-educated outsiders envision.

The Role of the State

The majority of our case studies describe the state, at least partly, as the enemy. Someshwar's essay is the major exception; his is primarily a critique of the populist perspective. To help poor people, he writes, they must be empowered by forming mediating organizations, such as cooperatives, that can assume responsibility for the comanagement of community forests. It is virtually the identical proposition that Freudenberger makes with regard to the Senegalese Maures and that Massaro describes in his study of the Shambaas. In all these cases, the recommendation is for strengthening local institutions. But this strengthening requires the support of the state, or it will not come about.

A similar dependence on the state can be observed in other cases. To make the concept of extractive reserves in the Amazon possible, the state must designate certain areas and use its police power to enforce their inviolability. It was the state that incorporated the squatter settlements of Los Belvederes after a prolonged citizen struggle. And CRAB activists in Brazil quite obviously needed an agency of the state with which they could negotiate their future in the Uruguai River Valley.

Ideology cannot be allowed to blind us to the realities of existing environmental struggles. These struggles may be a case of organized civil society against the state, but in the final analysis, what people want is not an anarchist utopia but a better state—one that takes the claims of its disempowered citizens seriously and is willing to tip the balance in their favor. What disempowered people want most is to be given a fair hearing and to have their rights as citizens and human beings acknowledged. There is no genuine alternative to a reformist state. Revolutions may emerge to destroy a state that is unwilling to reform itself, but they rarely succeed in changing the institutionalized structures that persist.

Conclusion

There is still a lot of unfinished business in the regions described. In Tanzania, the government proposal to resettle some 30,000 farmers in less densely populated areas currently lacks the resources for implementation. The fate of the impoverished Maures still hangs in the balance: Another drought or a further decline in world markets for gum arabic may disperse the remnants of this hardy people into the coastal cities of the region. In Brazil, the struggles against dams and for just indemnification continue, increasingly on a national scale. Rubber tappers' continued access to the forest is by no means guaranteed by the official proclamation of certain areas as extractive reserves. And even though the threat of squatter removal may have receded in Los Belvederes, other battles for land are beginning, almost on a daily basis, in this sprawling metropolis. The forests of the Garhwal Himalayas continue to be contested and redefined, despite increasing marginalization of local groups and communities living in the region. The fuel and biomass needs of poor peasants in Kolar are increasingly subordinated to the control of larger economic and political forces.

In these contested localities, foreign experts, movement activists, and idealistic university students come and go, their time perspective is rarely more than the few years of an engagement. But Shambaas, Maures, Brazilian peasant farmers, rubber tappers, and communities in Garhwal and Kolar are there to stay. They have no ideological battles to win, but they do have a stake in their localities. If human agency and action in relation to locality are not seen as the central issue for planners and policymakers, debates about sustainability, development, or the environment may well be only the armchair musings of those who hold economic and political power in different parts of the world. Localities and communities can hope for little more than to hold on and continue to struggle for the rights and entitlements that have been steadily stripped from them. Toward this end, they will focus their energies for as long as they can.

References

Buttel, Frederick, and William Sunderlin. 1988. "Integrating Political Economy and Political Ecology: An Assessment of Theories of Agricultural and Extractive Industry Development in Latin America." Presented at the 46th International Conference of Americanists, Amsterdam, 4–8 July.

Cleary, David. 1991. "The 'Greening' of the Amazon." In *Environment and Development in Latin America: The Politics of Sustainability*, edited by David Goodman and Michael Redclift. Manchester and New York: Manchester University Press.

Daly, Herman. 1991. "Sustainable Growth: A Bad Oxymoron." *Grassroots Development* 15(3): 39.

Dodwell, David. 1992. "GATT Issues Warning against Environmental Imperialism." *Financial Times* (London), 12 February.

Guha, Ramachandra. 1989. *The Unquiet Woods: Ecological Change and Peasant Resistance in the Himalaya*. New Delhi: Oxford University Press.

Hecht, Susanna, Anthony Anderson, and Peter May. 1988. "The Subsidy from Nature: Shifting Cultivation, Successional Palm Forests and Rural Development." *Human Organization* 47(1): 25–35.

Hecht, Susanna, and Alexander Cockburn. 1989. *Fate of the Forest: Developers, Destroyers and Defenders of the Amazon*. London: Verso.

Humphries, Jane. 1990. "Enclosures, Common Rights, and Women: The Proletarianization of Families in the Late Eighteenth and Nineteenth Centuries." *Journal of Economic History* 50(1): 17–42.

Meegan, Richard. 1992. "Liverpool—Sliding Down the Urban Hierarchy: From Imperial Pre-eminence to Global and National Peripherality." Presented at the Conference on New Urban and Regional Hierarchy, University of California, Los Angeles, 23–25 April.

Mitlin, Diana. 1992. "Sustainable Development: A Guide to the Literature." *Environment and Urbanization* 4(2): 111–24.

Peattie, Lisa. 1990. *Ecological Movements*. Unpublished.

Redclift, Michael. 1987. *Sustainable Development: Exploring the Contradictions*. New York: Methuen.

World Commission on Environment and Development. 1987. *Our Common Future*. Oxford: Oxford University Press.

ONE

BEYOND PARTICIPATION

*Empowerment for Environmental Action in
Tanzania's West Usambara Mountains*

RICHARD J. MASSARO

FOR MUCH OF THIS CENTURY, the West Usambara Mountains
in northeastern Tanzania's Tanga Region, Lushoto District, have been
known for environmental crises and failed conservation programs.
The Soil Erosion Control/Agroforestry Project (SECAP), begun in 1981
as part of the Federal Republic of Germany's aid to the Tanga Integrated Rural Development Program, may change that reputation. The
project is a community-based, integrated, ecologically sustainable,
economically viable effort to increase people's capacities to meet their
livelihood and development needs as well as an effort to control and
reverse the processes of soil erosion and environmental degradation
in the region.

History of the Region

Understanding the nature of the challenge in the Usambaras—and
SECAP's degree of success—requires an analysis of the origins and
evolution of its various crises. Into the 1800s, the Shambaa, the West
Usambaras' main inhabitants, adapted to the major social and technological changes taking place and devised ecologically sound production systems and a stable social organization. Factors that generated a
need for soil erosion control programs unfolded over more than two
centuries as a result of local, regional, and colonial political economy.
Trade penetration, colonization, promotion of plantation economies,
and, later, the policies of the Tanzanian government all combined to
produce the environmental crises in the Usambaras. This study traces
the evolution of those crises, describes SECAP's efforts to root effective

technical assistance in Shambaa history and socioeconomic conditions, and presents a critical summary of lessons from that experience and their implications for the prospects of sustainable development.

Usambara Lands

Mainland Tanzania is a land of rich diversity and striking contrasts with widely varying topography and ecosystems and 120 ethnic groups, "a bowl of fairly harsh environments at the centre, surrounded by a series of better-watered and relatively more fertile areas along the broken rim" (Sheriff 1980, 13). In the northeast, Mt. Meru and Mt. Kilimanjaro jut from wide grassland and woodland plains. South of Kilimanjaro, the plains meet the escarpment of the North and South Pare and West and East Usambara Mountains, a 225-kilometer barrier between the plains and a thin Indian Ocean coastal strip.[1] The escarpment is abrupt, a virtual wall up to 800 meters above the plains. Unlike volcanic Meru and Kilimanjaro, these mountains are "an uplifted block of metamorphosed, folded and faulted volcanic and sedimentary rocks. . . . Slopes are steep and level land limited" (Cliffe, Luttrell, and Moore 1975a, 148). The extremely irregular mountain terrain appears as intersecting systems of ridges and valleys, with valleys stretching 100 meters to a kilometer wide, and a few hundred meters to five kilometers long, before meeting another ridge. Elevations average 1,000 to 2,000 meters and reach 2,300 meters on some peaks (see Figure 1.1).

Cool climate and abundant regular rain produce thick forest cover. Most of Tanzania has long rains from January or February to as late as June, and then short November and December rains. Usambara also has August rains. Amounts of rainfall vary with elevation and relief, but the mountains are far moister than the plains and have a more lush, diverse plant population—some forty-three tree species, forty-three herbs, and fifty-seven other plants, almost all indigenous—including commercial species such as teak, mahogany, cedar, ebony, camphor, nutmeg, black pepper, wattle, and vanilla. Usambara has five soil types: laterized red soils with shallow organic topsoil, non-laterized red loams, grey loamy mineral soils, grey-to-black fresh mineral soils, and valley colluvium (Milne, in Cliffe, Luttrell, and Moore 1975a, 147). Types vary greatly over very short distances; the fragile, marginally fertile types 1–3 are usually found on mountain slopes, and the richer types 4–5 are in the valleys (TIRDEP 1985, 161).

Evolution of Human-Environment Symbiosis

For millennia these forests and soils were undisturbed. The earliest culture and technology involved hunting wild savannah animals and

Figure 1.1 Tanzania and Tanga Region

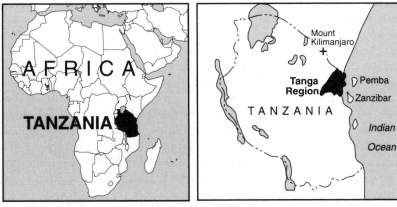

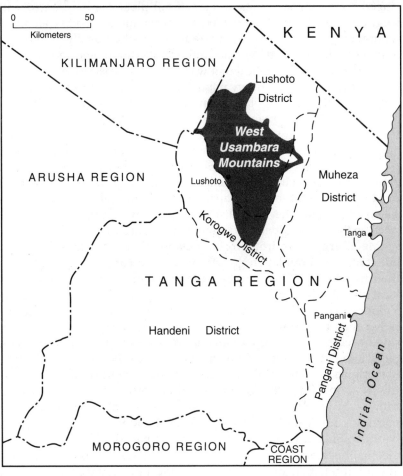

harvesting plants. About 1000 B.C., North African innovations (domesticated animals and cultivated crops) enabled a shift to food production (Munson 1986). Only when ironsmithy and bananas—"tools to clear the forest, and suitable crops to grow" (Sheriff 1980, 22)—reached Africa from Asia (likely through Arab traders plying the Indian Ocean) could Shambaa ancestors—the Proto-Bantu who spread out from Central Africa—colonize the highlands around 500 A.D. The mountains provided superior health, production, and security: They were malaria free and had more fertile soils, better rains, few predators, and rugged terrain to impede human invasions. The Shambaa adapted production and social systems to the environment and increased production by combining new and old methods and crops. The population grew, prompting new relations among people and with the land. By 1500, the Shambaa had permanent settlements ringed with banana groves and small hill plots nearby planted with sorghum, millet, pulses, and tubers to accommodate soil type, mimic natural cover, check erosion, and reduce risk of crop failure. Fertilization, field rotation, and lowland shifting cultivation renewed the soil.

The basic spatial, political unit was a village or oasis town, "in a zone so rich it can support a heavy population, and whose crops exhaust the soil so little that the population can be permanent" (Feierman 1974, 31). Siting towns on mountain rims aided other survival strategies. Additional farm plots on the plains and farming systems based on lowland and upland harvest times produced food year-round. Kinship, "blood partnership," and trade with plains peoples ensured against East Africa's recurrent famines. Shambaa men also kept cattle and goats for meat and milk, but their principal use was to indicate wealth, compensate medical and other specialists, pay fines, and secure wives. Grazing stock on the plains added to lowland spatial and social links.

Metallurgy gave iron-working clans initial political dominance, but continued population growth made land control more important than technology. The Shambaa adapted and created kinship-based local chiefdoms to maintain social stability and ecological harmony. Villages had multiple clans, but one with superior administrative, rather than technical, skills became dominant. Hereditary chiefs allocated access to communal banana groves and distributed outlying plots. Land access shifted from open usufruct to household and hereditary rights (Sheriff 1980, 22–23). Chiefs received produce and labor tribute to maintain chiefly courts and communal fields and vied for tribute within neighborhoods of villages associated, by lineage and marriage, for trade and defense. Some 1,100 years after the Proto-Bantu colonized Usambara, the Shambaa had developed a prosperous, sophisticated, and ecologically sound system and were adept at exploiting their rich environment and knowledgeable regarding its preservation.

Initial Challenges and Successful Adaptations

Starting in the 1500s, this system faced increasingly frequent and serious challenges. Two Cushitic groups pushed out from Kenya by the Maasai migrated to Upare and Usambara. The Nango gradually assimilated into the Shambaa as another clan in all but village and neighborhood allegiances. They, and later Mbugu herders who settled in areas that were drier and less accessible but fit for pastoralism, had transterritorial allegiances of lineage, common rites of passage, and a paramount ritual leader. Not competing for land, the Mbugu were a threat only if joined by clans in nearby Upare. The Nango threat was immediate and internal. In the late 1600s, Chief Mbegha resolved tribute disputes by fusing southern neighborhoods into a centralized state. When he died, a Nango ritual leader claimed political power. Rival Nango allied with Mbegha's son, killed the usurper, and further integrated the two cultures. The son and a grandson expanded the kingdom in Usambara and to coastal towns and hinterlands. From 1815 to 1862, a great-grandson, Kimweri, integrated the kingdom territorially by placing a son or grandson in charge of virtually every subchiefdom (Feierman 1974, 106) and creating a structure to identify and discipline oppressive chiefs, exiling recalcitrants and potential rivals to non-Shambaa areas of the kingdom.

Food tribute from subjugated neighbors supported population growth without expanding or intensifying land use that would risk ecological balance. This tributary kingdom arose from internal tensions but also integrated the Nango and contained the Mbugu. It centralized political organization, increased stratification, and made the Shambaa typical of 1800s Tanzanian societies: "politically independent . . . [their] economic and social development was closely in tune with their political development. Their economy was symmetrical and internally integrated. . . . [They] produced what they consumed and the surplus was retained within the community to support the development of non-agricultural crafts and social differentiation" (Sheriff 1980, 36). There were conflicts, even conquests. More common were coexistence and trade for scarce resources and locally specialized products. The Shambaa traded bananas and tobacco for Zigua metal implements, game meat, and salt; for Maasai livestock; and for coastal traders' cowrie shell beads and other goods.

Effects of Arab Trade

By 1200 A.D., Arabs had coastal settlements in East Africa, trading gold from Zimbabwe and ivory from throughout the interior; by 1500, they had regular caravan routes (Coulson 1982, 21). Leaders along the routes exacted tribute to enhance wealth and solidify power, but trade was marginal to most mainland political economies until the late 1700s and into the 1800s, when European, then American, expansion drastically changed the scope and role of trade and helped transform the organization and relations of many societies. Portuguese reached East Africa in 1498 and controlled virtually all Indian Ocean trade by 1650. In the late 1600s, the Sultan of Oman reasserted Arab dominance and developed Zanzibar into the empire's most important outpost. Sultan Seyyid Said moved his capital there in 1840 and set up clove plantations on Zanzibar and Pemba, opposite Pangani and Tanga, towns from which the Shambaa took tribute.

Until the late eighteenth century, the mainland's principal export was ivory to India, and the main imports were cloth and metal goods. By 1850, trade with Europe and America surpassed that with India and vastly increased demand, depleting supplies near the coast. Hunting and trade moved further inland. Arabs built caravan staging posts in central Tanzania in 1845 and at Lake Tanganyika in 1860 (Coulson 1982, 28). Trade's impact increased with its scale and range. Trade route control became vital to local rulers' wealth, power, and prestige as well as a source of conflict. Two other developments had more profound effects: slave export and firearms import. Traditionally, East Africa imposed slavery on debtors, criminals, and war prisoners (Feierman 1974, 174–75). Slave export, common in earliest Arab trade (Shorter 1974, 24), grew slightly in the 1600s to supply Omani date plantations but remained minor. In the late 1700s, demand for slaves exploded with French plantations on Mauritius and Reunion and higher American demand (Sheriff 1980, 38). The other development made slave extraction easier, more attractive, even necessary. As slaves were increasingly exported, firearms became the predominant import, giving a clear advantage in trade route control and in the capture of yet more slaves to buy still more arms and ammunition (Iliffe 1979, 50–51).

Mountains protected but isolated Usambara. Trade "was peripheral to the political economy of the early kingdom, tribute central. The Kings used tribute wealth to acquire the trade goods they needed rather than using trade to acquire political followings" (Feierman 1974, 123). Trade became crucial and helped destroy the kingdom when Semboja, chief of Mazinde—a trade center at the escarpment base—used firearms and alliances with Zigua, who traded for guns in the 1830s and took control of the Pangani Valley, to challenge Kimweri's son. Unable to raid better-armed neighbors, rivals raided each other and even sold their own subjects (Feierman 1974, 140–84). The Shambaa people rejected a centralized state and leaders who rewarded loyalty with slavery. Brutal evidence justified mistrusting, resenting, and resisting centralized government and outside interference; made political orientation local and isolationist; and embedded these attitudes in the cultural ethos. Leaders, having destroyed their power base, restructured the political economy. "At the heart of the political transformation was a shift from livestock to trade goods as the most important form of chiefly wealth" (Feierman 1974, 172). Pemba and Zanzibar clove plantations, absorbing 10,000 slaves a year by the 1860s, more than made up for lost markets when Britain expelled the French from Mauritius and Reunion and moved to abolish slave trade. Guns and slaves fed Shambaa conflict until German colonists forced submission in 1888 (Iliffe 1979, 66).

Trade also spread American maize, a coastal crop for centuries, inland. With higher yields for less labor than native sorghum and millet—though far less drought resistant, less suited to Tanzania's irregular rains and recurrent shortfalls, and slow to mature in upland environs—maize began to replace bananas as the Shambaa staple by 1877 (Iliffe 1971, 8). The Shambaa made it a staple by adapting technology. They planted in three zones—plains, mountain rims, and high interior mountains—according to the maturation rates and rainy season in each zone to produce year-round harvests (Feierman 1974, 25–26). Maize held another challenge: "Even as a mature crop, the leaf and root structures of the plant do not protect the soil from erosion. However, when it is intercropped, the erosion potential in areas where it grows decreases" (Lewis and Berry 1988, 103). The Shambaa met the challenge by intercropping and using stone walls and terraces to prevent erosion (Coulson 1982, 16). For added insurance they grew cassava, also from America, which was very drought resistant and suited to plains and dry mountain areas where maize, bananas, and other crops failed. Writing in 1890, Baumann noted:

> On the slopes one sees thick clumps of banana palms and in between these fields of sugar cane, maize, beans, pumpkins, and tomatoes . . . extremely well tended. In the pastures numerous well-fed cattle graze. . . . All the settlements and inhabitants of this delightful area display a certain prosperity. (Iliffe 1971, 33)

German Colonial Conquest: Balance Destroyed

Colonialism altered the pace and direction of change. By 1880, the industrial revolution caused fierce competition for raw materials, export markets, and settler enclaves to bind colonies to home countries. In 1884, Bismarck chartered the Karl Peters' Society for German Colonization. The 1884–85 Berlin Conference carved Africa into "spheres of influence," and Peters' armed expeditions got mainland chiefs to sign treaties giving Germany sovereignty over customs and settlement rights. These treaties were used to declare East Africa a

German protectorate (Arnold 1980, 67–77). The Society, now the German East Africa Company (DOAG by its German acronym), expanded its control (Coulson 1982, 35). In 1888, the sultan ceded coastal town customs rights, which DOAG took to mean direct rule (Temu 1980, 95–96). Arabs and Swahilis, joined by Africans, rebelled. The Shambaa, decimated and divided by their own wars, gave only token support to the rebellion. The Germans crushed the resistance (Iliffe 1979, 95–102). In 1890, they set up a station at Mazinde and gave Semboja a monthly salary for his acquiescence (Feierman 1974, 202–4). When he died in 1895, they executed his heir and installed their own chief "not as an independent sovereign but as a German agent especially for the recruitment of labour for German planters" (Temu 1980, 101).

German settlement focused on Usambara; it was fertile, temperate, richly forested, near Tanga and Pangani ports, and depopulated in large areas by Shambaa war (Iliffe 1979, 126). The Germans ended the war but made other changes that helped create later crises. DOAG "bought" land with token fees to chiefs and made farms and pastures, plantations, settler estates, and forest reserves. A commission of Germans and local headmen concentrated the Shambaa people on part of the land and alienated the rest of it. Land was soon scarce. In 1912, Usambara was closed to settlement. Scarcity forced Shambaa farmers to abandon traditional practices. Hill soils need three years of fallow for each year of crop use to maintain fertility and soil stability (Cliffe, Luttrell, and Moore 1975a, 147). But by 1912, "more than half the cultivatable land then remaining to Africans was said to be cultivated at any time, fallow periods were falling to destructive levels and food production was declining" (Iliffe 1979, 143).

Next, the Germans introduced taxes and monetization "to make people use money, sell surplus crops, work for Europeans, and obey a distant government" (Iliffe 1979, 133). Those in fertile areas near towns, plantations, estates, or road and rail construction sold food. Others were encouraged, and forced, to grow traditional and new crops for export: cotton, beeswax, rubber, coffee, and groundnuts. Those in remote or less fertile areas sold their labor as porters or construction workers and on plantations, which absorbed the most labor. Sisal from America did well in the climate and soils of the plains below Usambara and became the most important plantation crop.

Africans reluctant to enter wage labor were coerced and overtly forced, often by other Africans. "Each settler entering Usambara in the late 1890s was allocated several villages whose headmen had to provide a fixed number of workers each day" (Iliffe 1979, 152). This differentiated Africans into petty commodity producers and migrant wage laborers, and the colony into labor-absorbing and labor-exporting regions, except Usambara. The Shambaa had trouble entering the cash economy in either way. Reluctant to leave the mountains, they were abundant estate labor, which resulted in severely depressed wages; nor could they sell food or export crops. "European mixed farms produced their own food, no successful cash crop was ever found" (Iliffe 1971, 15). For coffee, "the lower land was too hot and dry, while West Usambara was too wet and cold. Both had shallow acidic soils which produced only low yields, a quarter of those later obtained on Kilimanjaro" (Iliffe 1979, 128). Low yields, land shortage, and depressed world prices reduced the number of estates in Usambara to forty-one by 1911. When the rail line reached Kilimanjaro in 1912, settler focus shifted there and to Mt. Meru. Like trade routes, the rail line isolated and marginalized Usambara and pushed the area further toward stagnation and peripheral involution (Cliffe 1977, 215).

British Administration: Crisis Intensified

Germany's colony was entrusted to Britain after World War I. Export-led development continued, but investment remained limited because the British colony, Kenya, took precedence during the financially difficult times of the depression and World War II. They extended rail lines and roads, but "the lines of communication of the colonial economy had bypassed Usambara, once one of the most sophisticated political and economic units in the country, and it had consequently become underdeveloped" (Iliffe 1971, 33). British policy for African agriculture intensified Usambara isolation and involution. Elsewhere, they encouraged and imposed cash cropping, but when the Shambaa began growing coffee in 1921, the policy was one of "nonencouragement," so as to maintain labor reserves and prevent competition with European growers (Iliffe 1979, 289).

The constant of British agricultural policy—applied across the territory but especially in Usambara—was erosion control,[2] "an issue of growing concern among technical and administrative officers in Tanzania since the 1920s" (Rapp, Berry, and Temple 1972, 105). British administrators felt that

> African agriculture was inefficient . . . systems of land tenure [lead] to an impersonal attitude to land with no incentive to improvement, and . . . systems of land use . . . [lead] to reduction of soil fertility and decreasing yields. It was the attitude of Europeans who believed that European capitalist methods of cultivation adopted since the agricultural revolution were a model for the world. (Bowles 1980, 170)

Hence, they promoted existing exports—sisal and coffee—and planned capital-intensive projects for new crops such as cotton and groundnuts. The infamous Groundnut Scheme, an experiment in large-scale mechanized peanut farming that ended in colossal failure, showed that "capital and technology alone made little impression on Tanganyika's environment" (Iliffe 1979, 170). To improve yields and colonial profits from African farms, "during the 1920s agricultural experts developed systematic extension techniques, emphasized the virtues of mixed farming, and became obsessed with soil erosion" (Iliffe 1979, 348), which they blamed on traditional farming and grazing.

After 1930, some officials began to admit that the lost equilibrium between the environment and traditional farming and herding may have been externally induced, with systems "breaking down under novel and increasing stresses: soil or pasture damage was a symptom rather than the disease itself" (Watson 1972, 222). Later conservation was based in part on "the awareness that agricultural change in the earlier years of colonial rule had in many areas disturbed the balance between men, animals, and the land" (Iliffe 1971, 34). Instead of addressing causes of stress, though, they retained a technical approach to solving the problem. Lacking funds for extensive schemes to prevent erosion or check it in already affected areas, the British chose to "persuade" people to improve land use methods (Rapp, Berry, and Temple 1972, 105–6). Persuasion took the form of fines or imprisonment. "Indirect rule" made local leaders enforce erosion control: closing steep slopes to farming, protecting watercourses and cultivated slopes, introducing new cover crops, and building bench terraces. Agricultural officers acted as police and prosecutors in courts presided over by chiefs, discrediting both (Coulson 1982, 52). Force, in fact, became the mainstay of policy toward African farming (Bowles 1980, 128). The Shambaa objected to and resisted—with good reason—the measures used to induce compliance. "[It] is now clear that the agricultural and economic logic behind many of the rules was wrong, so that the farmers were absolutely correct in opposing them" (Coulson 1982, 53).

Neither resistance nor failure daunted the British colonial government. Usambara justified erosion concern. The Shambaa population doubled between 1914 and 1948 (Iliffe 1979, 350) as land remained scarce. The government sold some German estates to Greeks and Asians, allowed some Germans to return, and evicted farmers who encroached on forest reserves when the Germans left (Johansson 1988a, 7). Hereditary rights controlled access to remaining land and fed differentiation. In 1930, of 250 Shambaa coffee growers, five, all in the former kingdom's capital, owned 20,788 of 35,324 trees (Iliffe 1979, 293). Most escape options were gone. Plains once farmed and grazed by the Shambaa were now sisal estates. Lowland population growth and interethnic animosity from slave raids precluded migration beyond the plantations. Limited land and uneven distribution perpetuated declining fallows and more extensive and intensive grazing, making fertile land even more scarce and fragile. Mlalo was the first target for erosion control. In the 1930s, the Agriculture Department called it seriously eroded, with farming and grazing laying slopes bare. Tree cutting for domestic fuel and hillside burning to increase and maintain pasturage were stripping away protective cover. The Forest Department began reforestation campaigns, and the Agriculture Department introduced bench terracing and—when this proved too unpopular—contour hedges.

A 1942 report again blamed Usambara erosion on farming and grazing practices and human and animal population growth. It recommended demonstrating a system of remedies on a 2,000-acre plot, forcing expanded fallow, and closing and reforesting the worst areas. "But neither the manpower, resources, nor the official will were adequate to ensure the implementation of this scheme at the time" (Watson 1972, 223). In 1944–45, F. J. Nutman offered even more ambitious proposals, in effect a comprehensive integrated development scheme combining erosion control, diversification (vegetables and fruits for the coast and wattle for a tannery), and agroforestry with processing activities and new village industries (tanning, brick making, logging and planing, ceramics, fiberboard and carton manufacture). To Nutman, the problem was not just technical but also economic and structural. Land degradation was caused by too many people solely dependent on agriculture on too little land. Reducing pressure on the land meant providing other options for economic activity.

Nutman's plan was rejected by government and local officials as impractical and out of touch with Usambara's reality. A revised proposal identified activities such as market gardening to increase cash incomes and reduce exported staples, planting wattle to control erosion and supply a tannery, creating leys, destocking, and moving people from Mlalo basin. A commission rejected the revision and followed the 1942 report. The 1946 colonial ten-year development plan made rehabilitating eroded land a priority for the whole mainland (Iliffe 1979, 473). That same year, Mlalo was chosen for a pilot scheme involving ten villages and some 360 people and 150 cattle. "The principal aims were to restrict cultivation on steep slopes, to curtail grazing by imposing stall-feeding, to prohibit the burning of plant residues and to introduce soil conservation measures" (Cliffe, Luttrell, and Moore 1975a, 162). Steep slopes could be planted only with bananas or made into forest reserves. Moderate slopes were to be terraced or ridged.

The pilot scheme met with immediate rejection. Anticolonialism and opposition to the ruling clan—unpopular since Semboja and now seen as British stooges—intensified. Still, in 1950, the Mlalo program was extended as the Usambara Development Scheme, despite recognition of major problems. Opposition spread and deepened because of resentment of cultivation, burning, and grazing limits; reaction to force; added labor in terracing; and fear that continued settler presence and relocation provisions in scheme legislation would mean forced migration and more land alienation (Cliffe, Luttrell, and Moore 1975a, 162–63). Officials increased compulsion and enforced the regulations; finally, some were abandoned in 1958, and others died at independence in 1961. "Perhaps the major cause of failure of the scheme, other than the unpopularity of its administration, was the absence of any immediate benefits associated with the new practices" (Cliffe, Luttrell, and Moore 1975a, 163). A tannery was built at Lushoto, the district's headquarters. Wattle seedlings were distributed throughout Usambara, but bark supply has never sufficed to run the factory at capacity. Further, since the conservation methods were not adapted to local conditions, some were actually destructive. Terracing caused loss of topsoil and fertility in Mlalo. The legacy of the scheme was deep resentment of and strong resistance to conservation programs. Land pressure persisted and, except for areas growing vegetables for Tanga and other towns and a small, highly concentrated area growing coffee, West Usambara remained marginalized, continuing the pauperization process begun earlier (Attems 1968, 140).

Early Tanzanian Administration: Stop-Gap Intervention

After independence, the government abandoned many unpopular and ineffective erosion control policies and instead, under popular pressure in 1964, opened 130 of 250 square kilometers of forest preserve to settlement and farming. Landless and land-poor farmers, chosen by lot, were to be given ten acres (Johansson 1988a, 7) to subdivide into six equal parts, protected by contour lines and managed with systematic crop, fodder, and fallow rotation. Farmers were also to grow fruits, tobacco, and vegetables in home gardens for consumption and market (Cliffe, Luttrell, and Moore 1975a, 163–64). This plan, too, met serious difficulties:

> Malpractices, or at least miscalculations, in administration have led to inequitable division of holdings . . . in part caused by the fact that local officials were withholding part of the ten-acre allotment from those settlers who already held land elsewhere but also using their influence over the distribution process for their own advantage. In other cases families who were allocated a plot sold all or part of it. In some localities land allotments varied from two to twenty acres. (Cliffe, Luttrell, and Moore 1975a, 164)

Further, it was not local farmers but Pare immigrants and forest wage laborers who got most of the new land. Local farmers instead encroached on additional forestland (Johansson 1988a, 7–8). According to missionaries present at the time, farmers resorted to wholesale burning of forests to clear and claim land, indicating the urgency and volatility of the issue.

Even ideal implementation would have provided only marginal relief. Land is both absolutely and relatively scarce. In 1957, there were 152,000 people in Usambara. From 1957 to 1978, population grew 3.2 percent a year to 200,000 in 1967 and 266,000 in 1978. The rate of growth then fell to 2.2 percent, and population stood at 330,000 in 1988—some 61,000 households averaging 5.4 persons each. Giving each a basic ten-acre (four hectares) allotment would require an area of 2,400 square kilometers with no allowance for grazing, forest, or other uses. Estimates of the total Usambara area range from 1,740 square kilometers (TIRDEP 1985, 162) to 1,971 square kilometers (TIRDEP 1975b, 38), or a maximum of 43,500 to 49,275 ten-acre farms.

Natural endowments and developed uses compounded the scarcity. Soils, terrain, and climate divide the mountains into four zones: humid/warm south, dry/cold west-central, dry/warm east-central, and dry/warm north (Taube 1988, 2). The humid/warm south zone has the most cash crops: coffee, fruits, vegetables, and, since 1962, tea—apparently the successful crop that eluded settlers (Cliffe, Luttrell, and Moore 1975a, 164). The other zones rely on subsistence farming and grazing but show the impact of the wider economy. Urban growth increased vegetable and fruit demand. Throughout Usambara, valley pastures have been irrigated to grow cabbages, potatoes, tomatoes, and other crops. This increased land competition has reduced grazing areas, put more stress on hillsides with grazing on fallow and crop residues, depleted stocks of nutrients returning to the soil, and further disturbed fragile soil structures.

There is relative scarcity as well, due to dictated land use and uneven distribution (Table 1.1). Recent estimates show little room for further redistribution. There is clearly just as little political will. None of the socialist policies, villagization, and nationalization schemes have altered uneven land distribution or the process of differentiation (Fleuret 1980, 69). Except for increased concentration, little has changed in Usambara since 1971, when 54 percent of 41,900 individual farms studied were under 0.5 hectares, far below the ideal and too small to sustain a household. Large farms occupied 64 percent of land individually held (1968–71 Regional Statistical Abstract, in TIRDEP 1975b, 58). Tanzanians themselves took over some estates and created new ones. Even scholars involved in policy formation and supportive of socialism advised against taking land from rich farmers, though they did suggest dividing church, estate, and forest reserve holdings among landless peasants (Cliffe, Luttrell, and Moore 1975b, 513).

Table 1.1 Land Use Classification

	Sq. km	Land Use Percent
Forest reserve	310	15.7
Tree crops	150	7.6
Irrigated crops	66	3.4
Dry land crops	1,135	57.6
Grazing/unused	310	15.7
Total	1,971	100.0

Source: Adapted from Lars Johansson, "Forestry Strategy: SECAP Phase III, 1988–1992" (Lushoto, Tanzania: TIRDEP-SECAP, 1988) 3.

Studies consistently show that Shambaa differentiation, rooted in tradition and reinforced by colonialism, intensified after independence. Land ownership now strongly correlates with age. In one area, men under forty had farms half the size of those who were forty-one to seventy-five years of age (Cliffe, Luttrell, and Moore 1975a, 167). Village interviews in 1989 suggest that for the young the problem is even more acute. Men under thirty had an average of 0.76 hectares, men thirty-one to fifty had 1.62 hectares, and older men had 3.24 hectares. Holding size is not solely a function of age, however. Wealthy farmers tend to belong to established "core lineage" families in villages. They expand holdings by purchase rather than inheritance and pass on farms intact to eldest sons instead of dividing them equally among sons and daughters as had been customary in the past (Fleuret 1980, 72–75). Large holdings create more surplus for further expansion. This increases landlessness and presses poor farmers to cultivate small and/or marginally fertile plots more intensively, reducing fallow and increasing erosion. Resources needed to address these and other rural development problems were made more scarce in the late 1970s by the combined effect of overall Tanzanian economic decline and increased investment in industry (Maliyamkono and Bagachwa 1990, 5). Cumulatively, Shambaa history and heritage, colonial penetration, Tanzanian policy, international economic conditions, and continued population growth have produced a situation in which

> the problem of diminishing resources is most distinct and serious. Various causes [are] self-reinforcing and bring serious stress [on] the environment, which in the final analysis leads to destruction of nature as a base of life . . . a successive transformation of fertile soil into barren land. To rehabilitate destroyed land and soil, decades or even centuries may be required. (TIRDEP 1985, 168)

Integrated Rural Development and Soil Erosion Control in the Tanga Region

The first steps on the long road to rehabilitation grew out of Tanzanian policy changes in the 1970s. Under "decentralization," Tanzania directed regions—subnational administrative units—to begin four-phased planning: baseline research, long-range plans, initial projects, and Regional Integrated Development Programs (RIDEPs). Foreign donors were invited to act as counterparts and funding sources in each Region. The Federal Republic of Germany agreed to aid the Tanga Region through its implementing agency, the Gesellschaft für Technische Zusammenarbeit (Technical Cooperation Services; GTZ). In 1972, GTZ began thirty months of phase-one research that resulted in the five-year Tanga Integrated Rural Development Program (TIRDEP).[3]

The second policy to affect GTZ's planning and implementation approach was the decree that villages be considered the basic political and planning unit. "Villagization" was a process by which scattered settlements and homesteads were regimented into clusters along roads. In Usambara and other highland areas, however, homes were left in traditional clan groups clustered on ridges throughout the mountains. Villagization there was more a matter of drawing village boundaries around existing homesteads, making many villages contiguous, with no space or obvious physical feature marking where one ends and the next begins. There was little impact on the spatial organization of Usambara beyond some nucleation as shops, bars, craft and service establishments, and some homes clustered around village centers and administrative offices. Villagization did, however, have a social impact. The influence of ruling clans had been steadily eroded, and government and party structures opened an alternative for local political organization. Each village has a democratic organ, an assembly of all village adults, and an executive organ, a village council consisting of a chair and twenty-four other elected members and a party-appointed secretary to monitor adherence to party policy. The council controls village political power (Asmerom 1986, 186). All households also belong to a structure of ten-house cells. Cells elect one member to voice concerns, organize participation in village projects, and meet regularly with the chair and secretary, if not the full council. This is not to suggest that clans have lost all influence. "The hierarchy of clan elders . . . involve themselves in social matters and the political offices of a village . . . deal with matters of general public importance and those matters . . . brought before them when no solution can be found by the elders" (von Mitzlaff 1988, 47). Clan and traditional influences are also widely represented in the new structures.

The integrated rural development program showed acute awareness of Usambara history and conditions. For all of Tanga, the goal
was increased agricultural output, but in Usambara, "The present
stagnation has to be broken. The task ahead is particularly difficult
since land productivity will have to be achieved while at the same
time soil protection and conservation measures will have to be carried
out in order to prevent a further deterioration of the ecological conditions" (TIRDEP 1975b, 444). Two projects were planned: a Livestock
Development Project (LDP) of fodder and tree nurseries, crop rotation,
and improved cattle breeding; and a Soil Erosion Control/Agro-
forestry Project (SECAP) to integrate cattle keeping, diversified farming, and planting trees on eroded land.

There was no implementation during the first five years. Rather,
GTZ continued its approach of thorough research, with discussion
papers from 1976 to 1978, prefeasibility studies in 1979, and full feasibility studies and plans of operation in 1980 (TIRDEP 1980, A1/15–16).
First efforts were to be small-scale and experimental. The livestock
project began in June 1980, and later merged with the soil erosion project in 1984 (Mdoe 1989, 4). Project staff (expatriates and Tanzanian
counterparts seconded from government service) selected villages that
were severely eroded, represented different agroecological zones, and
showed sufficient interest and cohesion to warrant inclusion. Staff
eventually introduced and tested a minimal technical package. On
hindsight, technologies by themselves proved far less important than
the process chosen for implementation.

Project Process

GTZ's research led to a project design aimed at building on the new
role of villages. Once staff selected villages, they asked leaders to call,
publicize, and convene meetings not to convince villagers to adopt
preset measures derived from research or mandate erosion control as
earlier efforts had, but to initiate discussion and dialogue. This was
central to project design and essential to long-term "self-determination
of people, ecological stability and sustainability, and economic viability" (TIRDEP 1985, 168). For about a year, the staff met with villagers to
discuss erosion and other problems, elicit village priorities, explore
advantages and disadvantages of possible project measures, and reach
consensus on problem causes and on types and amounts of participation needed for solutions.

Project documents and interviews with staff and villagers indicate
that the process of dialogue and consensus building, a distinctive feature of the program, has been key to project success. First, it gave the
basic orientation a significantly different nuance. Its goal of "stabilization

of the ecology of the West Usambaras" (SECAP 1988, 8) resembles aims of prior efforts, but the major issue is not defined simply or solely as erosion. The soil project focused on the human factor in the ecological equation. Villagers and staff placed erosion as the fifth factor in a chain of problems causing (4) lack of soil nutrients, organic matter, and moisture, causing (3) low and decreasing fertility; causing (2) low crop, fodder, and fuel yields; causing (1) the main problem, low farmer income (Huwe 1989, A1). Focusing on problems related to ecological degradation removed the conflict between the needs of the land and the needs of people, turned resistance into awareness that both sets of needs are interdependent, and enabled teamwork between staff and farmers to devise solutions to income problems that would protect and enhance the natural resource base. Second, the process brought consensus that the villagers themselves were responsible for their land and resources. As the dialogue continued, it became clear that success would require broad voluntary individual participation for on-farm components and village labor and land for others: closing eroded areas, establishing village woodlots, seedlots, nurseries, and demonstration plots. This led villagers and staff to create another structure under the village council, a Project Committee of six elected members to monitor participation, organize activities, and maintain dialogue with project staff. Insistence on village accountability reinforced the notion of responsibility. One policy, also agreed on by consensus, was to introduce no inputs unless participation was assured and to withdraw from villages that no longer met participation standards.

Project Components in Two Villages

In 1989, the dry/cold zone of Viti looked little like a target for both livestock and erosion efforts. Its four hamlets line ridges that frame a wide valley planted with vegetables and fed by a small channeled stream and irrigation ditches around each ten-meter-square plot. Mud dikes control flows where ditches join the stream, and a ridge rises into a forest reserve. Contour lines protect the slopes, and a village woodlot grows on a hill at one end of the village. It was only by touring the woodlot with the project's Zonal Extension Worker that evidence of former conditions became apparent. Grasses and creepers grew under thickly planted trees—some over ten meters tall and fifteen centimeters in diameter—but there were still patches of bare earth and rill and gully erosion scars to suggest how bad erosion had been and how long rehabilitation takes.

No radically new technologies were used to transform Viti. Instead of tie ridges or terraces to hold hill soils, SECAP used macro-contour lines (MCLs), permanent horizontal rows of crops planted twelve to sixteen meters apart on gentle slopes, six to twelve meters apart on moderate slopes, and four to six meters apart on steep ones. MCLs were planted with Guatemala grass to establish lines, slow runoff, and increase filtration rates (Scheinman et al. 1986, 20). Village meetings produced consensus that grazing livestock on post-harvest crop debris contributed to erosion by laying soils bare. Leguminous creepers and fodder bushes planted behind grasses in subsequent years to reinforce the lines gave MCLs a second function: to provide resources for zero-grazing (closing all fields and hills to grazing) and stall-feeding stock. This reduced the need to destock and helped integrate farming and animal husbandry, giving stock an alternative food source and providing farmers with a convenient fertilizer—manure from stalls.

To improve stock quality and milk yields while reducing cattle holdings, the livestock component supplied one purebred exotic bull per village and hybrid in-calf heifers to cross with local stock. The project also introduced animal traction and made oxen and carts available for purchase, to assist with transport needs. The bulls were funded by the project, but villages were required to provide labor, plant at least one hectare of fodder grass, and name a keeper to care for the bull and set breeding schedules before the project committed a bull and funded bull-pen construction. Farmers used cash or Tanzania Cooperative Rural Development Bank loans to buy heifers and cash to build stalls. Staff gave technical assistance in constructing bull boxes and stalls. The village, as a whole, attended village animal husbandry seminars and named trainees for Regional Livestock Institute seminars (SECAP 1988, 4). Those entering the animal traction component had to first make a down payment of 4,500 Tanzania shillings (Tsh.), commit to repay a 20,000 Tsh. loan in two years, and provide an ox of their own before receiving another ox and a cart (SECAP 1988, 16, 24).

To meet other needs, the project helped organize and stock seedling nurseries for lumber, domestic fuel, and fruit trees. Through the council and Project Committee, villagers set aside nursery land, designated severely eroded land for village woodlots, and named some members to be trained as nursery attendants and others as erosion-control extension workers. Cell leaders organized production and distribution of seedlings, which were then planted in the village woodlot, at homes, and as farm-plot borders. Fruits have since been added as local food sources and are sold in local periodic markets and to outside wholesalers for urban markets in Dar es Salaam, Tanga, Moshi, and Arusha. Pineapples and sunflowers were introduced as new cash crops, and maize cultivation seminars were held to increase yields and assist in pest control.

Areas on the road to Mbwei, another target village in the dry/ warm east-central zone, showed why erosion control and afforestation are concerns in Usambara. Hills were bleak and baked. Ridges, streaked with deep red erosion scars, had few if any trees. In contrast, well-tended streams one or two meters wide ran through the valleys, irrigated crops, and made startling strips of green that were fifty meters to two kilometers wide. The impact of the project on Mbwei was clear. On the road, women and children head-carried grass and fodder to cattle, sheep, and goats tethered beside their homes. MCLs lined some ridges. The village has a two-hectare woodlot planted with trees, interspersed with Guatemala grass seed plots and experimental maize plots, and fenced to keep out grazing stock and wood poachers. There is a nursery near the village office and a clean but empty cement bull shed at the large, well-maintained school. The bull had died of unknown causes.

According to those interviewed, village enforcement of district law has virtually halted open grazing and firewood harvesting. First offenses draw warnings. Second offenses bring pressure from village elders and officials. Third and later offenses become court cases with progressive fines—300 Tsh., 600 Tsh., and, if needed, a jail term in addition to fines and possible stock confiscation. The same sanctions apply to rules on reducing livestock numbers. Grazing was a particular problem in Mbwei. Large numbers of stock and added hillside stress from converting communal valley grazing lands into irrigated farm plots prompted project officials to add a range rehabilitation component. By 1988, work had advanced far enough to make plans to turn range management entirely over to the village, with project officials providing advice when needed (SECAP 1988, 26).

Project Progress

Overall, SECAP has made impressive gains. The project has developed a strategy of moving villages through five stages. Stage I villages have no project efforts. Stage II, forestry extension, begins with dialogue meetings and involves setting up a nursery, conducting agroforestry campaigns, establishing village leader cooperation, introducing project committees, and training nursery attendants. Stage III, two-year low-extension input, institutes zero grazing, a bull center, a fodder grass nursery, stall construction, and MCL components. Stage IV, five-year high-extension input, brings intensive extension on cropping systems, new crops, green manuring, and MCL improvement. Stage V post-project villages manage their own development, with monitoring and evaluation aid, low-extension input, and ad hoc SECAP support (SECAP 1988, 6).

The project was implemented in thirty-five villages during 1988—twenty-four Stage IV, nine Stage III, and two Stage II. In addition, eighty villages and seventy primary schools had seedling plots served by large zonal nurseries to ensure propagation, increase the variety and number of available tree and fodder species, and reduce transport time and cost (SECAP 1988, 2). The project forecasts that by 1992, twenty-seven villages will be at Stage V, thirty-one at Stage IV, and twenty-one at Stage III. All 126 villages were expected to reach Stage V by the year 2000 (SECAP 1988, 6, 37). In 1989, five more villages were already added. More importantly, the GTZ director and Tanzanian counterpart for the project stated that the impetus for participation had taken root and was spreading on its own. Stage I villages have adopted tree planting, contouring, and other methods without project aid.

Project Lessons

The project experience confirms the critical importance of the consensus process. It enabled people with a long history of resistance to develop not only common awareness of a problem and agreement on measures they were willing to try, but also a common commitment to and ownership of project efforts. SECAP overcame a problem in much of Tanzania's "participatory" planning. As one regional planning officer said, "Villagers taught us a lesson: You plan, you implement!" At the same time, dialogues helped staff appreciate the complexity of addressing environmental action in the context of peoples' survival strategies. Project components and inputs were tailored to local conditions, to competing demands for villager labor and resources, and to the broader economy.

After a 1987 review and in preparation for a comprehensive evaluation in 1990, project officials called for far more intensive two-way communication and training in communication and listening skills for all staff, especially village workers. Further, an expanded monitoring and evaluation unit was to put major emphasis on recording farmers' views and expectations (SECAP 1988, 13–14). The intent is to have all extension agents replace lecturing with dialogue and gear all meetings to monitoring "opinions, rumors, problems, and questions of the target group" (SECAP 1988, 37–38). In addition, the plan recommends farmers' defining and organizing themselves into interest groups (nonlivestock farmers, lowland farmers, pupils, and others) for specialized production measures and recommends creating subgroups by hamlets within villages to intensify extension contact.

Patience and rigorous research were perhaps as critical as building consensus. The project began with a premise that no problem so long in the making would yield to quick-fix efforts or could be adequately understood with solely technical assessments of its causes and dimensions. This was the reason for delaying implementation for five years of added, in-depth research. The scale and experimental nature of early efforts, an estimate that project implementation would take twenty years, along with changes in both inputs and methods during this period showed the flexibility and effectiveness of an "informed trial and error" approach. Supported by studies, reports, and evaluations, this approach highlighted another crucial lesson from SECAP's experience—the need to be rigorously self-critical.

In addition to this process, progress in implementation is also due to technical expertise in designing effective and carefully integrated inputs and methods that yield tangible and fairly immediate benefits. A 1989 study confirmed project assumptions and observations. In all zones and every aspect tested—various food and cash crops, dairy and other livestock products, fodder, and fuel wood—project methods and inputs significantly increased yields both per unit of land and per unit of labor. An MCL of a single grass line increased yields by 65 percent per hectare and 17 percent per labor unit. Full MCLs, no grazing, and manuring increased yields 85 percent per hectare and 34 percent per labor unit. Planting fruit trees increased gross output with almost no additional variable costs or labor inputs (Taube 1988, 13–15).

Selecting inputs that could be reproduced in villages or within the Tanga Region—village and zonal nurseries, local ox-cart production, shallow-well hand pumps—enhanced prospects for long-term sustainability, increased local capacities, and reduced the need for expensive foreign technologies and goods. Except for consultants needed for specific studies and evaluations, only three expatriates are planned as project staff—an administrator, an extension officer, and an agriculture officer. Each of these has a Tanzanian counterpart responsible for task completion. All other staff are locally trained and working in villages (SECAP 1988, 30). Since the main "staff" are the villagers themselves, the project has produced a detailed illustrated manual designed for village use (in Swahili, with an English version for use by audiences and development workers elsewhere) in addition to village seminars and extension services. To increase local capacities not only to manage existing components but also to establish an ongoing process for flexible and creative problem solving, the project is making a greater effort to assist village committees and councils to sharpen analytical, planning, and monitoring skills.

Challenges to Sustainability

Despite its effective approach, the project has not been perfect. In Mbwei in 1989, slopes yet to be contoured or planted still seemed to outnumber those rehabilitated. Work at Mbwei was difficult from the start. First efforts failed because farmers grazed stock in closed and newly planted areas. In 1982, SECAP started over with sociological and range studies and new dialogues before renewing implementation (Mdoe 1989, 6). Full village support has not yet been secured. In the nursery, each of the fifty-three ten-house cells is to keep and renew a ten-by-one-meter row of seedlings. Yet in August 1989, fewer than half the assigned rows had seedlings at all, and one-fourth of those were poorly tended. Asked how the village, in general, discusses and plans development, four elders said that besides mandated council, committee, and assembly meetings, villagers have to call meetings when people fail to report for nursery work as assigned by cell leaders and the Project Committee. Elsewhere, following its insistence on accountability, project work was halted in three villages where support was lacking, and three other villages were chosen (SECAP 1988, 3).

In Viti, challenges came from traditional influences. One clan flatly rejected all project activities and defied grazing restrictions. Their homestead borders the village woodlot. The zonal extension worker said that they graze stock in closed areas at night and erect thorn barriers to block government vehicles trying to pursue and apprehend them. In fact, new barriers had to be cleared to make a tour of the woodlot possible. Another clan waited until the village had cleared a valley plot for a communal farm, irrigated, manured, and planted it as a source of village development funds before claiming traditional title to the land. A court upheld clan ownership and gave the village no compensation.

Other problems arose. The regional ranch delivered poor-quality heifers (SECAP 1988, 16). A staff person stated that the project received culls and low-quality animals while prime stock went to people in other parts of the region and country with wealth, political influence, or ties to ranch personnel. High purchase and transport costs and loan defaults further prompted the end of the heifer component in 1987, and the focus shifted to the bull program to achieve stock improvement more reliably and at lower cost (SECAP 1988, 45). The project continues to address other technical problems, notably, discovering and developing a variety of MCL fodder, food, cash, and tree crop mixes to accommodate the broad range of soil and climate conditions and farmers' socioeconomic needs throughout Usambara (SECAP 1988, 5; Mdoe 1989, 22–25; Taube 1988). The emphasis on flexibility and experimentation has led the project to develop its own extensive research component, in addition to cooperating with the University of Hohenheim, the Silviculture Research Institute at Lushoto, the Tanzania Agricultural Research Organization, the Southern African Development

Coordinating Conference, and the Centro de Agricultura Tropical (Huwe 1989, 5).

A serious problem is uneven benefit distribution along class and gender lines, reflecting the continuing influence of the historical, structural roots of the crisis. In Viti, out of nineteen men who were asked who benefited from the project components, only five (two of whom were village officials) acknowledged the entire community. There was little agreement regarding the nature and distribution of project benefits. One man stated, "People say the leaders 'ate the money' but projects failed because people had no expertise."

Project studies confirm the uneven distribution of benefits. Although stating that it aimed at "virtually all farmers . . . [n]everthe-less, Project activities had to be biased initially toward the livestock component . . . and . . . attracted those farmers who could take risks more easily. Therefore, the livestock bias turned out to be a handicap in the communication with farmers with varying resource endow-ments" (SECAP 1988, 2). Finding a correlation between SECAP compo-nent adoption and farmer age, education, wealth, and social standing, a 1987 study concluded that "[o]nly those who can survive failure, both socially and economically, consider taking the risk" (Woytek 1987, in von Mitzlaff 1988, 53). Interviews suggest that wealth and willingness to take risks are also linked to positions of power that do, in fact, give privileged access to benefits. A former vil-lage chair was the first bull attendant, among the first in the heifer program, and the first to acquire an ox and cart. Interviews and other research also suggest that traditional power, prestige, and wealth give access to power within government structures, making the vil-lage council and the programs and resources it oversees vehicles for wealthy, traditional, party, and government elites (Asmerom 1986, 191–92).

Even among those who cited uneven distribution of benefits from the livestock component, there was agreement that erosion control and tree planting benefited all villagers. Thirteen of nineteen men inter-viewed said that they had fruit trees as a result of the project. Of the six remaining, four had government jobs or craft or service occupa-tions to supplement farm income and demand labor. For women, the impression and reality of uneven distribution of benefits were greater. Of twenty-one women in Viti interviewed in 1989, only six stated that SECAP benefited all villagers. More importantly, although nearly all men named some personal benefit from the project, eight women said that they received none at all, and eight said that they gained from more work and better rains. One person bought land with the stipend earned from working as a research assistant in a study on women's participation in the project. Only one very articulate, industrious, elder widow benefited directly from the project; she was able to buy a heifer, build a modern stall, and become keeper of Viti's second bull.

Many of these responses are consistent with studies and evaluations of the project. Colonial and postcolonial changes have intensified women's traditional disadvantage in the control of land and capital. They no longer inherit land (Fleuret 1980, 73), and young women who work on family plots to add to household income or their dowries do not have access to parental land once they marry (von Mitzlaff 1988, 24–25). The Shambaa still farm scattered plots to reduce risk of crop failure. The plots given to women for household subsistence are most often on steep slopes; the men farm moderate slopes for food and valley bottoms for cash crops (von Mitzlaff 1988, 40). Women farm smaller, more remote, and less fertile plots on steeper slopes, requiring MCLs at closer intervals, which increases labor and decreases crop areas. They own few, if any, cattle, have less incentive to grow grass and fodder, and—with manuring done mostly on valley and more proximate plots where profit margins are much higher—have less access to additional labor or capital inputs for plot improvement (Taube 1988, 20). Cultural mores further impede women's participation, in that they are not expected to speak out in mixed public meetings or argue with men. Only four of twenty-six project villages have women as extension workers, and since it is considered improper for men to visit unmarried women or to visit married women in their husbands' absence, they generally receive less information from extension sources. With little access to formal education and political participation, women are effectively excluded at the individual level (von Mitzlaff 1988, 47–53).

There are other challenges to sustainability. Villagers do not yet have the planning and administrative skills to carry forward on their own, despite manuals and intensive training for village councils and project committees (SECAP 1988, 37). Although the structure for integration with other government activities exists through a project steering committee, it is not fully functional. The project is unique in that it has its own planning process, budget, and schedule. Thus its relative autonomy from other government programs adds tensions and creates expectations that are often unrealistic. Government planning is dominated by national priorities that are linked to the agendas of international funding institutions and aid agencies. Given this context, national-level planning and budgetary processes provide little room for careful scrutiny of local needs.

Tanzanian economic conditions and the residual impact of long-term factors further challenge the project. Those with the most to gain from erosion control and other components—poor farmers, particularly women—have the least margin for risk and are the last to adopt innovations. Attems found it "incomprehensible" that Shambaa farmers did not work longer and harder to increase yields and reduce erosion by timely weeding and terracing, and concluded that they were apathetic and bound to tradition and needed the incentive of a profitable crop to break stagnation (Attems 1968, 163–70). The GTZ's analysis is less simplistic. It recognizes that even profitable crops must be hauled to urban markets on poor roads that are impassable during the rains, in vehicles owned by outside wholesalers who keep prices low (TIRDED 1985, 172). Lack of transport and adequate markets have already led some farmers to uproot fruit trees and plant subsistence crops. A mid-1980s national maize self-sufficiency campaign made things worse when farmers uprooted bananas as well.

Crop choice and labor allocation reflect a deeper problem. GTZ studies note high labor migration rates—50 percent of Usambara males aged seventeen to thirty-five (TIRDED 1985, 168). The project has yet to examine the impact of migration on household income strategies, wage labor, labor availability for erosion control, and plot improvement and incorporate these new realities into its programs. It may well be that high participation rates of wealthier farmers occur because poorer farmers are hired to work on their wealthy neighbors' lands, thereby neglecting their own plots. Problems are compounded for women, in that husbands and grown sons who migrate or seek wage labor leave behind additional work on the plots. Even "successful" examples from the project involve more work for the wives whose husbands adopt project components. They need to carry fodder and water for cattle as well as work harder to harvest and process higher crop yields (von Mitzlaff 1988, 60).

The project addresses labor and income issues only indirectly by noting the lack of linkages between agriculture and industry. It proposes experimentation with simple processing activities—manufacturing jams, wine, and spirits—and better use of labor and skills in carpentry, brick making, and local production of agricultural tools, seed, and other inputs, similar to Nutman's 1945 proposals for the region. In some ways, Usambara is an extreme case of the structural disarticulation of Tanzania, with no alternatives open for nonfarm employment other than a few entrepreneurial endeavors—tailoring, shopkeeping, shoe repair, and carpentry for men; basket weaving, pottery, and retailing at periodic markets for women. Although these are important survival strategies for households, they provide no deeper link to the national economy.

Summary

Strictly speaking, SECAP is not a case of spontaneous, self-directed, local mobilization to protect the environment and meet local livelihood needs. It may be something more unusual: an example of external agents—a foreign donor working with host government structures and personnel—functioning as a limited resource and effective catalyst for grassroots communal and individual action to undo centuries of ecological abuse and dysfunctional political and economic development. Nothing in Usambara's protracted history of marginalization, involution, and intensifying differentiation suggests that such action could have arisen internally. Nor did Tanzanian development policy and performance show much promise. Effective action to address the crisis in Usambara ecology and economy could have come only with outside assistance. Though external in origin, the project is an effort that genuinely aims at local determination, self-reliance, mobilization, and social learning. Project practice does adhere, within limits, to its participatory rhetoric.

The soil erosion control project has a number of strengths. Throughout its history, it remained experimental and flexible to meet local needs and conditions. It was thorough and realistic in assessing economic, political, institutional, cultural, and ecological opportunities and constraints and recognized the need for a long-term approach to complex issues with deep historical roots. Local needs were the starting point, and local participation and responsibility are project cornerstones. Rather than trying to ignore or supplant existing traditional and state structures, the project attempted to make the best of opportunities opened up by these institutions and, when possible, to limit or correct for areas in which structures impeded broad-based participation and popular support. Party and government structures served as entries to villages. Traditional influence gave added weight to communal decisions but in some cases undermined project efforts. Despite its focus on farmers and villages, the project recognizes that it is far from finished in establishing its local base and institutional capacities. It is aware that sustainability depends on dialogue not just to begin the program but to give it an enduring foundation.

Project officials appear to be aware of the many obstacles to long-term sustainability and have incorporated that awareness into the current plan of operation. In 1989, a Tanzanian woman was hired as project officer and an expatriate consultant was put in place to address program deficiencies in women's participation. Project staff are aware of other gaps. To date, there has been almost no collaboration with churches and other private voluntary or nongovernmental organization groups, which have longer experience in the villages, deeper roots in the communities, and a number of completed and ongoing development efforts.

SECAP may yet fail. Issues of population pressure and land distribution have yet to be addressed in any meaningful way. The government proposal to resettle 30,000 farmers in less densely populated areas lacks the resources for implementation, including new roads, schools, water supplies, and health care facilities. Even with adequate resources, relocation would be no less a palliative than the 1964 forest reserve opening. Nor would population control without economic diversification and restructuring correct root causes of undue pressure on fragile land. Considering erosion control and livelihood needs apart from traditional social formations and national political and economic conditions and structures would be a return to the isolationism and analytical myopia that caused involution in Usambara through internal politics and colonial and postcolonial development policies. The project already recognizes it may have intensified gender and class differentiation through its actions.

Ironically, even the short-term sustainability of the project was in question in 1989. Prior to German reunification, a delegation from Bonn informed GTZ that due to domestic economic conditions and political pressures, the home government was requesting a five-year timetable for withdrawal from long-term development aid commitments. This leads to the more urgent issue of not what the project may teach GTZ or outside observers, but what Usambara villagers and leaders and Tanzanian officials and development workers have learned, how deeply the commitment to local responsibility has penetrated, and how self-reliant and self-directed the people meant to benefit have become. The best hope for people who have participated in the project is that the awareness, dialogue, cohesion, and confidence developed by taking promising first steps toward ecological rehabilitation will grow into a foundation for social, economic, and political change.

Notes

Research for this study was conducted in 1989 as part of a Fulbright Dissertation Fellowship study of Tanzanian regional planning. Sources include Tanzanian and expatriate background, planning, and evaluation documents; site visits; and interviews with villagers and project and government officials. The generous cooperation and warm hospitality of Tanzanians and expatriates, all doing more than could have been expected, made the research possible and personally and professionally rewarding.

1. In addition to sources cited, data on Usambara topography, ecology, and soils are taken from Johansson (1988a, 1988b) and Johansson and Msangi (1988); regional development plans for Tanga; Operational Navigational Chart ONC M-5 (St. Louis: Defense Mapping Aerospace Center, 1981); and field observations.
2. The main source for British policy in Usambara is Watson (1972).
3. In an anomaly of Tanzanian regional planning, urban centers were "integrated out" of regions and placed under another government ministry,

primarily because of their projected role in expanded and diffused industrial development. For an analysis of Tanzanian industrial policy, see Luttrell 1986.

References

Arnold, David. 1980. "External Factors in the Partition of East Africa." In Kaniki 1980, 51–85.

Asmerom, H. K. 1986. "The Tanzanian Village Council: Agency of Rural Development or Merely a Device of State Penetration into the Periphery?" *Cahiers du CEDAF* 2(4): 177–97.

Attems, M. 1968. "The Agriculture in the Usambara Mountains, Tanzania: From Subsistence to Market Production." In *Smallholder Farming and Smallholder Development in Tanzania*, edited by Hans Ruthenberg. Munich: Weltforum-Verlag.

Bowles, B. D. 1980. "The Political Economy of Colonial Tanganika 1939–1961." In Kaniki 1980, 164–91.

Cliffe, Lionel. 1977. "Rural Class Formation in East Africa." *Journal of Peasant Studies* 4(2): 195–224.

Cliffe, Lionel, Peter Lawrence, William Luttrell, Shem Migot-Adholla, and John S. Saul, eds. 1975. *Rural Cooperation in Tanzania*. Dar es Salaam: Tanzania Publishing House.

Cliffe, Lionel, William Luttrell, and J. E. Moore. 1975a. "The Development Crisis in the Western Usambaras." In Cliff et al. 1975, 145–73.

———. 1975b. "Socialist Development in Tanzania Agriculture—Its Application to the Western Usambaras." In Cliff et al. 1975, 505–37.

Coulson, Andrew. 1982. *Tanzania: A Political Economy*. Oxford: Clarendon Press.

Feierman, Steven. 1974. *The Shambaa Kingdom: A History*. Madison: University of Wisconsin Press.

———. 1990. *Peasant Intellectuals: Anthropology and History in Tanzania*. Madison: University of Wisconsin Press.

Fleuret, Patrick. 1980. "Sources of Material Inequality in Lushoto District, Tanzania." *African Studies Review* 23(3): 69–87.

Huwe, Claus. 1989. "Description of the Research Section of SECAP." Lushoto, Tanzania: TIRDEP-SECAP.

Iliffe, John. 1971. "Agricultural Change in Modern Tanganyika: An Outline History." *Historical Association of Tanzania Paper No. 10*. Nairobi: East African Publishing House.

———. 1979. *A Modern History of Tanganyika*. Cambridge: Cambridge University Press.

Johansson, Lars. 1988a. "The Chambogo Programme: An Evaluation of Early Implementation." Lushoto, Tanzania: TIRDEP-SECAP.

———. 1988b. "Forestry Strategy: SECAP Phase III 1988–1992." Lushoto, Tanzania: TIRDEP-SECAP.

Johansson, Lars, and T. H. Msangi. 1988. "Management Plan for the Chambogo Forest Reserve." Lushoto, Tanzania: TIRDEP-SECAP.

Kaniki, M. H. Y., ed. 1980. *Tanzania Under Colonial Rule*. London: Longman.

Lewis, A. L., and L. Berry. 1988. *African Environments and Resources*. Manchester, Mass: Allen and Unwin.

Luttrell, William J. 1986. *Post-Capitalist Industrialization: Planning Economic Independence in Tanzania.* New York: Praeger.

Maliyamkono, T. L., and M. S. D. Bagachwa. 1990. *The Second Economy in Tanzania.* Eastern and Southern African Universities Research Programme, Dar es Salaam. London: James Curry.

Martin, Phyllis, and Patrick O'Meara, eds. 1986. *Africa.* 2d ed. Bloomington: Indiana University Press.

Mdoe, Michael. 1989. "Report on the Mbwei Scheme." Lushoto, Tanzania: TIRDEP-SECAP.

Munson, Patrick J. 1986. "Africa's Prehistoric Past." In Martin and O'Meara 1986, 43–63.

Rapp, Anders, Len Berry, and Paul H. Temple. 1972. "Soil Erosion and Sedimentation in Tanzania—The Project." *Geografiska Annaler* 54 A(3–4): 105–9.

Rodney, Walter. 1980. "The Political Economy of Colonial Tanganika, 1890–1930." In Kaniki 1980, 128–63.

Ruthenberg, Hans. 1964. *Agricultural Development in Tanganyika.* Berlin: Springer-Verlag.

Scheinman, David, Charles Mchome, Tina Eames, and Alice Gomes. 1986. "Caring for the Land of the Usambaras: A Guide to Preserving the Environment Through Agriculture, Agroforestry and Zero Grazing." Lushoto, Tanzania, and Eschborn, Germany: TIRDEP-SECAP and GTZ.

SECAP. 1988. "Plan of Operation: Phase III 1988–1992." Tanga, Tanzania: Tanga Regional Development Office and TIRDEP.

Sheriff, Abdul M. H. 1980. "Tanzanian Societies at the Time of Partition." In Kaniki 1980, 11–50.

Shorter, Aylward. 1974. *East African Societies.* London: Routledge and Kegan Paul.

Taube, Guenther. 1988. "An Economic Analysis of SECAP's Basic Recommendations for Soil Erosion Control." Lushoto, Tanzania: TIRDEP-SECAP.

Temu, A. J. 1980. "Tanzanian Societies and Colonial Invasion, 1875–1907." In Kaniki 1980, 86–127.

TIRDEP. 1975a. *Tanga Regional Development Plan 1975–1980, Volume 1: Summary.* Tanga, Tanzania: Tanga Regional Development Office.

———. 1975b. *Tanga Regional Development Plan 1975–1980, Volume 2: Analysis of Existing Situation and Outline of Development Strategy.* Tanga, Tanzania: Tanga Regional Development Office.

———. 1975c. *Tanga Regional Development Plan 1975–1980, Volume 3: Appendices.* Tanga, Tanzania: Tanga Regional Development Office.

———. 1980. *Experience with Regional Planning and Project Implementation in Tanga Region.* Tanga, Tanzania, and Eschborn, Germany: Tanga Regional Development Office and Gesellschaft für Technische Zusammenarbeit (GTZ).

———. 1985. *Regional Development Strategy, Tanga Region.* Tanga, Tanzania: Tanga Regional Development Office.

von Mitzlaff, Ulrike. 1988. "Women Farmers or Farmers' Wives? The Soil Erosion Control/Agroforesty Project (SECAP) and the Problem of the Involvement of Women." Lushoto, Tanzania: TIRDEP-SECAP.

Watson, John R. 1972. "Conservation Problems, Policies and the Origins of the Mlalo Basin Rehabilitation Scheme, Usambara Mountains, Tanzania." *Geografiska Annaler* 54 A(3–4): 221–25.

TWO

REGENERATING THE GUM ARABIC ECONOMY

Local-Level Resource Management in Northern Senegal

MARK SCHOONMAKER FREUDENBERGER

POLICYMAKERS IN SAHELIAN WEST AFRICA are currently experimenting with ways of devolving resource management—a traditional prerogative of state institutions—to user groups in rural societies.[1] The assumption of both state and nongovernmental developmental organizations is that if control over natural resources is transferred from the central state administrative bodies to appropriate local-level institutions, the management of natural resources can be made more efficient, more sustainable, and more responsive to local needs.

Policymakers often assume that the sparse woodlands of the Sahel are ecologically degraded and economically marginal resources. From the perspective of the rural populations that live in and around these forested zones, these areas are in fact vital and diverse sources of food, construction materials, firewood, medicines, and forage for livestock. Within Sahelian developmental circles, it is still said that forest users are selfish, undisciplined, and rapacious exploiters of dwindling resources. Yet within the past few years, there has been a growing awareness that rural populations possess a considerable store of indigenous knowledge about managing their environment in an ecologically sound fashion (Dupré 1991; Richards 1985). The challenge for planners is to find ways of identifying and encouraging these local initiatives and making them the cornerstone of the new microterritorial approaches emerging in the Sahel.

This chapter explores the numerous constraints and limited opportunities confronted by a particular resource user group in trying to protect, conserve, and regenerate the *Acacia senegal*, a forest resource that is central to its livelihood strategy (Lawry 1990). The *Acacia senegal* produces gum arabic and a host of other by-products that are collected in many parts of northern Senegal by black Maures, descendants of captives who gathered gum 400 years ago for Arab-Berber merchants in southern Mauritania. This minority population in the Department of Linguere in northern Senegal (see Figures 2.1 and 2.2) continues to extract gum arabic using sophisticated and ecologically sound collection practices.

Today the Maures' once successful gum arabic collection is threatened by rapidly changing ecological, economic, and social conditions. This case study reviews the historical foundations of the gum arabic economy in the Department of Linguere, identifies the variety of forces that threaten its future, and suggests measures that might be taken to facilitate the Maures' own strategies to protect and indeed revive the gum arabic collection system.[2]

Gum Arabic and the *Acacia Senegal* Tree

The *Acacia senegal* is a small, scrubby tree found in a semiarid belt that runs eastward from Senegal through northern Nigeria into Sudan and south into parts of eastern and southern Africa. The leguminous nitrogen-fixing tree is a pioneer species that thrives on sandy soils and 150 to 850 millimeters of rainfall (von Maydell 1986). The hardy tree has been employed extensively in reforestation projects throughout the Sahel because of its ability to restore soil fertility and its multipurpose uses. During the hottest months of the dry season, a saplike gum exudes naturally from fissures and wounds in the tree and hardens over the course of a few weeks into shiny amber-colored globules. The physiological causes of exudation are not fully understood, though it appears that it is a response to various stress factors such as high temperatures, insect wounds, and cuts made into the bark (Mouret 1988). Higher and more regular yields can be induced by tapping the tree at precise periods in the dry season.

International Market for Gum Arabic

Rural populations have long used the *Acacia senegal* and its by-products for a wide variety of purposes ranging from fodder to food. The small amount of gum arabic presently sold in local West African markets is employed primarily to starch clothing, though gum is still consumed as a famine food in some parts of the Sahel. The majority of gum collected is exported to northern Europe. From the mid-eighteenth to mid-nineteenth centuries, gum arabic was an indispensable product for the European textile industry. Gum also entered into the production

Figure 2.1 West Africa

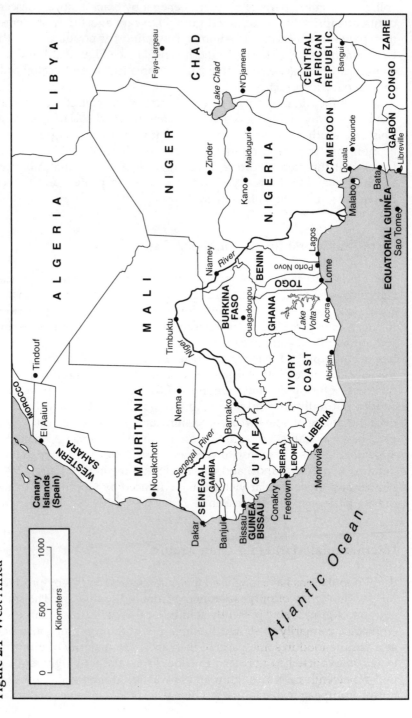

Figure 2.2 Northern Senegal and Department of Linguere

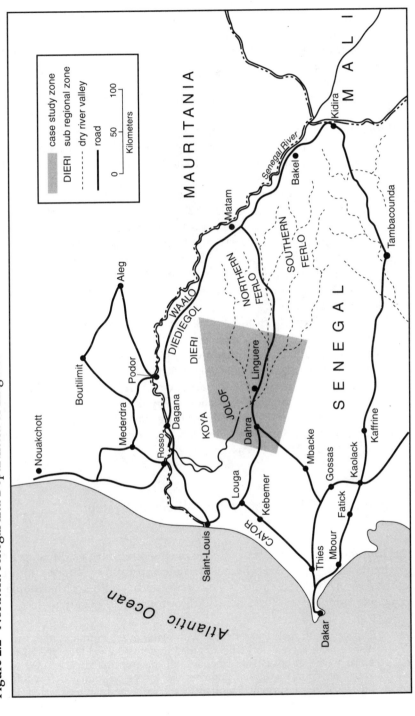

of paints, drugs, and certain foods (Glicksman and Sand 1973). Competition between the nascent industrial countries for access to the West African markets was so intense in the late eighteenth century that "Gum Wars" were fought off the coast of Mauritania between the navies of England, Holland, and France (Delcourt 1952).

In the early seventeenth century, European royal chartered companies started to barter for gum arabic collected in the Trarza and Brakna emirates of present-day southern Mauritania (Webb 1984). From the late seventeenth century until the 1870s, gum arabic was one of the most important exports of French trading interests stationed at isolated posts along the semiarid coast of Mauritania and along the banks of the Senegal river.

Exports increased from 500 to 600 tons a year in the early 1600s to around 2,000 tons a year by the 1830s. Gum arabic captured an even more significant share of the export economy after the Atlantic slave trade was halted in the early nineteenth century. Despite the emergence of the groundnut trade in Senegambia in the mid 1800s, exports of gum arabic from what is now Mauritania, Senegal, and Mali rose steadily throughout the colonial and early independence period to peak at an all-time high of approximately 14,000 metric tons in 1971 (Figure 2.3). Exports from Senegal fell dramatically after the drought of 1968–74 and now fluctuate between 500 and 1,000 metric tons a year, though official statistics are of questionable value (Figure 2.4). Seventy to 80 percent of the 50,000 to 60,000 metric tons of gum placed annually on the international market comes from the Sudan. For this reason, the marketing policies adopted by the Sudan and its principal North American and European trading partners strongly affect the dynamics of the Senegalese market and local production relations (U.N. Sahelian Office 1983).

Evolution of the Gum Arabic Collection System in Northern Senegal

From the early fifteenth to the late nineteenth centuries, Muslim merchants (*zawaya*) of Arab-Berber descent sent captive laborers into the interior of the Trarza and Brakna emirates in southern Mauritania to collect gum. The explorer René Caillié observed in 1824 that:

> The slaves fill their leather sacks with water every morning, and, furnished with a great forked stick, they traverse the fields in search of gum; as the gum bearing trees are all thorny, this stick is used to knock off from the higher branches the lumps of gum which would otherwise not be reached by hand. . . . The superintending *marabout*

Figure 2.3 Combined Gum Arabic Exports from Senegal, Mauritania, and Mali: 1860–1980

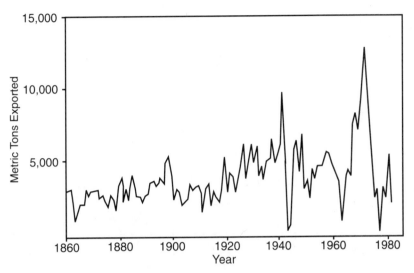

Source: Banque Centrale des Etats de l'Afrique de l'Ouest, *La Gomme dite Arabique* (Dakar: Banque Centrale des Etats de l'Afrique de l'Ouest, 1960); United Nations Sudano-Sahelian Office/International Trade Centre, *The Gum Arabic Market and the Development of Production* (New York: UNSO/ITC, 1983).

receives a portion of the gum; the slaves work five days for the master, and the sixth for the superintendent, who thus comes in for the greater part of the produce. (Caillié 1830, 49)

During its heyday in the eighteenth and nineteenth centuries, the trade in gum arabic dominated the political and economic affairs of the French and English commercial outposts along the coast of the West African Sahel. Much to the consternation of the French merchants in Saint-Louis du Sénégal, the Trarza emirs tightly controlled trade with the Jolof, a Wolof empire that is now largely encompassed by the Department of Linguere. In order to restrict the supply of gum arabic to the market and hence increase its price, the emirs set up camps of warriors to pillage caravanners attempting to engage in commerce in the Jolof. The French conquest of the Jolof in 1890 was undertaken principally to open the region to trade in gum arabic and other agricultural commodities (Barrows 1974; Charles 1977; McLane 1986).

Following the military pacification of the region, the colonial administration built an infrastructure of roads, wells, and a single-gauge railroad in an effort to draw the resident Wolof cultivators and Fulbe pastoralists into gum collection. Few were lured into the collection of

Figure 2.4 Gum Arabic Marketed in Senegal: 1940–88

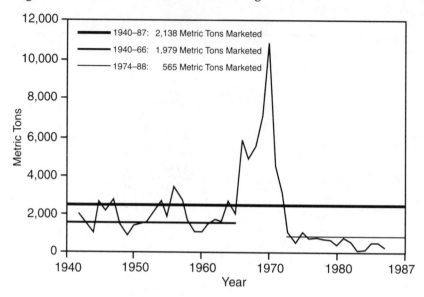

Source: République du Sénégal, Direction des Eaux, Forêts, et Chasse, *Rapports Annuels, 1942–87*.

gum until the administration instituted a policy of requiring taxes to be paid in cash. European merchants also coerced villagers to collect gum arabic through debt peonage. Villagers were required to pay back loans granted at usurious rates in gum arabic. By the 1910s, gum arabic had become one of the principal cash crops exchanged for overvalued imported items.

The expansion of the market for gum arabic stimulated the emergence of new labor and property rights regimes. While the colonial power and merchant interests created the market infrastructure, the Wolof political elite organized the collection of gum arabic. The *Acacia senegal* rapidly evolved from being a use-value species, long employed by the Fulbe and Wolof for livestock forage and timber, into an exchange-value species highly esteemed for the readily marketable gum. This brought about a transformation in labor relations and in the tree tenure systems that determined access rights and resource management practices.

Gum Arabic Collection System in the Department of Linguere

During the strife-torn decades of colonial conquest, gum collectors from the Trarza and Brakna emirates (many of them captives or descendants of the Bidan servile labor force) fled into the Jolof. In this new frontier, this population of what are now known in Senegal as black Maures replicated the traditional gum collection practices long employed in southern Mauritania. Even though the colonial administration had stripped the traditional Wolof leadership of much of its military authority, the last paramount chief (*bourba*) still controlled the allocation of many natural resources. The decisions of the *bourba* Bouna Ndiaye held sway not only among his own ethnic group but also over the resident Fulbe pastoralist populations and newcomers such as the Maures (Ba 1975; Santoir, 1983).

The Jolof *bourba* granted gum collection rights to the Wolof nobility, Wolof farmers, and—somewhat surprisingly—the newly arrived Maures. The densest concentrations of *Acacia senegal* located nearest to the market villages of Yang-Yang and Mbeuleukhé were reserved for the nobility. Teams of Maures were engaged by the Wolof patrons to harvest and transport gum arabic to the market centers. Wolof cultivators collected gum in a second zone found primarily around the villages of the Ferlo River Valley. Heads of lineages received gum collection rights from the *bourba* and then allocated subsections to relatives and dependents. In the far northeastern reaches of the Jolof (about seventy kilometers east of Yang-Yang, near the present-day village of Labgar), the *bourba* granted seasonal collection rights to the Maures. Without the intercession of Muslim clerics, who were advisors and religious counselors to the court of the *bourba*, the low-status Maure gum collectors could not have obtained access to the dense concentrations of *Acacia senegal* in this new frontier. In return, the clerics expected religious tithes from the gum collectors amounting to one-tenth or more of the gum harvest.

The expansion of the market for gum arabic stimulated the creation of seasonally determined rights to the *Acacia senegal*, a feature common to Sahelian tree tenure systems. At the start of the dry season in early October, the Maure gum collectors left their villages in the western Jolof to camp out in the eastern territories for the duration of the collection season. This seasonal migration did not interfere with the pastoralist activities of the Fulbe, who customarily occupied the area during the rainy season and used the *Acacia senegal* for firewood, poles, and occasionally as forage for sheep and goats. The Fulbe and their livestock had already vacated the zone by the time the Maures arrived, since the shallow rainy season pools (*mares*) used for watering livestock had dried up and the pastoralists had migrated either north to the Senegal River or south to the Sin and Saloum river basins. Within this seasonally "empty" space, the Maures found their occupational niche.

The first Maure occupants of the eastern Jolof divided the territory into sections that were then exploited by teams of *sourga* (tenants or sharecroppers) engaged to collect gum for the duration of the season. These first occupants were recognized as "patrons" vested with territorial rights of gum collection that had been allocated to them by the Wolof *bourba*. The *sourga* labor arrangement is a form of sharecropping found throughout much of the Sahel in which the head of the work unit provides food to dependent relatives, slaves, or migrant laborers in return for labor provided during a specified period of time.[3] Gum collecting *sourga* were generally young Maure men who turned over roughly three-fourths of the harvest to the patron or collected gum for him on five out of seven days in return for food and water for the entire season. *Sourga* returning to the same patron year after year gradually obtained permanent use rights to clearly delineated areas. The patrons tended to cede collection rights to relatives and friends as gifts, though trees were also loaned out on a seasonal basis.

The scarce factor of production was not the *Acacia senegal* itself but rather the supply of labor required for gum collection, the transport of water and gum by camel caravans to the distant gum collection zones, and the preparation of food. Although women and children rarely collected gum, they were essential to the smooth functioning of the system. Women were responsible for processing millet into a fast food known as *sahkal* (pounded and steamed millet couscous), drying meat, and sewing leather sacks used for the transport of water and gum. Women and children filled these water sacks for the camel caravans returning periodically to base camps for provisions. The collectors gave the largest gum balls to the women who had assisted them. The women in turn bartered this gum for milk from the Fulbe and merchandise from the itinerant traders who traversed the countryside.

Resource Management Practices of the Maures

Gum collectors tapped the *Acacia senegal* and used fire to induce higher yields and spread out the demand for labor.[4] Both these techniques were severely sanctioned by the colonial forestry service, yet a closer investigation of the practices shows a strong commitment by the Maures to resource conservation. The gum collectors had every reason to make judicious resource use decisions, since they depended on continuous exploitation of the same trees each season. Tapping consists of removing strips of bark with a long-handled ax and then waiting several weeks for the gum to exude from the wound. The Maures used fire to create two gum collecting seasons, one during the hottest weeks of the early dry season and another in the sweltering months before the arrival of the new rains. Fires were set in the early dry season when grasses were still somewhat green, especially in lowland depressions. Those trees singed by the fires were tapped in the first season: those left unburnt in the lowland depressions were tapped during the second season, thus dividing peak labor demand into two seasons.

The Maures employed a number of management practices (many of them still used today by experienced collectors) to conserve the *Acacia senegal* from the effects of tapping and bush fires. Proper tapping consisted of scraping off only the superficial layers of the bark without scarring the white wood. No branch was ever tapped in the same spot in consecutive years. Fires probably contributed to the regeneration of the pioneer species by removing the dense undergrowth of competing weeds and hence promoting the growth of tree seedlings. Colonial scientists were eventually forced to admit the validity of many of these practices. After several seasons of continuous exploitation, the *Acacia senegal* were placed in "reserve" so that the mature trees could recover from the physiological stresses associated with tapping and fire. Many of these techniques, reflecting centuries of experience, could be usefully employed in contemporary reforestation and natural forest management programs where sustainable management of the species has been a recurrent problem.

Introduction of Boreholes in Northern Senegal

Other than the gum arabic trade, the Jolof generated few other exports of commercial value. Groundnut exports were marginal due to the low and erratic rainfall of the region, and the Fulbe refused to sell their livestock. The scanty colonial records on the Jolof suggest that gum arabic exports ranged from 500 to 700 metric tons a year. Unfavorable climatic conditions, such as drought, reduced yields in some years; locusts sometimes consumed the harvest; unseasonably late rains dissolved the water-soluble gum in others. The lack of water during the long dry season kept the Jolof at the periphery of the colonial economy and effectively protected the niche economy that the Maures had so expertly developed.

All this was to change when, in the late 1930s, French hydrologists discovered the Maestrichtian aquifer, a massive and seemingly inexhaustible source of fresh water underlying a large part of northern Senegal. Following World War II, the administration built an extensive network of 200- to 300-meter deep boreholes, powered with diesel pumps, throughout northern Senegal at intervals of twenty-five to thirty-five kilometers, roughly the distance livestock could walk in one day. Ever since the conquest of the Jolof, the administration had tried to force the Fulbe to sell livestock to the rapidly growing urban markets of the colony. The Fulbe had successfully resisted most attempts to commercialize the sector. The authorities initially foresaw the construction of the boreholes as a way to facilitate the transport of livestock by hoof to urban centers. As one administrator recalled:

> [W]e recognized straight away that the deep boreholes were the dream technology which would permit all the animal trails in the sylvo-pastoral zone of the Sahel to be bordered by modern, well-equipped drinking troughs. One can imagine the borehole as destined to satisfy the water needs of these transhumance herds in much the same way that train station cafeterias or drink stands meet the needs of rail travelers. (Territoire du Sénégal 1956, 41)

The boreholes also promised to resolve a burgeoning conflict over natural resources. Colonial development policies had long favored the expansion of groundnut cultivation zones into the sparsely populated though higher-rainfall areas of eastern Senegal. This put pastoralists, who had a long tradition of grazing this area, in conflict with the Islamic Mouride sect, who moved into the same region to cultivate groundnuts (Pélisser 1966; Barral 1982; Copans 1988). Suddenly the administration found itself drawn into violent disputes between the Fulbe and the Mourides. By constructing boreholes in what was considered to be the largely unoccupied desert of the northern Jolof, the authorities had hoped to open the region to year-round pastoralist exploitation, which would in turn reduce land use competition in the new groundnut cultivation zones further south. Within a couple of years after the construction of the boreholes, the Fulbe did indeed radically alter their transhumance and settlement patterns. Small Fulbe camps sprouted up during the dry season within a radius of fifteen to twenty-five kilometers of the boreholes (Barral 1982).

For the Maure gum collectors, however, the introduction of the new water technology was disastrous. The complementary relationship between pastoralism and gum collecting rapidly disintegrated as the Fulbe opted to remain year-round in the northern Jolof. Young Fulbe herders now traversed the territory during the dry season after the Maures had tapped their trees, and some began furtively to collect the tempting amber-colored balls. Although initially this was not a serious issue, it foreshadowed events to come as the competition for resources increased.

Transformation of the Maure Collection System
during the Great Sahelian Drought

Exports of gum arabic from Senegal averaged roughly 1,300 metric tons a year from 1962 to 1970, not substantially different from amounts exported in the late colonial era. The Great Sahelian Drought of 1968–74 profoundly altered this relatively stable situation. Average annual precipitation plummeted (Figure 2.5). Throughout northern Senegal, the severe drought led to a major die-off of the *Acacia senegal*. Studies conducted by the International Biological Program at Fété-Olé and elsewhere in northern Senegal showed that between 1969 and 1972, roughly 70 percent of the *Acacia senegal* perished (Poupon, 1973, 1977).[5] The commercial impact of the die-off was spectacularly reflected in government statistics. From 1940 to 1988, roughly 2,000 metric tons of gum arabic were marketed annually in Senegal. Between 1974 and 1988, the average dropped to a mere 565 metric tons (see Figure 2.4).

By the late dry season of 1974, four dry years had taken a severe toll on the pastoralists. In northern Senegal, as much as 40 to 60 percent of the livestock population, which had risen dramatically between 1950 and 1975, perished from lack of forage (Santoir 1986). Throughout the northern Jolof, the Fulbe responded to the crisis by diversifying their income-generation strategies: Some sent household members to Dakar or the groundnut basin in search of wage employment; others moved into petty trade, increased sales of their remaining livestock, or sold wood collected from dying forests. For the first time, a large number of Fulbe moved into the collection of gum arabic, encouraged by exceptionally favorable gum prices, which had skyrocketed just when the pastoralists faced their greatest threat to survival. The international price of gum arabic rose from $650 per metric ton in early 1973 to $5,000 per metric ton in May 1974 as a result of supply shortfalls in the Sudan gum zone, which was also hit hard by the drought. The local price rose less dramatically, though still over 280 percent in one season (Figure 2.6). The Fulbe shouldered their distaste for what had long been considered a culturally demeaning livelihood and reluctantly entered into this highly lucrative income-generating activity. To the Maures, this represented outright expropriation of historically determined use rights.

Breakdown of Resource Management Institutions

The Maures attempted to enforce rights of exclusion against the newcomers, engendering a bitter struggle between the two resource user groups for control over the diminishing populations of *Acacia senegal*. Beatings and knifings reflected the depth of animosity that suddenly erupted between the two formerly compatible ethnic groups. By the time of the drought, the traditional institutions that might have been able to mediate the disputes had been largely abolished.

The few remnants of customary institutional mechanisms for mediating conflict between the Maures and the Fulbe—village-level

Figure 2.5 Cumulative Annual Rainfall, Linguere: 1934–89

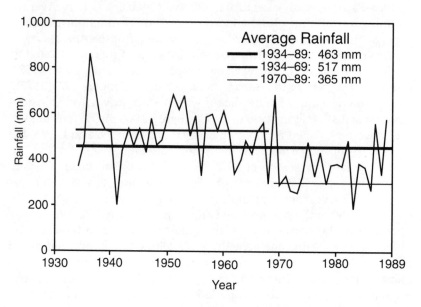

Source: Republic of Senegal, National Meteorological Service Statistics, 1934–89.

councils of elders from both ethnic groups—were incapable of resolving the tenure disputes over the gum trees. The Maures feared that by granting concessions to the Fulbe, they risked permanently losing access to the best concentrations of gum trees. The Fulbe were faced with the intractable stresses of their struggle for immediate survival. The conflict reached an impasse; no customary authority could solve this deep-seated tenure crisis.

The failure of traditional dispute-resolution mechanisms reflected the breakdown of traditional governance institutions, namely the Wolof *bourba* and his coterie of subregional chiefs (*kangam*), and the Fulbe *ardo*. The French colonial administration imposed *chefs de cantons* and later, during the postcolonial period, the state vested considerable administrative powers in *préfets* and *sous-préfets*. These centralized and hierarchical institutions, using Western juridical concepts, took over many of the dispute-resolution functions once handled by traditional governance bodies. Yet in the case of the violent disputes over the gum arabic trees, there were no legal precedents to guide the judicial and administrative bodies to an equitable resolution of competing interests.

For the first time in the history of the gum economy of the Jolof, the Senegalese administrative authorities and technical services

Figure 2.6 Comparison of Free-on-Board Price vs. Quality of Exports of Gum Arabic "Ferlo": 1970–88

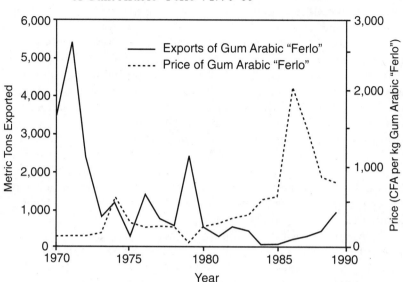

Source: République du Sénégal, Ministère des Finances et des Affaires Economiques, Commerce Extérieur Spéciale, *Statistiques Douaniers*, 1970–88.

became arbitrators in the tenure disputes over the contested gum arabic trees. New tenure rules were created by the state, reflecting what the administration considered fair and equitable. Rather than side with the interests of the Maures, the administration decreed that since the gum trees were a resource held in the public domain, all citizens had equal rights of access. The state forestry service granted the Fulbe permits to collect gum from *Acacia senegal* found within the immediate vicinity of their scattered encampments. This doctrine, reflected in the following justification for a tapping permit, is still very much in force today:

> Mr. Amadou, who has lived in the said locality for nearly 34 years is entitled to exercise his use-rights in accordance with the legal articles cited as follows. . . . Because of the conflicts and quarrels that arise from this exudation business in the Fulbe milieu, we have limited gum collecting forays to an area of approximately one square kilometer in order to avoid any eventual clashes with neighbors in the zone. Marks are to be placed on the tree to delineate the perimeter in question.[6]

Since the Fulbe were widely dispersed in seasonal encampments throughout the gum belt of northern Senegal, this policy gave the pastoralists government-sanctioned rights to collect gum throughout most of the Jolof. In effect, the Maures were prohibited by the forestry service from collecting gum arabic in many of their former prime gum collecting zones.

The Maures could not muster political opposition to this policy stance, since they no longer maintained reciprocal relationships with Muslim *zawaya* clerics who, in the past, might have protested and negotiated on the gum collectors' behalf. Confronted by the continued threat of violence and the reality of being a minority population possessing almost no political influence, the Maures saw little promise in continuing to press their case and instead decided to migrate to the more peripheral and inhospitable regions in the southeastern part of the Department of Linguere, near the villages of Tiel and Velingara (Figure 2.7). Here they were better protected from competition with the Fulbe, since the region was not used extensively by pastoralists during the dry season due to a chronic lack of wells and boreholes.

Once again the Maures pioneered gum collecting among the extensive, but relatively underexploited, stands of *Acacia senegal*. As in the past, the first arrivals divided the new territory among themselves and replicated the technical and organizational features of their ancient livelihood system. Although the Maures experienced few difficulties in acquiring initial use rights to the gum arabic trees from the Fulbe living in the vicinity of Tiel and Velingara, they have encountered difficulties in holding on to the prime gum collecting zones.

Theft of gum has been a critical problem, especially within the dense thickets (200 to 300 *Acacia senegal* per hectare) found scattered throughout the area (Lawesson, Freudenberger, and Tybirk 1989). As in the past, thievery became rampant when gum prices increased dramatically. During the last "gum boom" of 1984–86 (gum prices once again rose after the 1983–84 drought, this time to over 1,500 CFA per kilogram), the Maures lost control of the dense thickets near Velingara to the Fulbe residents of the area and struggled to maintain rights of access elsewhere.

In contrast to the pre-borehole gum collection system of northern Senegal, the new gum belt of the southeastern part of the department is used year-round by several different resource users. Charcoal producers illegally gather wood for charcoal; pastoralists graze cattle, sheep, and goats; and other villagers collect various forest products, such as "gum mbepp" (*Sterculia setigera*) and the fruit of baobabs (*Adansonia digitata*).[7] Each user group profits by stealing the exuding gum of the Maures whenever it can. Gum collecting has thus become an increasingly marginal activity, especially at a time when international prices have fallen precipitously from 1,500 CFA per kilogram in 1986 to about 350 CFA per kilogram by mid-1991.

Figure 2.7 Migration of Maure Gum Collectors: 1970–90

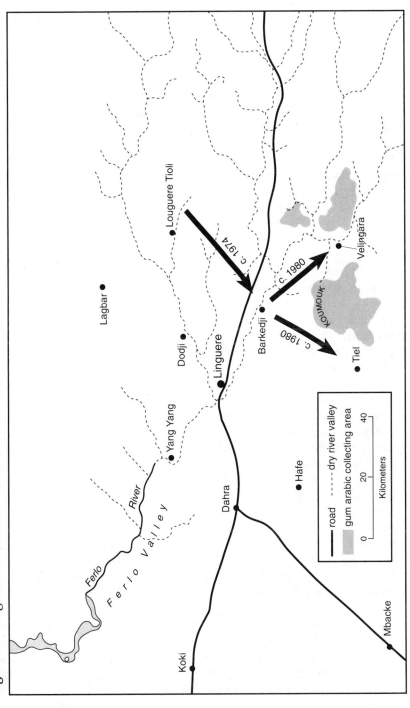

The Maures themselves clearly recognize that the future of the gum arabic economy is precarious. Interviews with collectors demonstrated a sophisticated understanding of the causes behind the deteriorating market conditions and the factors constraining collection at the local level. If the Maures are to continue to earn a substantial part of their household income from gum collecting, then costs of gum gathering must be brought down substantially through a reduction in the amount of labor expended in controlling theft. A solution suggested by the gum collectors is to create rules that, in effect, mimic the seasonal spatial separation of gum collectors and pastoralists characteristic of the pre-borehole era. Only this strategy, they believe, will reduce the high labor costs associated with the protection of gum harvests from theft. Yet, as will be seen in the following section, legal, administrative, and political factors all cast hurdles in the path of efforts to create a new resource management system.

Senegalese Land Laws and the Comanagement of Natural Resources

Comanagement of natural resources is a concept gaining popularity in the Sahel. It builds on the idea that local populations have vast substantial knowledge concerning the management of resources in their communities and should have a much greater say in how they are exploited. This is in contrast to the highly centralized, paternalistic patterns of decisionmaking that have prevailed since colonial times. Comanagement implies a two-step process in which the state first cedes part of its authority for resource management to local communities, which then negotiate rights of access to and responsibilities for protecting natural resources among competing interests. Although this process is characterized by myriad legal, administrative, and political complexities, it may offer the only hope of protecting fragile niche economies, such as the collection of gum arabic, that depend on the enforcement of local use rights that are both highly articulated and flexible. Such arrangements can evolve only when user groups are active participants in a decisionmaking process that builds on their intimate knowledge of local resources and their intense concern for maintaining resource productivity.

In contrast to other Sahelian countries, Senegal possesses a legislative framework that would allow the resource user groups of the Department of Linguere to reconstruct key elements of the pre-borehole gum collecting system. In principle, the body of laws and edicts associated with the 1964 *Loi relative au domaine national* (Senegal's core land use legislation) permits the decentralized, microterritorial management of natural resources. This legislation is an illustration of how Sahelian states currently interested in local governance might craft a comanagement relationship that allows the state to retain considerable control over the use of natural resources, yet also grants resource user groups latitude in devising appropriate and innovative local-level arrangements. However, the Forest Code, a vestige of colonial forestry policy, maintains state control over tree resources and severely constrains the devolution of resource management control from the state to local user groups.

The impact of three laws affecting comanagement arrangements are addressed below: The first two empower local users, and the third maintains critical controls in the hands of the state and partially negates the effects of the other two.

User Control

In the mid-1960s and early 1970s, Senegal enacted a series of laws permitting user-based governance of natural resources. The 1964 *Loi relative au domaine national* is founded on the precept that most land is held in the national domain, but the state can grant use rights to those who render it economically productive (*mettre en valeur*) in conformity with national and local development criteria. The 1972 *Loi relative aux communautés rurales* vests in 318 locally elected rural councils the responsibility for allocating land to individuals and groups residing in the administrative district (*communauté rurale*) "as a function of the capacity of the beneficiaries to assure, either directly or with the aid of their family, the development of their lands conforming to a program established by the council" (Article 3). Officially, all land transactions, such as the inheritance of fields, must pass through the rural council.

The *Loi relative au domaine national* and the *Loi relative aux communautés rurales* grant rural community councils the right to allocate land, plan local development activities, employ as much as 75 percent of the rural tax for these development projects, and resolve land disputes (République du Sénégal 1984, 1988). Several provisions in the original legislation give rural community councils the right to express resource use preferences. One provision allows the community council to determine all rights of usage in the interior of its territory and to express its wishes on regulatory measures that would be useful in order to obtain a judicious exploitation and an effective protection of resources. The community council leadership is authorized to establish land use plans and to determine local rules and regulations governing many forms of resource exploitation. A subsequent amendment gave the rural councils jurisdiction over and responsibility for fighting forest fires, determining access to water, creating and installing livestock paths, and planning for the exploitation of all forest gathering products and wood cutting.

Forestry Service Control

The 1964 *Loi relative au domaine national* and the 1972 *Loi relative aux communautés rurales* create the statutory framework that would facilitate the emergence of innovative resource management arrangements. Yet the laws associated with these two acts clash with the Forest Code, a vestige of French colonial forestry policy. The Forest Code gives the forestry service extensive powers to enforce a wide array of regulations pertaining to the exploitation of the forest domain. Many techniques used by gum collectors to manage the *Acacia senegal* are illegal under the code. For instance, gum collectors often lop off thorny branches that hinder the tapper's approach to the tree. A gum collector could face a stiff fine and up to two years in prison if caught trimming the tree by a forest agent. The Forest Code states that since the *Acacia senegal* is a legally "protected" species, it is subject to numerous interdictions against any "felling, pulling up, or mutilation" of the species unless authorization is granted by the forestry service. This provision justifies the requirement of an annual permit to collect gum. Even though the permit is free, the transaction costs of obtaining it are high, since the collector must often travel great distances to locate the forestry agent responsible for issuing the permit.

There are legal ambiguities between the Forest Code and the *Loi relative au domain national*. The code states that exploitation of trees and tree crop products for commercial purposes falls under the jurisdiction of the forestry service. From the perspective of the forestry service, the community council does not have the right to legislate regulations affecting commercial exploitation of forest resources such as the *Acacia senegal*. Revisions in the Forest Code are currently being discussed. If the revised version of the code passes legislative and bureaucratic hurdles, it may give resource user groups the right to manage forests collectively on the condition that the association employs conservation practices determined in collaboration with the forestry service.

Administrative Impediments to Comanagement Arrangements

The community councils possess considerable authority to craft local resource use arrangements, yet the administration of the Ministry of the Interior may in fact veto any of their decisions. Although this provision is intended to provide "checks and balances" between the state and the community council, the provision has been abused by the administration on many occasions. Several cases have been reported in northern Senegal, where community councils controlled by Fulbe have attempted to create pasture reserves as a way to block the northward advancement of Mouride groundnut cultivators. These attempts have been vetoed by *préfets* who supported the more powerful external interests served by groundnut cultivation, which provides a major foreign exchange–earning commodity (Juul 1991).

The Senegalese government has resisted devolving true governance powers to community councils perhaps because the state development bureaucracy would lose many of the prerogatives it has enjoyed for so long. Most international development aid in Senegal is channeled through centralized ministries that design and implement projects without significant consultation with the community councils. Donor aid creates jobs for the bureaucracy and provides substantial per diems to those who venture briefly into the hinterlands. Foreign aid translates into vehicles for project managers, international travel, and academic scholarships to the West. Little of this aid flows down to the regional and subregional levels. Local-level extension agents, for example, see only a meager portion of the millions of dollars of aid funds flowing into Senegal, and almost none filters down as far as the development budgets of the community councils.

The donors are also at fault for failing to improve the managerial capacity of the rural community councils. In the past, multilateral and bilateral donors have preferred to support large parastatal development organizations rather than work through community councils. Donor projects have financed large-scale gum arabic plantations managed by the forestry service instead of working with the host of user groups involved in exploiting not only gum arabic but many other forest resources. Smaller, nongovernmental development agencies have frequently created parallel structures to manage development projects within their own agencies rather than reinforcing local administrative structures. Both the concentration of major development resources at the national level and the creation of parallel structures by local projects have undermined the institutional capacity at the base that is vital to territorial management of natural resources.

Local Political Constraints on Comanagement Arrangements

Comanagement of resources implies the redistribution of responsibility for resource use decisions between state and local authorities. This, in turn, creates both the opportunity for and the responsibility of local communities to negotiate use rights among diverse and perhaps competing local interests. It may or may not lead to policies that are more equitable than the state-imposed strictures. However, history suggests that traditional resource management systems, which allow for more seasonally flexible arrangements and a more dispersed allocation of the "bundle" of use rights around resources,[8] often protect niche economies and minority interests better than the blunter management regulations that characterize modern legal frameworks based on private ownership of particular parcels of land.

Groups like the Maures are clearly minority interests. As newcomers to the southeastern part of the Department of Linguere, they are a largely "invisible" and economically marginal population living within the broader Fulbe and Wolof cultural and political milieu. They lack the political power and legal skills to promote their economic interests. Yet the development of new resource management arrangements hinges on the community's recognition of the Maures' seasonal rights to collect gum in particular territories. In the early twentieth century, the Jolof *bourba* allocated seasonal use rights; today the state, through the aegis of the community councils, must do the same. However, neither the government nor the leadership of the community council is likely to act unless forced to do so by the Maures themselves—a problem for such a distinct minority population. In such cases, government development agencies, nongovernmental organizations, forestry projects, and committed individuals can play a key role in strengthening the hand of minority user groups. The external actors could help the Maures organize themselves into legally recognized associations such as Economic Interest Groups (*Groupements d'Intérêt Economiques;* GIEs). GIEs are legally constituted groups of two or more individuals involved in commercial activities; they are entitled to receive bank credit and could request officially recognized use rights to the *Acacia senegal* from the community council.

The history of the gum arabic economy in northern Senegal suggests that the reallocation of rights usually takes place during periods of rapid environmental and economic dislocation, such as those caused by drought or rapid price changes. A window of opportunity is opened each time the value of gum arabic suddenly increases on the international market. During these moments, disputes tend to break out among competing interest groups over access to the *Acacia senegal*. These disputes mark critical junctures in the evolution of the resource management regime. It is precisely at these points that the community councils, backed up as needed by higher administrative authorities, might intercede to help negotiate new agreements. The next section presents an example of what that process might look like in practice.

A Comanagement Scenario

Although the impediments to instituting effective comanagement arrangements should not be underestimated, neither should they be seen as hopelessly intransigent. Legislative changes to liberalize the Forest Code are already being discussed, some community councils have begun to stand up for local interests against higher state authorities, and development organizations increasingly recognize the indigenous knowledge of user groups such as the Maures. It is perhaps worth considering how a comanagement arrangement could be negotiated in an area like the southeastern corner of the Department of Linguere, where disputes over gum arabic have caused bitter divisions in the community over the last several years and losses through theft threaten to undermine any rational exploitation—and hence long-term management—of the resource.

The community councils of Tiel and Velingara could, in theory, devise ways to manage the forest resources of the area in a fashion that incorporates the interests of the Maures without jeopardizing essential interests of other local user groups. The history of the gum economy in northern Senegal provides many valuable hints about what such an arrangement might look like. Two features of the past gum collection system need to be revived: (1) the reconstruction of an arrangement that allows temporary exclusion of livestock and herders from gum collecting areas at key times during the early dry season, and (2) the creation of suitable resource management institutions that have sufficient authority to control the movement of people and animals.

The community councils in southeastern Linguere have the authority to convene the principal users of the gum collecting territories to discuss and implement measures to revitalize the gum collection economy. The forestry service, under the auspices of the government extension service (the *Centres d'Expansion Rurale Polyvalents,* or CERP), could provide necessary technical support. The council could begin with various measures to reduce theft. It could legislate regulations excluding the passage of livestock through particularly dense concentrations of *Acacia senegal* during the first weeks of the gum collecting season. Since roughly 75 percent of gum exudation occurs during the early months of the dry season, seasonal restrictions on the entry of livestock and herders into particular gum collecting areas would facilitate unhampered collection by the Maures. Once the harvest is brought in, the zone would be opened up to grazing. Such an arrangement could provide considerable benefits for the pastoralists, since it would create a late dry season pasture reserve. The council could encourage the Maure and Fulbe users of the gum collecting areas to practice proven resource management techniques. In collaboration with the forestry service, appropriate times and frequencies for setting bush fires might be established for the district. Fulbe and Maures would then be responsible for setting and controlling bush fires in predetermined locations. As both scientific studies and rural populations note, such fires not only help regenerate vegetation but also eliminate pests that are harmful to livestock production. Other proposals would certainly emerge from the forum organized by the community councils.

Problems may arise if local institutions are not strong enough to enforce locally devised rules and regulations; the state may need to help enforce such arrangements. "Free riders" tend to shirk responsibilities to the broader community and break community conventions. For those caught stealing gum or illegally cutting *Acacia senegal* for charcoal making, a system of fines could be instituted, payable to the rural council. The gendarmerie or the forestry service might enforce local sanctions against gum theft when notified of transgressions by the community council. Revenues from fines collected by the council could then be used for community-initiated projects. Although these options are not exhaustive, they provide a small indication of the great potential in Senegalese land laws for creating new comanagement systems.

Conclusions

The prognosis for the future of the gum arabic economy in northern Senegal appears bleak on many accounts. Botanical studies indicate that the *Acacia senegal* in the northern half of the Department of Linguere have not fully regenerated in the wake of droughts (Lawesson in press). International demand may be declining rapidly as synthetic substitutes such as xanthum gum displace gum arabic in the international market (Robbins 1987). It is easy to believe that the gum arabic collection system will disappear entirely as a result of the declining international demand for gum arabic and that the export gum economy will simply cease to exist.

However, the lessons of this historically important commodity are important for the host of niche economies that flourish across the Sahel and other marginal ecological zones. Whether producing jojoba oil or shea butter for European cosmetics or baobab fruit for local markets, these economies provide a vital share of the livelihoods of rural dwellers. Like gum collecting, they are critical to the myriad risk-aversion strategies employed by rural households struggling to recoup from crop failures, sudden death of livestock, or other threats to household survival. Policies to protect these tree crop economies clearly have positive social benefits to the poor who depend on them. But broader conservation interests are also served by such policies. The best way to conserve and regenerate Sahelian forest resources is to assure that the minority populations who depend on collecting tree crops continue to exploit—on a sustainable basis—the resources upon which their livelihoods depend. As this case study has shown, those who depend on the *Acacia senegal* tend to conserve the tree, provided they have sufficient incentives—including firm rights of access to the resource. Hence, the maintenance of these tree crop resources provides a continuing source of revenue for poor and sparsely scattered populations, and the perpetuation of such diverse microeconomies may offer the most productive and sustainable use of semiarid regions of the Sahel.

The development community in the Sahel has recently begun to experiment with new and innovative local-level rule-making arrangements. In most Sahelian countries, the forestry service is turning some management control of state forest reserves over to contiguous communities. In these pilot projects, the state defines the broad framework for local participation and works with the community to create joint use rights agreements within spatially delineated zones. In a sense, the state provides the "protection" required by local groups to develop locally adapted resource management arrangements.

The case of the gum arabic tree crop in the Department of Linguere provides a sobering picture of the factors that inhibit the development of new comanagement arrangements around commonly used forest resources. Although rural Sahelian populations like the Maures may possess the knowledge and skills to manage resources on a sustainable basis, numerous legal, administrative, and political constraints hinder the emergence of collective actions to protect and restore forest resources like the *Acacia senegal*. The history of the gum arabic collection system in northern Senegal illustrates how these factors impinge upon the Maures' efforts to maintain a traditional source of livelihood and the difficulties they face in adapting their management strategies to changing socioeconomic and ecological conditions.

The devolution of resource management control to specific user groups requires a very different planning orientation from the top-down "master plan" approach that has dominated the practice of rural development planning for so long. Protecting and nurturing a complex array of niche activities (as opposed to government schemes to promote ranching or monocrop plantations of gum arabic trees) require an intimate knowledge of the diverse physical and social particularities of specific places. The systematic participation of local communities—including minority populations—in crafting and implementing rules regulating local uses of natural resources is essential to the success of this new approach. Yet as this chapter has shown, the state plays an important part in creating the legislative and administrative framework under which such comanagement arrangements might be encouraged.

Notes

1. For a comprehensive discussion of microterritorial development approaches (*aménagement/gestion de terroires villageoises*) in francophone West Africa, see Painter 1991 and Thomson et al. 1989.
2. For a detailed presentation of field research conducted in Senegal from 1987 to 1989, see Freudenberger 1992.
3. For a more complete historical discussion of the *sourga* labor system, see Searing 1988.
4. Studies conducted during the late 1950s at the Gum Arabic Research Station at Linguere showed that only 52 to 80 percent of trees yielded gum in any one season and that average annual yields ranged from a low of 57 grams per tree to a high of 190 grams per tree (Territoire du Sénégal 1952/1955).
5. For an in-depth study of the impact of the drought on the ecology of northern Senegal, see the series of articles in *La Terre et la Vie* 26(1–3) 1972; and 28(1) 1974.
6. "Authorisation gratuite d'exudation sur essences protégées," of 13 December 1980, by the Chef de Brigade Forestier of Dahra, M. El Hadji Malick Dieye.
7. "Gum mbepp" is a water-soluble gum used as a cooking ingredient in Senegal, but it is also exported and employed in many dietary products. (See Robbins 1987, 61–66).
8. A "bundle of rights" refers to the "possession or holding of the many rights associated with each parcel of land . . . that can be broken up, redivided, passed on to others" (Riddell 1987, 2).

References

Ba, Oumar. 1975. "Les Peuls du Diolof au XIXième siècle." *Bulletin de l'IFAN* Série B 37(1): 117–36.

Barral, Henri. 1982. *Le Ferlo des forages: Gestion ancienne et actuelle de l'espace pastoral.* Dakar: ORSTOM.

Barrows, Leland. 1974. "The Merchants and General Faidherbe: Aspects of French Expansion in Senegal in the 1850s." *Revue française d'histoire d'outre-mer* 61:236–83.

Caillié, René. 1830. *Travels through Central Africa to Timbuctoo.* London: Henry Colburn and Richard Bentley.

Charles, Eunice. 1977. *Precolonial Senegal: The Jolof Kingdom, 1831–1858.* Boston: Boston University, African Studies Center.

Copans, Jean. 1988. *Les Marabouts de l'arachide: La confrérie et les paysans du Sénégal.* Paris: l'Harmattan.

Delcourt, André. 1952. *La France et les établissements français au Sénégal entre 1713–1763.* Dakar: Institut Fondamental Africain.

Dupré, Georges. 1991. *Savoirs paysans et développement (Farmer Knowledge and Development).* Paris: Editions Karthala et Editions ORSTOM.

Freudenberger, Mark Schoonmaker. 1992. *The Great Gum Gamble: A Planning Perspective on Environmental Change in Northern Senegal.* Ph.D. dissertation, University of California, Los Angeles.

Glicksman, Martin, and Ralf E. Sand. 1973. "Gum Arabic." In *Industrial Gums: Polysaccharides and Their Derivatives*, edited by Roy L. Whistler and James N. BeMiller. New York: Academic Press.

Juul, Kristine. 1991. "Problèmes fonciers et aménagement territorial en zone agropastorale: Le cas de l'arrondissement de Barkedji." Dakar: Centre de Suivi Ecologique.

Lawesson, Jonas. "Sahelian Woody Vegetation in Senegal." *Vegetatio* in press.

Lawesson, Jonas Erik, Mark Schoonmaker Freudenberger, and Knud Tybirk. 1989. "The Ecology and Economy of the Gum Arabic Tree (*Acacia senegal*) in Northern Senegal." Arhus, Denmark: Botanical Institute, University of Arhus.

Lawry, Steven W. 1990. "Tenure Policy toward Common Property Natural Resources in Sub-Saharan Africa." *Natural Resources Journal* 30 (Spring): 403–22.

McLane, Margaret O. 1986. "Commercial Rivalries and French Policy on the Senegal River, 1831–1858." *African Economic History* 15:39–68.

Mouret, M. 1988. "Gummosis of Acacias: Current Histological Research." *Bulletin of the International Group for the Study of Mimosoideae* 16:38–45.

Painter, Thomas M. 1991. "Approaches to Improving Natural Resource Use of Agriculture in Sahelian West Africa." Agriculture and Natural Resources Technical Report Series 3. New York: CARE.

Pélisser, Paul. 1966. *Les Paysans du Sénégal*. Saint-Yrieix: Imprimerie Fabrègue.

Poupon, Henri. 1973. "Influence de la sécheresse de l'année 1972–1973 sur la végétation d'une savane Sahélienne du Ferlo septentrional, Sénégal." In *La désertification au sud du Sahara*. Colloque du Nouakchott, 17–19 December. Dakar: Les Nouvelles Editions Africaines.

———. 1977. "Evolution d'un peuplement d'*Acacia senegal* (L.) Willd. dans une savane sahélienne au Sénégal de 1972 à 1976." *Cahiers ORSTOM*, série Biologie XII(4): 283–91.

République du Sénégal, Ministère de l'Intérieur. 1984. *Guide pratique du conseiller rural*. November.

———. 1988. *Guide de la planification du développement dans les communautés rurales*. October.

Richards, Paul. 1985. *Indigenous Agricultural Revolution*. London: Unwin Hyman.

Riddell, James C. 1987. "Land Tenure and Agroforestry: A Regional Overview." In *Land, Trees and Tenure*, edited by John B. Raintree. Nairobi and Madison: ICRAF and Land Tenure Center.

Robbins, S. R. J. 1987. *A Review of Recent Trends in Selected Markets for Water-Soluble Gums*. Overseas Development Natural Resources Institute Bulletin 2.

Santoir, Christian. 1983. *Raison pastorale et politique de développement: les peul Sénégalais face aux aménagements*. Paris: Travaux et Documents de l'ORSTOM.

———. 1986. "Peul et aménagements hydro-agricoles dans la vallée du fleuve Sénégal." In *Pastoralists of the West African Savanna*, edited by Hahdi Adamu and A. H. M. Kirk-Greene. London: International African Institute.

Searing, James F. 1988. "Aristocrats, Slaves and Peasants: Power and Dependency in the Wolof States, 1700–1850." *International Journal of African Historical Studies* 21(3): 475–503.

Territoire du Sénégal, Service des Eaux et Forêts. 1952/1955. *Rapports annuels de 1952, 1955*. National Archives of Senegal, 2 G 52 (35), 2 G 55 (21).

———. Inspection Forestière du Fleuve. 1956. *Eléments de politique sylvo-pastorale au Sahel Sénégalais*. Rapport Grosmaire. Saint-Louis.

Thomson, James T., Alfred Walstein, Sheldon Gellar, and Jerry Miner. 1989. *Options for Promoting User-Based Governance of Sahelian Renewable Natural Resources.* Associates for Rural Development. January.

United Nations Sahelian Office. 1983. *The Gum Arabic Market and the Development of Production.* New York and Geneva: United Nations Sudano-Sahelian Office and International Trade Centre.

von Maydell, H. J. 1986. *Trees and Shrubs of the Sahel: Their Characteristics and Uses.* Eschborn, Germany: Gesellschaft für Technische Zusammenarbeit.

Webb, James L. A. Jr. 1984. "Shifting Sands: An Economic History of the Mauritanian Sahara, 1500–1850." Ph.D. dissertation, Johns Hopkins University.

THREE

DAMS, DISPLACEMENT, AND DEVELOPMENT

A Resistance Movement in Southern Brazil

MARK D. MCDONALD

OFFICIAL ENTHUSIASM FOR DAM PROJECTS, especially large-scale projects, as the answer for various national and regional planning objectives has grown markedly in the last three decades. This enthusiasm has been a function of perceived national development needs, improved technologies, and the availability of financing. Perhaps the most common objective of large-scale dam projects is to obtain the cheapest supply of energy.[1] Compared to thermal and nuclear energy, hydroelectricity can be generated at significantly lower cost and is sometimes defended as a "clean" energy source as well.[2] Following the oil shock of 1973, developing countries with abundant water resources such as Brazil increasingly turned their planning attention to hydroelectric projects as an alternative energy source and as a means of reducing their import burdens while fostering energy independence.[3]

However, the enthusiasm with which dam construction was advocated during the 1960s and 1970s has waned as serious social and environmental costs have come to be associated with these projects. For instance, large, standing bodies of water are breeding grounds for disease-carrying insects and thus can lead to the spread of malaria, hepatitis, schistosomiasis, and river blindness (Michaels and Napolitano 1988). In heavily forested regions, the loss of flora and fauna from flooding can be enormous; where water circulation is poor, anaerobic decomposition of the forest may occur, releasing gases that can endanger human health.[4] Other environmental costs include the loss of productive agricultural land due to flooding, salinization, and the lack of siltation.[5]

In many cases, the building of dams—particularly medium- and large-scale projects—disrupts people's lives by displacing the populations residing in the construction and reservoir areas. Dams are frequently associated with the destruction of communities and a reduction in the living standards of the displaced. One author summarizes: "[c]on-struction of dams usually means the exploitation of resources for the benefit of one group at the expense of another" (Williams 1986, 10). Dam construction in Brazil has been plagued by precisely such problems. Communities facing displacement are often not only excluded from the benefits of projects but also regarded by project officials as merely obstacles to be removed at the least possible cost.

The Uruguai River Basin project (Figure 3.1) exemplifies this lack of concern for local communities. The technocratic and authoritarian approach of the government project company, ELETROSUL, in dealing with the local population led to a regional social movement against the project that eventually blocked construction and forced major and costly adjustments. Beginning with simple demands for more information about the proposed project, the movement evolved into a highly organized and sophisticated force in the region. It not only effectively battled a powerful state-owned company but also raised important questions about environmental degradation, development priorities, and the need for more democratic forms of policy formulation and implementation.

This chapter explores the evolution of this resistance movement and the sources of conflict between ELETROSUL and local populations. It highlights the stress suffered by local populations that are faced with the threat of displacement and the deeply felt attachments of communities to their territorial space. The account is based on interviews conducted from 1989 through mid-1991 with leaders of the movement and members of the rural communities in the project area as well as documents and newsletters produced by the movement and local newspaper accounts from 1979 to mid-1991.

The lessons of the Uruguai River Basin project highlight the need for a much more thorough accounting of the social and environmental costs of dam projects, especially regarding displacement. The case study also emphasizes that where dam construction is inevitable, early, detailed resettlement planning—with the genuine involvement of affected communities—is critical and is the best way to guarantee that the project represents development for all citizens involved.

Historical Setting

The conflict that arose in the Uruguai Basin can be properly understood only in the context of the authoritarian political climate in Brazil that emerged from the military coup of 1964. The populist government

Figure 3.1 Uruguai River Basin

of João Goulart was overthrown, and General Castelo Branco was installed as president of the republic. The regime soon came to be dominated by extremist elements within the military. After 1968, the authoritarian state system was characterized by what Thomas Skidmore has called "the alliance of hard-liners and technocrats": The military depended on the technocrats for economic policy, and the technocrats and managers depended on the military to keep them in power (Skidmore 1973).

Strengthening the state in order to guarantee national security was the primary goal. For the military, this meant enforcing social stability and creating the conditions for capital accumulation, with significant state intervention in the economy. The economic model implemented after 1964 called for the centralization of resources in large state enterprises; they, in turn, would provide the basic infrastructure for massive investments of foreign capital. Military leaders promoted the ideology of "Brasil Grande," initiating enormous projects such as the Trans-Amazon Highway, the Itaipu Dam, and the Carajás mining project (Santos and Nacke 1988). This agenda was accomplished at the expense of much needed investments in education, public health, and housing and contributed to an increasing disparity between social classes.

The model pursued by the military assumed high and steadily increasing rates of energy consumption over several decades. Massive expenditures in energy production would become one of the principal areas for state investment as hydroelectric projects took on a new significance. Since that time, many of the assumptions about energy need have been challenged as overly optimistic; however, during the dictatorship, no room existed for public debate of such issues.

Military leaders no longer believed that economic growth, at least in the short run, could be achieved in an open political system. Political and economic decisionmaking in Brazil was hidden from the public and highly centralized, removed from any pressure generated by popular demands and protests. Labor union activities and rural organizations were severely repressed, as were most forms of popular mobilization. Through the late 1970s and into the 1980s, the Brazilian regime managed a controlled return to democratic institutions, culminating in a new constitution and direct elections for president in 1989. It was during this transitional decade of the 1980s that the project in the Uruguai River Basin progressed.

The Project and the Region

After the military wrested power from the civilian government in 1964, a restructuring and expansion of the energy sector took place. A systematic approach was undertaken to determine Brazil's exploitable energy resources, part of which was a study of the hydroelectric potential of the southern region. This initial study was carried out during 1966–69 by the Comitê de Estudos Energéticos da Região Sul (ENERSUL), under the technical supervision of Canambra Engineering Consultants Limited. Just before this, in 1965, the state electrical energy agency, the Centrais Elétricas Brasileiras S.A. (ELETROBRAS), had created the Centrais Elétricas Do Sul Do Brasil S.A. (ELETROSUL), which would assume the primary responsibility for electrical energy development in the south.

The ENERSUL study underwent revisions beginning in 1976. In 1979, ELETROSUL published a revised study proposing the construction of twenty-five dams: twenty-two dams in the Uruguai River Basin, which lies in the states of Santa Catarina and Rio Grande do Sul, and three dams on a stretch of the Uruguai River dividing Brazil and Argentina. ELETROSUL initially estimated that the twenty-two dams would displace 35,900 people, of which nearly 30,000 resided in rural areas or small villages.[6] These numbers would be sharply criticized by the region's inhabitants, who put the number of people affected at 200,000.[7]

The scale of the project came as a shock to the region's residents, including the state legislative assemblies. In fact, as the *atingidos* (the Portuguese word for those who were affected by the project) pointed out, the methods adopted for estimating Brazil's future energy needs raised many doubts and questions. The *atingidos*, with help from the local university and the union headquarters in Erexim, argued that Brazil was not even consuming its current energy production, and that projects such as the massive Itaipu Dam were not operating at their full potential.

The impact area of the project in the Uruguai River Basin is vast. The Uruguai River extends over 2,000 kilometers, forming Brazil's border with Argentina to the west and separating the states of Santa Catarina and Rio Grande do Sul to the north. However, this particular case study focuses on a much smaller area where the first two dams of the project— Machadinho and Itá (designated Region 1 by the movement)—were to be installed (Figure 3.2). The area is densely populated, especially near the Machadinho site, where there is an average of thirty-one people per square kilometer (Sigaud 1986). A large majority of these residents are farmers, with small plots of fifteen to thirty hectares, who produce a wide variety of agricultural products. Soybeans are the main product, constituting 32 percent of the region's agricultural production; corn is the second largest product (23 percent), and the raising of pigs and poultry is also quite common (16 percent) (Canali, Munoz, and Schwab 1986). Other products include wheat, manioc, potatoes, rice, and beans.

Figure 3.2   Uruguai River Basin Projected Dam Sites

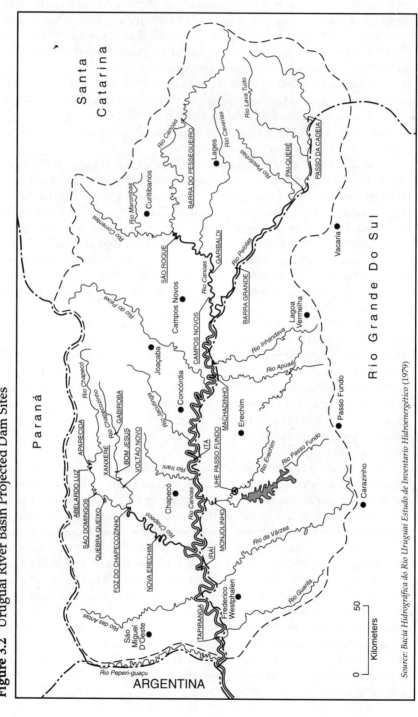

Source: Bacia Hidrográfica do Rio Uruguai Estudo de Inventario Hidroenergético (1979)

Most of the people in the region are of European origin, descendants of nineteenth-century immigrants. Soon after Brazilian independence in 1822, the country began promoting immigration as a means of colonizing huge areas of the interior. Much of the southern part of the country was covered with forest; beginning in 1824, German, Italian, and later Polish immigrants began opening up the southern states for settlement (Santos 1974). Their present-day descendants have deep ties to the fertile land they now hold. Most have legal titles, although there is also a significant number of *sem-terras*, or landless renters and sharecroppers.

The fact that the area is densely populated has contributed to the strength of some local organizations that have flourished and provided the foundation for a mobilized response against the dam project. The principal institutions active in the region are the Catholic church (through both its local congregations and its Pastoral Land Commissions), the Evangelical Lutheran church, and rural unions (Sindicatos dos Trabalhadores Rurais, or STRs). It is the unions, along with the local university FAPES (Fundação Alto Uruguai Para a Pesquisa e o Ensino Superior), that have provided the most direct support for the *atingidos*. The vitality and direction of these unions, however, vary from *município* to *município*.[8] It is also significant that the Worker's Party (Partido de Trabalhadores) grew in strength in the region during the 1980s; many party activists contributed to the dynamism and strength of the movement against the dams.

The Birth of a Movement

The first years of ELETROSUL's work in the region were marked by both an extreme disregard for the stress suffered by local residents and authoritarian practices that quickly began to erode the company's legitimacy. ELETROSUL showed itself to be unsympathetic and unresponsive to the psychological and emotional impacts that the mere threat of its project imposed on the region. Moreover, it soon became clear to the local residents that ELETROSUL had no plan for resettling them and that the company was not willing to discuss the project with them directly. This was simply incomprehensible for many families, whose livelihood was wholly dependent on the land they worked. In response to the company's approach, a mobilization process slowly emerged in the rural communities of the project area, which began to solidify as an established movement by 1984.

The Early Years

Reports of the proposed dam project for the Uruguai River Basin began to surface in 1978. These first reports were made public by representatives of the Catholic church's Pastoral Land Commissions and by professors from FAPES, who learned of the project through contacts with ELETROSUL workers and through other informal channels. With the assistance of the university, a few rural union leaders, and members of the Catholic church, approximately 150 meetings were held in 1978 and 1979 to discuss the project in the rural communities. It is important to note that initial efforts to bring the population together around this issue were dependent on outside agents who had access to critical information.

Far from opposing the dams, the communities initially looked favorably on the project as important for the region's development, even considering themselves to be "allies" of ELETROSUL in the venture.[9] The principal concern of the *atingidos* was to receive fair and timely indemnification for all the losses they would incur. On 24 April 1979, at a meeting in Concórdia, Santa Catarina, 350 farmers along with representatives from the Catholic and Lutheran churches, rural unions, and FAPES created a commission for the purpose of protecting the interests of the *atingidos* (CRAB 1989, 1–2). This commission would come to be known as the Comissão Regional de Atingidos por Barragens (Regional Commission of People Affected by Dams), or CRAB.

By 1980, doubt and alarm began to surface, as accounts of widespread dissatisfaction filtered into the region from those affected by previous ELETROSUL dam projects at nearby Salto Santiago and Salto Osório. At a CRAB meeting in March 1980, those present produced a document that questioned the project, especially the lack of consultation with the population, and emphasized their rights of compensation (CRAB 1980). Later in the year, however, ELETROSUL published its viability study of the first dam to be built—Machadinho—in which the only mention of indemnification referred to one Indian reservation (Sigaud 1986, 73).

People were anxious about receiving adequate compensation, and the project was unclear about the location of the dams—specifically, which areas would be covered by reservoirs—and when construction would begin. Moreover, the company (a federal agency) clashed with state government institutions, which took offense at being excluded from the project.

Local newspapers captured the climate of apprehension and uncertainty that had descended on the region by 1981, principally due to ELETROSUL's reluctance to clarify the project or address the concerns of the local population. An article in *Folha da Tarde* (4 February 1981), titled "Agricultores em pânico: barragens" (Farmers in panic: dams), described the situation in the region as "completely chaotic." Another in *Zero Hora* (17 November 1981) stated, "Incerteza aflige as famílias que moram na região" (Uncertainty afflicts families living in the region). These were typical of the press coverage at the time and captured the collective fear.

The latter article highlighted the fact that ELETROSUL had been unresponsive to persistent requests for information by concerned *atingidos*. A state deputy of Rio Grande do Sul lashed out at ELETROSUL, complaining that although there was plenty of information about the energy-generating potential of the project, "there is no information whatsoever about any project for the resettlement of those to be displaced," and valuable time was being lost.[10] Even the president of the legislative assembly for the state of Rio Grande do Sul criticized the paucity of information concerning the destiny of the *atingidos*, emphasizing that in the *município* of Machadinho alone, 22,000 farmers would be dislocated.[11] In order to keep the *atingidos* better informed, in September 1981 CRAB began to publish, on an irregular basis, a bulletin called *A Enchente do Uruguai* (The Flood of the Uruguai). This publication became an important organizing tool through its ability to provide information to rural communities scattered across the affected region.

Finding themselves already on the defensive, the *atingidos* organized a regional meeting in Marcelino Ramos on 7 August 1981 to clarify their position and concerns to ELETROSUL. In addition to those who identified themselves with CRAB, there were representatives from seventeen rural unions, the Diocese of Chapecó and Erexim, the Lutheran Evangelical church, and the Catholic Pastoral Land Commissions for the states of Rio Grande do Sul and Santa Catarina, as well as advisors from FAPES. They set forth a document that demanded the immediate demarcation of the areas to be flooded and spelled out the conditions for resettlement or monetary compensation expected by the *atingidos* (CRAB 1981). It was slowly becoming clear that the local population would have to defend its own rights rather than trust local politicians. After meeting with ELETROSUL officials in May 1981, several mayors in the region started supporting the project and tried to convince the *atingidos* to trust the agency.[12]

In the beginning of 1982, the president of ELETROSUL, Telmo Thompson Flores, announced that work would begin on the Machadinho Dam in 1983 and that the second dam, Itá, would begin in 1985. Yet Flores's declaration conflicted with other reports circulating in the region that the project would never actually get off the ground, or that it was not scheduled to begin any time soon. In February 1983, the governor of Rio Grande do Sul announced that there would be no dam project,[13] and a state deputy testified before a special commission on dams of the legislative assembly that no dams would be built before the year 2000.[14] Even the federal government gave no coherent response: Contradicting Flores, the president of ELETROBRAS, General

José Costa Cavalcanti, responded in a letter to two state representatives that Machadinho would not begin before 1986 and that Itá, as well as two other dams, would not begin before 1992.[15] Residents became increasingly frustrated with all the confusion and mounting stress. Questioning the company's inconsistencies, a CRAB leader later reflected that ELETROSUL used its "machine of disinformation" in a "planned program to confuse the population."[16]

Only in May 1982 did ELETROSUL finally meet with the *atingidos* themselves, in what was supposed to be an encounter to calm the fears and answer the questions of the local population. In the hope that ELETROSUL would be prepared to give satisfactory responses to their concerns, CRAB sent a list of twenty-nine questions to the company several days before the meeting. However, from the *atingidos'* perspective, ELETROSUL sent only middle-rank technicians who did not even know whether the dams would be built and offered no clarification about the destinies of the thousands of families living in the project areas.[17]

Moreover, ELETROSUL argued that questions regarding resettlement would have to be taken up with the National Institute for Colonization and Agrarian Reform (INCRA), apparently seeking to distance itself from all responsibility for the future of the *atingidos*.[18] The May meeting was typical of subsequent meetings in which ELETROSUL participated; not only did the company consistently fail to offer satisfactory answers to the legitimate concerns of the *atingidos*, but it also continually sought to justify the project with technical language that the local population could not understand.[19] On several occasions the company simply failed to appear.

Tensions in the region were reaching a boiling point, such that the legislative assembly of Rio Grande do Sul organized a special public forum in September 1983—the *I Encontro Estadual* (First State Conference)—to clarify the Uruguai River Basin project and its various social and environmental impacts. Yet again, ELETROSUL failed to confront the public's concerns: The company sent technicians who explained that they could not answer all the questions because they lacked proper authority. By the end of the special forum, delegates were calling for the resignation of Flores and expressing their opposition to the project (Assembléia Legislativa 1983, 25).

The *I Encontro Estadual* marked a shift in the *atingidos'* struggle. The absence of answers about the future of those to be displaced, the apparent stalling by ELETROSUL to present a resettlement plan, and the disregard for the affected populations—five years after the project became public—led to such a serious erosion of ELETROSUL's credibility in the region that CRAB decided to adopt the radical position of completely opposing the project. The slogan of the *atingidos* became "Não as Barragens" (No to the Dams). CRAB decided to circumvent ELETROSUL altogether and take the struggle over the company's head.

On 25 October 1983, CRAB launched a petition drive against the project that gathered 1,016,000 signatures over the next several months. (In addition to those fearing dislocation, people throughout Santa Catarina and Rio Grande do Sul signed the petition out of concern for the social and environmental impacts of the project that were not being addressed by ELETROSUL.) The Federation of Agricultural Workers (FETAG) backed CRAB's position and assisted in the petition drive; church leaders and several rural unions also took positions against the project. The bishop of Chapecó, Dom José Gomes, expressed the following widely held belief: "We know that in Brazil there is a surplus of energy. There is no necessity for the construction of these dams that will not benefit the people, but will benefit the owners of capital."[20]

The deterioration of ELETROSUL's legitimacy within the region was further displayed by CRAB's decision to deliver its petition signatures not to ELETROSUL headquarters in Florianopolis or even to ELETROBRAS headquarters in Rio de Janeiro, but directly to the Minister of Land Tenure Affairs, General Danilo Venturini, in Brasília. Venturini received them well, assuring them that he would take up the matter with ELETROBRAS, and he cautioned them not to sell their land.[21] On the way to Brasília, the CRAB delegation of thirty-three stopped at the ELETROBRAS headquarters in Rio de Janeiro to try to speak with the president and obtain clarifications about the project. However, they were met only by low-level aides who again offered little information and could not even tell them when the first dams would be built. The lesson CRAB learned from its struggle and from this trip is found in an article that appeared in *A Enchente do Uruguai*:

> It is not enough to promote or participate in negotiations to guarantee our right to remain on the land. It is necessary to broaden the fight, occupying all of the possible spaces in the newspapers, radio, television, local government offices, schools, in conclusion, to take our message everywhere of why we fight against the dams.[22]

From 1979 to 1984, as the struggle became more combative, CRAB evolved significantly as a regional movement. During the initial years (1979–82), activities focused primarily around the area of the Machadinho Dam, and even though thousands of families were threatened with displacement, CRAB itself had very few active members (CRAB 1989, 2). Led by concerned rural union leaders and members of FAPES, the first years were spent educating the rural communities and the wider public about the social and environmental threat posed by the project. The need for an organizational structure was not evident in the beginning, since the *atingidos* could not foresee difficulties with ELETROSUL, and they were only demanding what they considered to be obvious rights of compensation.[23]

Beginning in 1981, regular contacts began to be established with *atingidos* from the Itaipu Dam in the nearby state of Paraná, as well as with *atingidos* from Passo Real and other ELETROSUL projects at Salto Osório and Salto Santiago. The stories that the *atingidos* of the Uruguai Basin heard from those displaced by other dams stimulated widespread suspicion and a sense of urgency to seek guarantees from ELETROSUL. At every project, promises had been broken, whether they were for adequate resettlement or another form of compensation. Some *atingidos* traveled from other states to testify that they had been waiting for years for compensation, although they had long since lost their lands.[24] In 1983, a video was made about the experiences of those displaced by the Itaipu Dam, which showed people surviving in misery in the Amazonian state of Acre and others who failed to receive compensation for their lands. This video was shown by CRAB leaders throughout the countryside in 1983 and 1984 and proved to be a powerful communication tool, directly contributing to the growth of the movement.[25]

By the end of 1983 and through 1984, CRAB was establishing local and municipal commissions in the areas of the Machadinho and Itá dams as part of a structural expansion. The rural union headquarters in Erexim donated an office to CRAB so that volunteers could attend to the administrative duties of the movement.[26] Large assemblies were organized, including the First and Second *Encontros Interestaduais* (interstate conferences). At one protest against the dams organized by the Catholic church in 1983, 20,000 persons traveled from all over the region in a massive display of mounting distress over the project.[27]

During this initial period, ELETROSUL rejected the idea of consulting the *atingidos*. The agency's displacement policy was simply to pay off the legal landholders based on a pricing table set by the company. There was, in fact, no resettlement plan.[28] Dialogue with the *atingidos* was regarded as unnecessary and was not part of the historical practice of the company. ELETROSUL's approach to the project was succinctly expressed by a project official, who stated, "The time simply arrived for us to use the energy potential of the Uruguai River Basin."[29] The position of the *atingidos* was equally clear:

No one is against the dams, but what we cannot tolerate is the disregard for the farmers who are expelled from their land without receiving other land to continue their activities.[30]

The Turbulent Years

After the *I Encontro Estadual* in 1983 and the subsequent hard-line position taken by CRAB, ELETROSUL consistently showed itself to be ineffective in dealing with the mounting social tension. Rather than seeking to open lines of communication with the movement, the company hardened its position against CRAB, creating an explosive situation by 1987. CRAB grew in numbers and organizational capacity and continued to demand collective negotiations and a resettlement plan in the region. Meanwhile, ELETROSUL challenged the movement's representative authority in the region and sought to indemnify legal title-holders on a case-by-case basis.

ELETROSUL was adamant in avoiding any direct negotiations with CRAB, and in some cases it simply failed to show up for discussions with the *atingidos*. Those interviewed were unanimous in their comments that even when ELETROSUL officials appeared at meetings to explain the project, the farmers could not understand their technical jargon, which was always presented in terms of energy need and employment generation but avoided issues of relocation. The *atingidos* had learned from other projects that the possibility of losing their land was real, and it was clear to them that ELETROSUL had no resettlement plan. ELETROSUL's strategy of indemnifying only legal titleholders made no provisions for renters or sharecroppers (*sem-terras*), and the standard formula was always cash for land and assets. The movement, however, consistently fought against this strategy for three reasons: (1) Based on the experience of *atingidos* from other projects, they had learned that the money was almost never enough to begin again elsewhere—most farmers compensated in this manner ended in misery; (2) farmers negotiating prices with ELETROSUL on an individual basis, rather than collectively, ran the risk of not being indemnified fairly—with Brazil's persistent inflation, price negotiations could be quite complicated; and (3) compensating merely the legal titleholders overlooked the more complex social system of the region, which included a substantial number of *sem-terra* families. Furthermore, several broken promises of indemnification had already left the company with some powerful critics. The Bishop of the Diocese of Vacaria, Dom Orlando Dotti, angrily announced that "regarding 'dialogue' with ELETROSUL, we are against it, since their promises are never fulfilled."[31]

Besides attempting to buy out farmers on an individual basis—which most *atingidos* regarded as both a means of trying to cheat them and a way of avoiding the issue of the *sem-terras*—ELETROSUL sought to work through local mayors, leaders of the cooperatives, and other local officials whom the *atingidos* did not consider their spokespersons. These individuals argued for the benefits of the dams at local meetings, in the newspapers, and on the radio, urging everyone to trust ELETROSUL. CRAB regarded this strategy of coopting local leaders as a means of polarizing communities.

With at least the tacit blessing of ELETROSUL, a commission was established in support of the dams. Its intention was to challenge CRAB's authority as representative of the *atingidos*. This commission, *O Equipe de Justiça e Trabalho* (The Group for Justice and Work), had the support of several local mayors, presidents of four rural unions,[32] directors of the principal cooperative—COTREL—and the president of the Association of *Municípios* of the Alto Uruguai. In a letter to the public, CRAB accused the *Equipe* of being in the service of ELETROSUL and explained that COTREL was involved because it would benefit directly from the dam project: The cooperative was responsible for a colonization program in the state of Mato Grosso (CRAB 1984). Because positions taken and decisions made by the *Equipe* were not discussed with the *atingidos*, they lacked local support, and the *Equipe* soon dissolved.

Since ELETROSUL seemed unwilling to ameliorate the stress and anxiety of the *atingidos*, CRAB began to take a more aggressive posture toward the end of 1984 as the conflict approached the boiling point. Soon after the Rio-Brasília trip, a small group of CRAB leaders decided to make a trip to Brazil's northeast to learn from the experiences of the *atingidos* there. The fate of those who had failed to organize in time came as a shock to the CRAB leaders, who visited the Itaparica, Paulo Afonso, and Moxotó dams on the São Francisco River. At Itaparica, the dam was less than a year from actual operation, yet nearly 7,000 families had still not been compensated; the experience "showed clearly with whom we were fighting" and impressed upon the leaders the need to secure guarantees before the dams were built in the Uruguai Basin.[33] The *atingidos* from the northeast counseled their southern colleagues to undermine ELETROSUL's control in the region by destroying reservoir markers, presenting their own resettlement proposals, and forcing a signed accord before it was too late.[34] This type of communication between grassroots organizations proved to be critical for CRAB's future successes.

Upon returning from the northeast, CRAB organized meetings in all the *municípios* of the Machadinho region to pass on the lessons learned. Many communities subsequently called for the destruction of all reservoir markers. In the *município* of Viadutos, two days were set aside for collecting the heavy markers. After a celebration and church service, the wooden markers were broken, doused with oil, and set on fire. To conclude the ceremony, all traces of the markers were thrown in the river.[35] At another meeting, nearly 2,000 farmers removed and destroyed markers in Sananduva after watching the film about the struggle of the *atingidos* of the Itaipu Dam.[36] Such acts of defiance would be performed by communities and individuals throughout 1985 and 1986.

In March 1985, the Minister of Mines and Energy, Aureliano Chaves, announced that the dam project in the Uruguai Basin had been suspended because of unresolved social concerns.[37] A senator from Rio Grande do Sul, who had met with Chaves to help influence his decision, proclaimed: "Enough of projects that only respect technical data, insensitive to people's dramatic situation. Regarding the treatment of dams, the number one priority is now the social aspect."[38] Nevertheless, and much to the dismay of the residents, ELETROSUL continued to plant markers, complete measurements, and undertake other studies.[39] To make matters worse, from the *atingidos'* perspective, ELETROSUL functionaries working in both the Machadinho and Itá areas were now entering properties without the permission of the owners.

Tense confrontations began to take place, and the protests became more aggressive. The slogan of the *atingidos* was still "Não as Barragens," and Brasília had announced the suspension of the project, yet workers were still entering farmers' properties. CRAB's newsletter alerted the population that workers were sneaking around in personal cars in order to accomplish their tasks undetected.[40] CRAB understood this to be a flagrant challenge to the resolve of the movement, and farmers began to expel workers from their lands. One *atingido* expressed the collective anger:

> Why is ELETROSUL invading the land of the farmers without permission, using the name of municipal council and the mayor of Viadutos? If the dam project on the Uruguai River is suspended, why is ELETROSUL trying to take land in the region?[41]

Protests in the region became much more dramatic during this period, such as the one at Tapejara on 12 October 1985 (National Day of Protest against the Construction of Dams and for Agrarian Reform). *Atingidos* gathered from dozens of *municípios* to complain that machines were still working in spite of Chaves's announcement of the project's suspension. They burned a coffin full of protest signs and then engaged in a long march during which fifteen people carried a heavy wooden cross to symbolize the suffering of the people. They reenacted the history of the dam project through a theater presentation and chanted, "ELETROSUL, ELETROBRAS, *quanta tristeza você me traz*" (ELETROSUL, ELETROBRAS, how much grief you bring me).[42]

In October 1985, Chaves reaffirmed that the dam project was in fact suspended until ELETROSUL completed a restudy concerning the necessity of the project and until resources had been secured for resettlement and the resolution of all land problems.[43] However, the restudy commission demanded by CRAB was not created; in its place, the minister called for two commissions, one each for Machadinho and Itá, to study the socioeconomic aspects of the project for the purpose of mitigating social costs. One CRAB leader expressed the disappointment of the movement, "it [Chaves's decision] is authoritarian, because it negates the re-study of the project and ignores data that the movement has presented."[44] Chaves intended that CRAB be represented on the commissions, but disappointed CRAB leaders said that the decision about whether to participate (now seen as legitimizing the project) would have to be made by the membership, and only after discussions could be held in every affected community.

Over the next several months, while ELETROSUL continued its work on the dams, CRAB organized over 100 meetings throughout the region to discuss the commissions and the implications of CRAB's participation. The thoroughness of CRAB's attempt to reach a democratic decision proved to be important in mobilizing the population and also boosted CRAB's legitimacy as the representative of the *atingidos*. The result of the local discussions was that the majority of the population now believed that the dams were inevitable, that ELETROSUL was too great an adversary, and that participation on the commissions would be the only way to guarantee their rights of compensation.[45] They elected representatives to sit on the commissions, but by August 1986 these members became disillusioned with the pace and lack of genuine discussion on the commissions and decided to withdraw their support.

Having abandoned the hope that participation on Chaves's commissions would bring them any benefits, CRAB began to demand a meeting with ELETROSUL's new president Wilmar Dall'Agnol. According to the *atingidos*, a meeting was finally arranged for 15 August 1986 in Carlos Gomes; Dall'Agnol was said to have agreed to attend this meeting on three separate occasions,[46] but when the day came, he sent three functionaries in his place, who again offered few concrete answers to questions about resettlement. Dall'Agnol's absence was taken as the most direct affront yet suffered by the movement. The CRAB representatives refused to let the ELETROSUL workers leave the meeting until they had spoken with Dall'Agnol by telephone and arranged for him to meet personally with them on 26 August, at which time he was to bring concrete answers to their questions.[47] They continued to hold the functionaries for several hours while they produced a document stating that no work would be permitted in the region until satisfactory answers had been received from the company and that the *atingidos* would not be responsible for the safety of workers who entered the region (CRAB 1986b).

Dall'Agnol, however, had no intention of appearing at the meeting. On 24 August, he sent a letter to the press stating that ELETROSUL would not be coerced into meeting CRAB's demands and that the actions of the *atingidos* were "totally condemnable . . . anti-democratic and criminal."[48] After the scheduled meeting on the twenty-sixth, when Dall'Agnol did not appear, the *atingidos* marched en masse and blocked a local highway for several hours as a symbol of their protest. In the following months, Dall'Agnol became embroiled in a political scandal and was replaced as president of ELETROSUL. Meanwhile, none of the social questions regarding the project had been resolved.

In a general assembly on 5 May 1987, the frustrated movement decided on a more conciliatory approach of permitting workers into the region to demarcate the margin of the reservoirs for the Machadinho and Itá dams. Conditions were spelled out, however, including demands that ELETROSUL provide a resettlement plan by 15 July 1987, that *atingidos* accompany workers performing the demarcation at ELETROSUL's expense, and that no *atingido* be pressured into negotiations (CRAB 1987a). The May 1987 issue of *A Enchente do Uruguai* also contained a list of denunciations of ELETROSUL, such as its failure to indemnify 300 families in Aratiba as promised, the total exclusion of the local population from discussions concerning their displacement, and ELETROSUL's failure to present even one area for resettlement of the *atingidos* (CRAB 1987a).

As the company's demarcation work resumed in the region, the federal government signed a decree for the expropriation of the work site and diversion canal at the Itá Dam, prompting a strong reaction by the movement. In a special publication, CRAB declared:

> In this decree, the government expropriates land of the *atingidos* without presenting land for resettlement, proving once again their disregard for the social question. For this and for other attitudes of the government of the New Republic and of ELETROSUL who do not favor the affected population, we must unite to defend our land. (CRAB 1987b)

A group of more than fifty farmers from the Itá Dam area decided that they had had enough by June 1987. They entered the Itá work site and captured one of the chief engineers. Marching him through the construction areas, they forced him to order a complete work stoppage that lasted one week.[49] Such acts were important for the resolve and confidence of the movement; they had little impact, however, on the project overall.

As the 15 July deadline for a concrete resettlement plan passed by, ELETROSUL workers continued to enter the region, but by now the situation had become explosive. Functionaries were captured in the *município* of Paim Filho on 16 and 19 July. On the first occasion, a worker captured while placing markers for aerial photographs was "delivered" to ELETROSUL's project headquarters in Erexim by truckloads of angry residents. *Atingidos* interviewed by local television stations warned the company that in subsequent captures, they might not be so restrained. CRAB leaders regarded the July conflicts as consequential because they proved to ELETROSUL that they were not "playing around"—they believed that ELETROSUL had specifically sent the workers into the region after the 15 July deadline to test their resolve.[50]

On 24 July, CRAB organized a mass protest in Erexim, where 5,000 to 7,000 farmers surrounded ELETROSUL headquarters and demanded that a meeting be arranged with the company's president immediately. When employees said that such a meeting was impossible, the demonstrators began to press in on the building and threatened to burn it to the ground. After a tense couple of hours, a small delegation of *atingidos* was allowed into the office to speak with the president by telephone. He agreed to meet representatives from CRAB at his office in Florianopolis on 7 August. For the first time since the news of the project hit the region, ELETROSUL and CRAB were to sit down for genuine discussions regarding the future of the *atingidos*. The 7 August meeting would lead to a series of additional meetings and the signing of a resettlement accord on 29 October 1987.[51]

The Agreement

The accord called for separate discussions for the Machadinho and Itá dam areas, in which representatives from CRAB would meet with ELETROSUL officials to iron out the details for resettlement. Discussions for Itá began as scheduled in January 1988, but ELETROSUL has since claimed an inability to fulfill its part of the accord due to resource limitations. Tensions again mounted to the point that *atingidos* occupied the ELETROSUL office in Erexim for several days in July 1991 as a sign of protest.

The situation with the Machadinho Dam became even more conflictual. In June 1988, when the Machadinho resettlement negotiations were scheduled to begin, ELETROSUL called CRAB into its Erexim office to announce that due to financial constraints the company would have to suspend negotiations until a later date.[52] On 1 July, eight ELETROSUL workers were captured and expelled from the *município* of Getulio Vargas (Machadinho area).[53] Furious with the company, CRAB called an assembly in Erexim on 4 July in order to decide how to deal with the ELETROSUL announcement. Its earlier strategy had been to force a signed accord in order to guarantee the *atingidos'* rights; now that the accord had clearly been broken, CRAB's options were few. The *atingidos* of the Machadinho Dam decided that the company had been given enough chances and that if the conditions of the signed accord were not met immediately, CRAB would demand the definite cancellation of the dam. They further proposed that the Machadinho site be given to resettle some of the families from the Itá Dam.

In a second assembly on 25 July, after no advances had been made by ELETROSUL, the *atingidos* voted unanimously to launch a campaign for the permanent cancellation of Machadinho. The new slogan became "*Machadinho Nunca Mais*" (Machadinho never again). After the assembly, with the participation of the bishop of Vacaria, 2,000 *atingidos* burned the newly placed reservoir markers and copies of the Machadinho construction schedule in front of ELETROSUL's Erexim office.[54] Since this demonstration, ELETROSUL has not attempted to resume operations on the Machadinho Dam, citing financial constraints and the hostile social climate as its reasons.[55] As one local leader stated, "Now, we are letting no one from ELETROSUL enter the region . . . here, no one even sets foot."[56]

Summary of CRAB's Evolution

By the time the accord was reached in 1987, CRAB had evolved into a democratic and highly organized social movement.[57] From a small group of committed leaders in the early 1980s, the movement had expanded its organizational base by promoting local and municipal committees in all the affected regions. In 1984, an Executive Committee was formed to meet and discuss the movement's business on a regular basis, and in 1985, a Secretariat was created—and a full-time director hired—to carry out administrative functions, including the publication of *A Enchente do Uruguai* and the training of local leaders. Neither the Executive Committee nor the Secretariat was given decisionmaking capacities—decisions were always made by discussions and voting at the base level (local committees) and then passed up through local representatives at regional meetings. In the first years of its existence, CRAB depended quite heavily on help from outsiders (especially concerning information from both FAPES and the union headquarters in Erexim), but it eventually developed into an internally strong and democratic organization, marking a shift from past movements' dependence on charismatic leaders.

In 1985, CRAB divided the impact area of the twenty-five dams into five regions; this helped organize activities over a vast area and expand membership.[58] To facilitate decisionmaking even further, CRAB instituted the General Assembly in 1986. Important decisions are now made by this body of local representatives after the discussion process at the base level. The publication of *A Enchente do Uruguai* also became more regular and more sophisticated. In addition to informing communities of meetings and news related to the dam projects, it also began to feature articles on the environmental impacts of dams and the economic and energy policies of the Brazilian government. CRAB meetings began to incorporate discussions of these topics as well.

CRAB also showed itself to be an effective player in the international arena. Leaders traveled abroad to participate in environmental conferences and to foster ties with nongovernmental organizations such as the U.S.-based Environmental Defense Fund. Through these connections, CRAB has been able to exert pressure on institutions such as the World Bank to provide assurance that any loan made to Brazil's energy sector deals adequately with the social and environmental costs of proposed projects. In one case, when representatives of the Inter-American Development Bank came to the region to meet with officials of ELETROSUL, CRAB was told that it could not be part of the meeting, since the discussions would be technical. CRAB called the Environmental Defense Fund in Washington, D.C., which then called the bank's headquarters, and a meeting with the *atingidos* was soon arranged.

The movement became an integral part of the lives of many farmers, a means for the defense of their families and land. For most of the leaders, it was the first time they had ever experienced conducting meetings, dealing with the media, and negotiating with an adversary.[59] The signed accord was seen as a victory of their struggle, a victory earned through sacrifice and hard work. Far from being a gift from ELETROSUL, the accord was "a conquest by the *atingidos*."[60]

Conclusion

As of July 1991, over a decade since ELETROSUL entered the region, there is very little to show for the Uruguai River Basin project. On paper, the *atingidos* have agreed to allow the construction of the Itá Dam on the condition that all residents facing displacement have a choice of resettlement or monetary compensation. The movement even demanded that the *sem-terras* be the first families to be resettled. This resettlement process began in August 1989, when thirty-two *sem-terra* families were moved to plots of twenty to twenty-five hectares in Marmeleiro, Paraná.[61] An ELETROSUL official conceded that this is the first resettlement project that includes *sem-terras*.[62] A second resettlement effort was completed in April 1990 that benefited fifty additional families from the Itá area. However, continued progress at the Itá site is being threatened by ELETROSUL's insistence that funding constraints will force the company to postpone future scheduled resettlement programs. The *atingidos'* patience may be wearing out, as witnessed by the July 1991 occupation of ELETROSUL offices in Erexim.

The Machadinho Dam, which was slated to be the first constructed, has been completely suspended. In areas I visited, all signs of ELETROSUL have been removed and replaced with signs reading "Machadinho Nunca Mais." At Campos Novos, scheduled to be the third dam after Itá and Machadinho, local CRAB committees confronted ELETROSUL workers entering the region in September 1988, insisting that no work would be permitted until all problems were satisfactorily resolved at the Machadinho site.[63] Now that CRAB is well organized in all five regions of the Uruguai Basin, ELETROSUL's difficulties in Campos Novos are being repeated at other sites as well. Clearly, the company underestimated CRAB's organizational strength and communications network.

The strongest complaints of the *atingidos* were their complete exclusion from the project and the withholding of information by ELETROSUL. Project officials have since admitted that the failure to establish an effective communication system with the public was a major cause of the company's loss of credibility (Canali, Munoz, and Schwab 1986).[64] Closely associated with these concerns was the resentment created by the authoritarian practices of the company, such as entering lands without permission, not appearing for meetings, missing indemnification deadlines for groups of families, continuing to work while the project was suspended, and finally breaking the signed accord. At several points in the history of the project, the company missed valuable opportunities to work with, instead of against, the movement. At various stages, the company could have cut its losses and mended its relationship with CRAB, thereby utilizing the movement's organizational resources and legitimacy with the *atingidos* to overcome resistance and assist in the process of relocation.

The changes in policy that occurred after 1986—direct negotiations with the *atingidos*, the establishment of accords concerning the displacement process, the resettlement of *sem-terras*—were the result of pressure on the company rather than social learning. Through protests and demonstrations, through the media and public forums, through international alliances, and by capturing company workers and occupying offices, the movement successfully forced the debate over the dams into the public arena and, in the end, had an impact on the policies of ELETROSUL.[65]

Due to a conjunction of factors, especially after the mid-1980s, it became increasingly difficult for ELETROSUL to ignore CRAB. The democratic opening in Brazil over the last decade has allowed popular groups progressively more political space in which to organize and protest. At the same time, rural movements have dramatically increased their communication skills: With the assistance of rural unions and the Catholic church, both of which can call upon well-established organizational networks, groups fighting against dam projects traveled across states to trade experiences, made videos exposing the threat of the dams, and shared organizing skills and strategies.

This increased level of mobilization and cooperation between popular organizations has led to the recent formation of a national movement of *atingidos*, the National Movement of Workers Affected by Dams. This movement is beginning to coordinate activities related to enforcing signed accords, guaranteeing the solution of all social and environmental problems at existing dam projects, and ensuring a proper accounting of these costs in all future projects. Forcing reforms within the energy sector and protecting the territorial rights of indigenous groups are also objectives of the new movement. The newly formed National Committee contains representative members from all regions in Brazil (except for the center-west region, where the *atingidos* are not organized on a regional level) as well as representatives from several indigenous groups and the Central Unica dos Trabalhadores (CUT; Central Workers' Union). This new movement will surely affect how future dam projects are implemented.

Accounts from other dam projects in Brazil (such as Tucuruí, Itaparica, and Itaipu) confirm that the poor treatment of the *atingidos* in the Uruguai Basin was not an isolated case, suggesting that policies related to the displacement of populations in Brazil are in serious need of reform. First, it is necessary that an accurate system of estimating the social and environmental costs of dam projects be implemented. This should include providing options for those who will be displaced: either resettlement under conditions at least equal to their present situation, or adequate monetary compensation for their land and assets. Implicit in such a policy is the assumption that all persons affected by a project will experience improved living conditions or, at a minimum, will not suffer worse conditions. In addition to those displaced, considerations must be made for families living near the riverbanks below any dam, since they are likely to be affected by changes in water quality and the inconstant river level (Vianna 1989). Such an accurate and comprehensive accounting of all social and environmental costs will certainly mean that many projects designed for populated areas will not be economically viable.

Projects that remain viable even with full accounting of all costs need to be much more inclusive of local populations in the planning and implementation of displacement. Project officials should consult with affected communities at early stages of the project and communicate with them fully regarding their plans and schedule (Brokensha and Scudder 1968). This would include showing them the expected margin of the reservoir and genuinely involving them in discussions and decisions concerning displacement: amount of compensation, location of land for resettlement, housing, infrastructure, timing of the move, and additional details. Such community involvement would necessarily involve an approach to resettlement that regards the relocation of communities as a form of development, not just as clearing the project area.

The lessons of the Uruguai River Basin project demonstrate the capacity of local populations to resist threats to their land and livelihood and their desire to be included in decisions that affect their future. CRAB's struggle (and the struggle of the newly formed national movement) has been to guarantee that the farmers in the Uruguai Basin will not be the victims of a development policy meant to benefit only other groups. The farmers are asserting their identity and demanding to be heard. As Sherer-Warren and Reis (1986) have noted, social movements in Brazil such as CRAB are establishing new relations with the state, creating new historical subjects in the process, and redefining the meaning of citizenship.

Notes

1. Other objectives for dam projects include improving agricultural productivity through irrigation, controlling seasonal floodwaters, and improving river navigation.
2. For example, Budweg refers to hydropower as "non-polluting" and calls for its use in Brazil "as much as possible" (Budweg 1983, 29). However, although hydroelectric projects do not pollute in a conventional sense, recent research highlights the environmental destruction and polluting effects of reservoir creation (Goldsmith and Hildyard 1984, 1986; Farvar and Milton 1972).
3. A registry of Brazilian dams includes 684 dams. Of the 104 larger dams (those over 50 meters high), 97 were built after 1960 (Comitê Brasileiro de Grandes Barragens 1982, 251–79).
4. For the Tucuruí case in the Brazilian Amazon, see Monosowski 1986.
5. The most thorough examination of the environmental impacts of large dam projects is found in Goldsmith and Hildyard 1984, 51–230.
6. The estimates also included 710 Kaingang and Guaraní Indians.
7. Letter from CRAB to the Minister of Mines and Energy, July 1985.
8. A *município* is an administrative district, usually containing an urban center, several small towns or villages, and the surrounding hinterland.

9. Interviews with Raimundo Pedroza and Henrique Stempkowski.
10. "Barragens: encontro em Erexim," *Zero Hora*, 18 October 1981.
11. "Aldo Pinto quer informações sobre as barragens do Uruguai," *Zero Hora*, 10 December 1981.
12. "Prefeitos recomendam aos agricultores que confiem apenas na palavra oficial," *Voz da Serra*, 10 November 1981.
13. "Barragens: informações desencontradas," *Zero Hora*, 19 February 1983.
14. "Colonos protestam contra o que chamam de tática do desmentido," *Zero Hora*, 14 May 1983.
15. Letter from ELETROBRAS president, José Costa Cavalcanti, to Rio Grande do Sul state representatives Adylson Motta and Marino Andrade, 4 March 1983.
16. Interview with Ivar Pavan.
17. Interview with Ivar Pavan.
18. *A Enchente do Uruguai*, no. 3, September 1983, pp. 3–4, and interviews with Raimundo Pedroza and Reinaldo Pertile.
19. Interview with Mauro Postal.
20. *A Enchente do Uruguai*, no. 6, March 1984, p. 5.
21. *A Enchente do Uruguai*, no. 8, August 1984, p. 6.
22. *A Enchente do Uruguai*, no. 8, August 1984, p. 5.
23. Interview with Raimundo Pedroza.
24. "II Encontro Interestadual de Barragens," *Voz da Serra*, 3 March 1984.
25. *A Enchente do Uruguai*, no. 7, June 1984, p. 6.
26. Interview with Raimundo Pedroza.
27. "O Protesto dos colonos contra as barragens," *Zero Hora*, 16 February 1983.
28. Interview with Pedro Paulo Voltolini Jr., ELETROSUL Division Director for the Implantation of the Reservoirs on the Uruguai River.
29. "Empresa diz que nao vai alterar projeto," *Zero Hora*, 20 December 1984.
30. "Documento a Figueiredo: Barragens no Rio Uruguai desalojarao 200 mil," *Gazeta Rural*, July 1984.
31. *A Enchente do Uruguai*, no. 10, April 1985, p. 8.
32. CRAB considered unions participating in this *Equipe* to be *sindicatos pelegos*, or lazy, insignificant unions, which do not represent the will of the people, as opposed to the *sindicatos auténticos*, or authentic unions, which actively defend the rights of their members. Both types of unions are found in most *municípios* in the region.
33. Interview with Luis Dalla Costa.
34. Interview with Reinaldo Pertile.
35. Interview with Reinaldo Pertile.
36. *A Enchente do Uruguai*, no. 14, March/April 1986, p. 7.
37. "Aureliano garante: barragens não vao mais ser construídas," *Zero Hora*, 24 March 1985. The announcement prompted the immediate resignation of ELETROSUL president Thompson Flores, who claimed political reasons were behind the suspension and argued for the southern region's energy needs ("Presidente da ELETROSUL renuncia e expoe razoes," *Gazeta Mercantil*, 3 April 1985).
38. "Aureliano garante: barragens nao vao mais ser construídas," *Zero Hora*, 24 March 1985.
39. "Aureliano prometeu suspender as obras. Mas elas continuam," *Zero Hora*, 1 October 1985.
40. *A Enchente do Uruguai*, no. 11, July 1985, p. 3.

41. Quoted in "Apesar da proibiçao, ELETROSUL nao para," *Zero Hora*, 23 August 1985.
42. *A Enchente do Uruguai*, no. 13, November/December 1985, p. 3, and "Agricultores prometem continuar a campanha," *Zero Hora*, 14 October 1985.
43. "Aureliano reafirma que a ELETROSUL já suspendeu as obras," *Zero Hora*, 2 October 1985.
44. *A Enchente do Uruguai*, no. 14, March/April 1986, p. 5.
45. Interview with Luis Dalla Costa and Mauro Postal.
46. Interviews with Henrique Stempkowski and Reinaldo Pertile.
47. "Técnicos da ELETROSUL presos por colonos em Getulio Vargas," *Zero Hora*, 16 August 1986.
48. "ELETROSUL—Nota Oficial," *Diário da Manha*, 24 August 1986.
49. Interviews with Nilo Brandt and Luis Dalla Costa.
50. Interviews with Henrique Stempkowski and Alberto Cervinski.
51. Interview with Henrique Stempkowsksi and *A Enchente do Uruguai*, no. 19, January 1988. The Minister of Mines and Energy (Chaves) also signed the accord on 6 November 1987.
52. Interviews with Ivar Pavan and Luis Dalla Costa; also *A Enchente do Uruguai*, no. 23, July 1988, p. 3. Although Brazil's energy sector has been having a difficult financial time recently, the movement has opined that this is being used as a stalling technique. ELETROSUL's position has also been challenged through constant complaints that if the company does not have resources to fulfill the signed accord, then there should be no money for other aspects of construction that have continued openly.
53. Interviews with Ivar Pavan and Luis Dalla Costa; also *A Enchente do Uruguai*, no. 23, July 1988, p. 3.
54. *A Enchente do Uruguai*, no. 24, August 1988, p. 3.
55. Interview with Pedro Paulo Voltolini Jr.
56. Interview with Henrique Stempkowski.
57. Ilse Sherer-Warren and Maria José Reis (1986) provide an excellent discussion of CRAB as a "new" social movement.
58. The five regions are Region I, Itá and Machadinho; Region II, Itapiranga and Iraí; Region III, Lages and Vacario; Region IV, Chapecó and Chapecozinho; Region V, Garabí and Roncador. Each area is named after the principal dams slated for its area.
59. Interviews with Luis Dalla Costa and Ivar Pavan.
60. *A Enchente do Uruguai*, no. 18, September 1987, p. 3.
61. According to CRAB, the families resettled in Marmeleiro are now producing 15,000 sacks of corn, 700 sacks of soybeans and 2,000 to 3,000 sacks of beans annually (*A Enchente do Uruguai*, no. 33, May 1990, p. 5).
62. Interview with Clodis Guimarães de Souza, ELETROSUL Appraisal Technician.
63. *A Enchente do Uruguai*, no. 24, August 1988, p. 6. The *atingidos* of Campos Novos met with ELETROSUL for the first time just two months after ELETROSUL broke the resettlement accord. They complained angrily that if ELETROSUL did not have the finances to comply with the Machadinho accord, what was it doing in Campos Novos? By December 1988, residents were removing markers set by the company (*A Enchente do Uruguai*, no. 26, December 1988).

64. Interview with Pedro Paulo Voltolini Jr.
65. Beyond the scope of the Uruguai Basin, the efforts of movements such as CRAB are also having an impact on broader policy questions. Vianna (1989) points out that movements of *atingidos* have had an influence on the development of Brazilian environmental legislation, although these movements have not used this legislation to their benefit to any great degree.

References

Assembléia Legislativa. Estado do Rio Grande do Sul. 1983. *Nossa terra vai sumir do mapa: Vamos deixar?* Encontro Estadual sobre Implantação de Barragens na Bacía do Rio Uruguai.

Budweg, F. M. G. 1983. "Water Resources and the Environment: Development Planning in Brazil." *International Water Power and Dam Construction* 35 (July): 29–36.

Brokensha, David, and Thayer Scudder. 1968. "Resettlement." In *Dams in Africa: An Interdisciplinary Study of Man-Made Lakes in Africa*, edited by Neville Rubin and William M. Warren. London: Frank Cass and Company.

Canali, G. V., H. R. Munoz, and M. A. Schwab. 1986. "Hydropower Development in Southern Brazil: Requirements for Solving Conflicts and Promoting Social Benefits." Paper presented at the International Symposium on the Impact of Large Water Projects on the Environment, UNESCO, Paris, October.

Comitê Brasileiro de Grandes Barragens. 1982. *Barragens No Brasil*. São Paulo: Editora Técnica.

CRAB. 1980. "Manifesto dos Agricultores do Alto Uruguai Gaúcho e Catarinense sobre Barragens."

———. 1981. "Comunicado." Marcelino Ramos: CRAB, August 7.

———. 1984. "Sobre a Equipe a favor das barragens." Erechim: CRAB, November 13.

———. 1986. "Assembléia dos atingidos pelas barragens." Getulio Vargas: CRAB, August 15.

———. 1987a. "Assembléia do movimento dos atingidos por barragens. Região 1–Itá e Machadinho." *Documento oficial dos atingidos*. Erechim: CRAB, May 5.

———. 1987b. "Enchente Urgente." no. 2. July.

———. 1989. "Breve histórico do movimento de atingidos por barragens." July 28.

Farvar, M. Taghi, and John P. Milton, eds. 1972. *The Careless Technology*. Garden City, N.Y.: Natural History Press.

Goldsmith, Edward, and Nicholas Hildyard. 1984. *The Social and Environmental Effects of Large Dams*. San Francisco: Sierra Club Books.

Goldsmith, Edward, and Nicholas Hildyard, eds. 1986. *The Social and Environmental Effects of Large Dams, Volume 2: Case Studies*. Camelford, United Kingdom: Wadebridge Ecological Centre.

Michaels, Pete S., and Steven F. Napolitano. 1988. "The Hidden Costs of Hydroelectric Dams." *Cultural Survival Quarterly* 12(2): 2–4.

Monosowski, Elizabeth. 1986. "Brazil's Tucuruí Dam: Development at Environmental Cost." In Goldsmith and Hildyard 1986, 191–98.

Santos, Silvio Coelho dos. 1974. *Nova história de Santa Catarina*. Florianópolis: Pedidos.

Santos, Silvio Coelho dos, and Aneliese Nacke. 1988. "Povos indígenas e desenvolvimento hidrelétrico na Amazônia." *Revista Brasileira de Ciencias Sociais* 3(8): 71–84.

Scherer-Warren, Ilse, and Maria José Reis. 1986. "As barragens do Uruguai: a dinâmica de um movimento social." *Boletim de Ciencias Sociais*. Universidade Federal de Santa Catarina, Centro de Ciencias Humanas 42: 24–48.

Sigaud, Ligia. 1986. "Efeitos sociais de grandes projetos hidrelétricos: as barragens de Sobradinho e Machadinho." Comunicação No. 9, Programa de Pos-Graduação em Antropología Social. Universidade Federal do Rio de Janeiro, Museu Nacional.

Skidmore, Thomas E. 1973. "Politics and Economic Policy Making in Authoritarian Brazil, 1937–71." In *Authoritarian Brazil*, edited by Alfred Stepan. New Haven: Yale University Press.

Vianna, Aureliano. 1989. "Hidrelectricas e meio ambiente: informações basicas sobre o ambientalismo oficial e o setor eletrico no Brasil." Rio de Janeiro: Centro Ecumenico de Documentação e Informação (CEDI). July.

Williams, Philip. 1986. "Introduction." In *The Social and Environmental Effects of Large Dams, Volume 2: Case Studies*. Goldsmith and Hildyard 1986, 9–14.

FOUR

THE STRUGGLE OF THE SERINGUEIROS

Environmental Action in the Amazon

MICHELLE A. MELONE

AN URGENT TELEGRAM FROM ACRE was received during the third day of the seminar. Two rural union members had been shot. Both were dead, and officials refused to investigate—attributing both casualties to drunken accidents. The seminar, entitled "The Planning and Administration of the Creation of Extractive Reserves in Amazonia," was being held in Curitiba, the capital of the southern state of Parana, far from the area of actual conflict in the Amazon. Gathered were rubber tappers, local government officials, researchers, representatives of international environmental organizations, and local community members who were working in isolated Amazonian extractive communities.[1] Seminar participants had gathered to discuss and share ideas about bringing into reality extractive reserves, which are a special land reform program advocated by extractive workers. Their common purpose was to stop the very kind of violence that the urgent telegram announced—violence that had become commonplace in disputes over land and deforestation in the Amazon. Rubber tappers and government officials from Acre were tense as they made plans for an immediate return. Other participants in the seminar strove to continue their work, hoping that if a more comprehensive planning procedure could be defined, perhaps extractive reserves would become a reality more quickly. But the mood was heavy as a petition was drawn up asking for investigation into the deaths. Most likely, the petition would come to nothing.

Brazilian rubber tappers have lived in areas of the Amazon for decades, tapping rubber from wild rubber trees. Many are descendants of men brought into the region during the great Amazon rubber booms of 1870 and 1915. Some remain from recruitment during World War II—the last real attempt at reinstituting rubber production on a large scale in the Amazon. It is estimated that they occupy between 240,000 and 380,000 square kilometers of forest, an area roughly 8.4 percent of the Amazon (Environmental Defense Fund 1991). Tappers live within the forest and use its living resources to an extent that, except for indigenous populations, few can emulate. They often reside in isolated forest areas and employ a variety of production practices to gain their subsistence, including the gathering of forest products, hunting, fishing, and small crop cultivation (Weinstein 1983; Hecht, Anderson, and May 1988; Melone 1988). Their main cash income, however, comes from the sale of natural rubber latex tapped from trees in the forest. They practice what many view as a "sustainable" production system.

These rubber tapping populations of the forest, estimated at approximately 500,000 (Schwartzman 1987b), are caught up in a movement that is gaining recognition and support throughout Brazil and internationally. Their movement combines the broad notion of preserving the Amazon rain forest with their personal interest in finding a place for themselves amid the swirling forces of development that have been unleashed in the Amazon. Today, they see a place for themselves amid competing interests, and this place offers a sustainable development alternative for the region based on the rubber tappers' unique management skills and productive activities. Unfortunately, assassinations and deadly confrontations have become common occurrences.

The Amazon is the largest tract of rain forest ecosystem left on the planet. Its destruction stirs great concern because of its immense biological diversity (Wilson 1988) and increasing fears of the global climatic implications—ranging from global warming to less severe shifts in regional climate (Salati 1987). Current development options in the region not only threaten the rain forest environment but also imply repercussions for forest populations such as the rubber tappers who live within and use the rain forest to support themselves. Not surprisingly, the Brazilian government's policies to expand and economically develop the region's potential are the subject of much academic debate (Barbira-Scazzocchio 1980; Browder 1989; Bunker 1985; Hemming 1985a, 1985b; Hecht and Cockburn 1989; Lisansky 1990; Cleary 1991). Many of these discussions point to the need for more sustainable development options in the region.

The inhabitants of the Amazon could certainly benefit from new forms of sustainable development—especially ones incorporating their contributions. Until very recently, development efforts have conspicuously ignored the inhabitants' knowledge of the ecological limits and capabilities of the fragile rain forest ecosystem. Despite their considerable number, the very existence of these people has often been ignored. These oversights compound the difficulties of identifying successful methods of production in an unfamiliar environment. After thirty years of development efforts in the region, little economic stability exists, and few of the government-sponsored policies have brought their promised successes. Efforts to change these policies have given impetus to the rubber tapper movement.

This chapter tells the story of the rubber tapper movement in the Brazilian Amazon. It begins with a brief discussion of the development history of the Amazon region, using the history of one western state to illustrate the conflicts that ensue. A discussion of the history of rubber production follows to clarify the events leading up to the current situation. Next, I trace the beginnings of the rubber tapper movement and elaborate on its significance both to the tappers and to others who seek empowerment through organized actions against more powerful forces of society. I close with some remarks about the wider significance of environmental action in the Amazon.

History of Amazonian Development

Approximately two to three million inhabitants of the Amazon region could be classified as forest dwellers (Hecht and Cockburn 1989). Along with indigenous groups, these forest dwellers have consistently been the victims of the forces driving development in the region. Contemporary Amazonian development has been a relatively short yet complicated series of ambitious plans and disastrous failures. Investment and planning began in the early 1950s and 1960s in the hope of utilizing this vast region's potential, but by the early 1970s, the Amazon region still contributed only 4 percent to the Brazilian gross national product (GNP) and held only 8 percent of the population, despite accounting for 59 percent of the total area of Brazil (Gayley 1977; Kohlhepp 1982).

Long thought of as a wild frontier, the Amazon has held the fancy of Brazilian policymakers as a region of great unexplored potential. Excessive enthusiasm was curbed when the area's many geographical and social obstacles hindered its easy incorporation into the larger Brazilian economy. Not only did the Amazon have inadequate physical infrastructure for transport, communication, and energy, it also lacked an economic structure that could aid in easy exploitation of the region's resources. Up until the 1950s, the region's economy still depended primarily on extractive forest products such as rubber, Brazil nuts, and wood. The main commerce in the region was geared toward trade in these products, rubber being the predominant resource.

The push to develop and occupy the Amazon region began in earnest in the 1950s. A series of disruptive processes heralded these efforts and, as a result, the isolated lives of forest populations began to be threatened. In the minds of policymakers, the Amazon region was a vast uninhabited region; the actual presence of more than two million people living in the forest, subsisting on petty extraction, was bound to generate conflict. The "invisible" forest populations faced an onslaught of colonists and cattle ranchers brought in by new government policies. These newcomers were bent on cutting down the rain forest to create pastures and agricultural fields.

The rubber tapper movement began in the western Amazonian state of Acre (Figure 4.1), and Acrean contemporary history is a good illustration of how conflicts engendered by official development policies are playing themselves out. Acre has had a long history of tumultuous land conflict: Ownership has been claimed by Bolivia and by Amazonas (a neighboring Amazonian state), and it has been an independent nation; it was finally declared a Brazilian state in 1903. Despite playing a large part in the two Amazon rubber booms in 1870 and 1915, until the early 1970s Acre remained an isolated frontier with few ties to the rest of the country.

In early 1970, Acre governor Wanderley Dantas began to advocate development policies for the state, targeting out-of-state investors in land. These investments were further encouraged by Amazonian regional policies. The Superintendencia do Desenvolvimento da Amazonia (SUDAM) had been created in 1966 to channel fiscal incentives to the private sector, mostly livestock ventures. The Plan for National Integration (PIN) was initiated in 1971, focusing primarily on land investment for colonization and road building. These efforts proved successful and, by 1975, 80 percent of the land in Acre had been sold to new investors (Schwartzman 1987b).

Land was usually transferred from traditional rubber barons to new investors. The rubber barons controlled large landholdings as well as the extraction of rubber on these lands. They organized tappers (*seringueiros*) into rubber-producing estates known as *seringais*. Tappers set up households and remained on these *seringais*, tapping rubber and producing subsistence crops even after the major rubber booms had subsided. Although the rubber barons no longer controlled the labor or production of the tappers, they still maintained their claims on the land, which enabled them to sell or transfer property to investors. This put the rubber tappers in a tenuous position, since the land they lived on was virtually sold out from under them. The tappers did have certain legal claims to the land as *posseiros*, or squatters, based on their long-term tenure, use, and improvement of the land; however, few of them knew this fact.[2] With the rubber tappers occupying the lands, title claims were not straightforward, and the market value of the land hinged on possession of clear titles. When

Figure 4.1 The Brazilian Amazon: Major Areas of
Rubber Tapper Struggles

tappers attempted to claim their squatters' rights, the new "owners"
often resorted to violence to evict them. In actuality, the investors'
titles were problematic even without tappers' claims. Because of the
many changes in status of Acre's territory, land titles still existed from
each of its historical periods, and many of them were still considered
valid up until the late 1970s. Therefore, the majority of land in the
state had overlapping "legal" titles (Hecht and Cockburn 1989).

Until this period of increasing property ownership, land titles had
been of little interest or import in Acre. It was the resources on the
land—the trees and the right to exploit forest goods—that had value.
"Ownership" of areas was not determined by bounded lots but by
areas of exploitation that might overlap or be intertwined among several families. Thus, the imposition of property titles on this traditional

system of ownership and the ensuing desire to bound the land gave rise to many conflicts.

Under the new regime, land was converted to two predominant uses: cattle ranching and colonization for agricultural production. Ranching usually fueled the most violent clashes between newcomers and rubber tappers because of the need to clear vast areas of forest for conversion to pasture. Ranchers were typically wealthy investors from the south who were able to hire *pistoleiros* (gunmen) to intimidate those they deemed illegal occupants of their newly acquired lands. Violence escalated when the occupants began to challenge the ranchers. An alliance between ranchers, urban elites, and government officials strengthened the ranchers' position, and when violence occurred, it often went without legal repercussions. Such was the case in the incident recounted at the beginning of this chapter.

Land conflicts were also generated by the transfer of land to state-promoted or independently run agricultural colonization schemes. This was a more common experience in Rondonia, a neighboring state of Acre. In these projects, large tracts of land were subdivided into uniformly sized plots, usually 100 hectares, and allocated to colonizing families. Settlers would clear the land for agricultural plots, ignorant of the many valuable forest products existing there. As colonization plans overlapped with areas of traditional *seringais*, colonists and rubber tappers squared off over their competing uses and claims to the land.

Efforts to place rubber tappers within typical colonization schemes simply did not work. Exploitation of forest products involves an area delineated by the occurrence of tree and plant species, not by uniform boundary limits. An average rubber tapper family exploits between 200 and 500 hectares of forest, and the areas of several families often overlap. Even in areas where overlapping claims exist, respect for resource use and extraction is maintained. Uniformly bounded plots do not allow tappers to follow the system required for extracting rubber; consequently they are reduced to being subsistence cultivators, a status they neither desire nor are willing to accept.

When threatened by ranchers and colonists, the local populations had little legal or political recourse, especially since they were not organized into towns or central settlements but were scattered within the forest. During the early 1970s, it is estimated that 40,000 to 50,000 rubber tappers moved from Acre across the border into Bolivia (Allegretti and Schwartzman 1988; Branford and Glock 1985). Other tappers were forced into the quickly growing urban centers, where their opportunities for gainful employment were few (Hecht and Schwartzman, unpublished). As the prospects of halting development policies became less likely, rubber tappers were motivated to organize efforts to address their concerns. This organization was aided by several out-side actors and was fueled by charismatic leaders. It is clear that not until the rubber tappers came together as a group did they gain legiti-macy as a constituency with rights and claims to the forest.

History of Rubber Production in the Amazon

Natural rubber has been used in the Amazon since before the Por-tuguese "discovery" of the New World (Weinstein 1983; Dean 1987). However, it was not until the vulcanization process was perfected in 1844 that it gained global appeal. In the late 1800s, a major campaign was launched to promote the collection of natural latex as a result of its growing use in the industrializing world. It was increasingly used for machine belting and tubing, as buffers for railway cars, and for insulation of telegraph wiring (Dean 1987). During this period, men were recruited from other rural areas of Brazil and brought into the Amazon to tap rubber. The majority of them were recruited from northeast Brazil, an area racked by droughts and with limited employ-ment options for its many farmers and laborers. Desperate for income, men signed on as *seringueiros*.

Working conditions were harsh. Most often, rubber tappers arrived in the Amazon indebted to the rubber bosses or *serengalistas* who had recruited them. Too poor to purchase their own tools, the rubber tappers were given the necessary supplies to get them through their first season in the forest. In return, they were required to sell the rubber they collected to the *serengalistas*, who could manipulate the terms of trade in their own favor. Debt servitude persisted indefi-nitely, and few rubber tappers were able to earn enough to be released from this original debt. They remained trapped in debt peonage for years, unable to leave unless they escaped and became fugitives.

Severe conditions of production continued throughout the years of the Amazon rubber boom, roughly until 1910. It was then that plantation rubber from Asia swamped the world market and outcom-peted the natural rubber collected from Amazonian forests. Asian rubber was of better quality, offered more stable supply in terms of quantity, and was produced at a lower price.[3] Except for a brief period during World War II, rubber from the Amazon never again became a major product on the world market.[4] However, even after the decline in the international significance of rubber, its production in the Amazon did not halt completely. Various "valorization" plans to aid the industry were attempted during its period of decline—in 1906, 1908, 1911, and 1920 (Dean 1987). In 1930, rubber was still con-sidered a key product in the region, as evidenced by President

Vargas's suggestion to include rubber production as a component of a new development strategy.[5]

Over the ensuing fifty years, as rubber production slowed, some rubber tappers left the forest and returned to the northeast or other areas they had been recruited from. Some moved to the growing urban centers in the region. Others stayed behind, diversifying their production strategies to supplement dwindling cash income from rubber sales. The rubber bosses, finding their profits low, were also leaving. Some *serengalistas* simply abandoned the land, leaving the tappers to fend for themselves. Others held on until the land boom allowed them to cash in on rising land values and speculation.[6] The rubber tappers generally found themselves in a somewhat more independent position, although even today this varies greatly throughout the Amazon.[7] Although declining in profitability and monopolized by marketers and middlemen, rubber is still profitable enough to keep many families on the land.[8] Where rubber tappers remain, they simply fade into the forest, an unseen population that lives and produces within the rain forest.

The tappers remaining in the Amazon lead fairly isolated lives. Their household areas, called *colocações*, are small central clearings surrounded by forest and rubber trails, where one or two families live. The rubber trails extend outward and return to the *colocação* in a U-shaped pattern. The practice of tapping rubber is carried out by making a V-shaped cut with a special knife in the bark of the tree. A small can or container wedged into the tree at the base of the V-cut collects the liquid latex as it slowly runs out. Rubber trees are found scattered throughout the forest, occurring naturally at about one or two per hectare (Allegretti 1987). A tapper rises early in the morning to make the first round through the forest cutting the trees. Later that same day, the tapper returns along the same route collecting the rubber that has accumulated in the containers. That rubber is then prepared, either smoked into a round *pele* or ball of rubber or pressed into a square block of semicongealed rubber. A typical *colocação* has two to three rubber trails. The tapper alternates trails each day, thereby reducing the chances of abusing the natural productivity potential of the rubber trees. In this manner, the same rubber tree can be tapped for up to fifty years (Weinstein 1983).

All household activities—raising small livestock, cultivating small plots, and preparing the rubber for sale—are contained within the *colocações*. The isolation, however, is never absolute. Rubber tappers are always aware of their neighbors, who may live an hour's or even a day's walk from their homes. Communications occur in several ways. People use *varadouras*, or large paths through the forest, for travel. These paths usually pass by the *colocações* of all rubber tapper families within a given area. Any person passing by spreads news from one household to the next. More recently, communications also occur through shortwave radios, which are owned by many households.

Today, these producers are caught up in a rapid cycle of change. They were freed from an oppressive system of bonded labor, yet they were immediately cast against other oppressive forces: the influx of investors and colonists intent on cutting the forest in order to produce profits. Overlooked in the process of change, rubber tapper populations were forced to act to ensure their rights to remain on the land where they have subsisted for almost a century.

The Rubber Tapper Movement

The rubber tapper movement has a complex history: the first small, spontaneous acts of resistance and opposition; the support and critical participation of external actors; the coordination of a national association; and the eventual step into national policymaking (Weinstein 1983; Scott 1985). In its evolution, the movement has disseminated power to single individuals, then to small groups, and finally to larger constituencies.

Initial efforts at resisting the exploitative relations between tappers and rubber bosses were dealt with harshly. Those tappers who attempted to sell rubber to other traders for a higher price met with quick retribution. A common practice was to bind the tapper, put a ball of rubber around his neck, and set it on fire. Whipping and severe punishment were meted out to tappers who attempted to flee their positions without paying off their debts. In the face of this violence, rubber tappers devised small ways to resist. Some tappers continued to sell to smaller traders, or they would place stones in the smoked balls of rubber to increase the weight. These acts of resistance were not always successful, but they demonstrated the desperate desire of these men to survive in the face of declining rubber prices and oppressive production conditions.

It was not until a larger and more encompassing threat confronted them that an organized of the rubber tapper movement began. It sprang up in direct opposition to rapidly increasing deforestation for cattle pasture. As previously mentioned, livestock ranching is a favored development policy in the region. Generous government subsidies are offered for the creation of these ranching enterprises (Hecht 1985). Between 1970 and 1975, ranchers bought six million hectares of land in the region of Vale do Acre, using fiscal incentives (Mendes 1990). This same land had approximately ten thousand rubber tappers living on it. Setting up a ranch involves first clearing the forest to create pasture. Therefore, the tappers faced not only expropriation of their land but also destruction of their resources. Confrontations turned violent as the new land owners sought ways to move the tappers off their ranches.

The rubber tappers, however, developed a unique response to the deforestation: They entered the forest in groups and confronted the cutting crews hired by the ranchers, persuading them peacefully to stop felling trees and leave the forest. These confrontations are known as *empates*, or standoffs. Although their origin has been attributed to Chico Mendes, a former rubber tapper leader, *empates* actually began as a spontaneous response by a group of rubber tappers trying to oppose deforestation near Brasileia, Acre, in 1981. *Empates* have since developed into a sophisticated and well-coordinated strategy and played a major role in establishing the momentum of the rubber tapper movement. It is said that they involve hundreds of tappers and their families and represent a communal response to a shared threat (Revkin 1990).

Empates are conducted without weapons and are essentially confrontations based on class identification. A major part of an *empate* involves appealing to the common plight shared by the workers sent to cut down the forest and the rubber tappers. If these appeals fail to dissuade workers from felling, their temporary shacks are emptied and torn down. Workers' equipment is taken away, and they are left with little choice but to return to town. This method has proved effective in stemming the pace of destruction in the forest.

Despite the relative success of *empates*, rubber tappers realized that adopting such a strategy by itself would not ensure the survival of the forest or their livelihoods. Each successful *empate* represented only a short respite in a larger struggle. The same lands could be threatened repeatedly. Tappers realized that the larger threat required action to ensure a more permanent solution.

External Agents and Charismatic Leaders

In 1975, formal organization of the rubber tapper movement began with the assistance of outside actors.[9] This does not mean that the rubber tappers were encouraged or pushed into action by these groups. The links that these outside agents provided for the nascent tappers' organization merely allowed it to blossom into a full-blown resistance movement. The rubber tappers had few contacts with the state or the larger society. Their products were marketed through trading intermediaries, and because many of the tappers were illiterate, they had little access to their rights as Brazilian citizens. Because they did not directly participate in the functioning of the larger state society, the role of external agents was crucial. The external agents translated and channeled the energy of the rubber tappers into the formal structures of the larger society. However, without the vigor and honest courage of the tappers themselves, their desperate struggle for livelihood would not have succeeded.

The initial outside actor was the rural workers' union—CONTAG (Confederação dos Trabalhadores da Agricultura). The first such union was established in 1975 in Brasileia, a town in the state of Acre near the Bolivian border. These rural unions recruited rubber tappers and began training them in organizing and other community leadership roles. These skills proved extremely useful as their impact spread across the state. By 1978, there was already a statewide rural workers' union association. In three short years, these unions had begun to play an active role in organizing rubber tappers to act against ranchers, especially through *empates*.

Two rubber tappers who were dramatically affected by union activities became prominent leaders in the burgeoning movement. The first was Wilson Pinheiro, who is considered the first recognized leader of the rubber tapper movement. He was the president of CONTAG. When the popularity of *empates* increased and ranchers were forced to negotiate with the tappers, it was Pinheiro who argued that tappers had to remain in the forests; they could not give up their forest homes for money or small plots of land elsewhere. After taking this stand, Pinheiro became a direct threat to the ranchers who had hoped to "resettle" tappers into colonization projects or urban areas. Pinheiro became a visible target and was assassinated in 1980 by locally hired gunmen. Despite general knowledge about who his murderers were, the assassination was not investigated by the police. The rubber tappers in the area, angered by this lack of action, retaliated a week later. A group of tappers went out to the ranch of one of the organizers of the assassination and, after an impromptu trial, convicted and shot him (Hecht and Cockburn 1989). Police subsequently rounded up many of the rubber tappers and took them to jail. Some were tortured, and others were held for several months without being brought to trial.

Tragically, Pinheiro's fate was only an indicator of more violence to come. The second prominent rubber tapper leader was Francisco "Chico" Mendes. Chico Mendes gained a reputation as a leader and organizer in the community. In 1977, he started a workers' union in Xapurí, his Acrean hometown. He became president of this union and organized resistance actions in the *seringais* of Acre. Mendes was also active in publicizing the plight of forest peoples and eventually became the international spokesperson for the movement. Through Mendes, the rubber tappers had an outlet to the outside world, which was instrumental in increasing the coordination and direction of the movement.[10]

During the period of union organizing, Catholic priests practicing liberation theology moved into Acre and also began working with the rubber tappers. The Catholic church, through its CEBs or Comunidades de Base (base communities), has a long history of activism and organization in rural areas of Brazil, and its support further legitimized the struggle.[11]

Organizing efforts among local forest communities increased in the wake of accelerating development in the region. More roads were being built, the rate of deforestation was increasing rapidly, and more ranchers were moving into the area. Violent conflicts were becoming commonplace as ranchers brought in hired gunmen and assassins to "clear" their lands of tappers and others living in the forest. *Empates* began to occur frequently and expanded into large events. The most significant development, however, was that more and more people were becoming aware of the trials and tribulations of the rubber tappers.

One of these people was Mary Allegretti, an anthropology student working in the area. After completing her thesis research on *seringueiros*, Allegretti stayed on and worked in Acre for several years. Eventually she met and became closely allied with Chico Mendes. Allegretti's role in the emergence of the rubber tappers' movement as a national and international concern would prove to be pivotal. Her energy and efforts prompted the tappers to expand their struggle into new arenas.

Allegretti's first major project with the rubber tappers was Project *Seringueiro,* begun in 1981 and based on her own research. It was a program to establish schools in isolated *seringais* to teach illiterate tappers how to read and write. Illiteracy among tappers was very high; a few had been taught to sign their names, but few possessed literacy skills. Project *Seringueiro* was based on "appropriate" language models and Paulo Freire's principles of popular education using locally relevant examples to facilitate learning.

Allegretti's role continued even after she left the *seringais* in Acre to work with a nongovernmental organization in Brasília. While working there, she became aware of the academic ignorance and political apathy at the national level regarding the existence of rubber tappers. She suggested to Chico Mendes that he organize a meeting of rubber tapper leaders in Brasília, where they could publicize their struggle and educate people about their existence and lifeways. Tony Gross, another researcher who had been working with rubber tappers, was able to convince his sponsoring organization, Oxfam, to provide funding for this meeting (Revkin 1990).

The "Environmental" Connection

Meanwhile, Allegretti and Gross had been discussing strategies for generating funds and securing additional allies for the rubber tappers, indigenous populations, and human rights groups that were embroiled in conflicts throughout the region. One of the options they discussed was to involve U.S.-based environmental groups that enjoyed large support and access to financial resources. Gross convinced Allegretti to travel with him to Washington, D.C. Building on the popular fascination with tropical rain forests, Allegretti was able to find support from U.S. environmental groups.[12] Driven by concern for the international implications of rain forest destruction, the environmental groups enthusiastically joined the alliance, which was envisioned as a combination of the ideas of social justice and environmental protection and conservation—a complicated match.[13] Upon their return to Brazil, Gross and Allegretti met with the rubber tappers to discuss the new alliance that would bring their plight to the attention of the world.

Allegretti and Gross returned in time for the first national forum of rubber tappers, held in Brasília during October 1985. Although originally planned for a small group of participants, the meeting was attended by more than 120 rubber tappers from different parts of the Amazon. The agenda for discussion exceeded all expectations of its planners, and two important decisions were made. First, a national organization—the National Council of Rubber Tappers (Conselho Nacional dos Seringueiros)—would be formed to create a clear national voice for the movement. From this point onward, the role of external agents, although still important to the coordination and funding of organizing activities, was paralleled by the coordinated governing body of rubber tappers. Second, an alternative approach to agrarian reform based on extractive activities was proposed—the creation of extractive reserves. The proposal delineated areas that would be reserved for extractive activities such as rubber tapping and collection of Brazil nuts and medicinal plants. Modeled on the idea of indigenous reserves, extractive reserves rapidly became the newest development alternative in the region. Expansion of these first two ideas eventually led to rubber tappers' full-scale involvement in the politics of regional development.

It was also at Brasília that the idea of the "environment" was articulated into the movement, as Allegretti and Gross explained the new international interest in helping rubber tappers conserve the rain forests. The North American concern for saving rain forests was a new perspective for the tappers to comprehend, since to them, the "environment" was not an entity separate from their lives in the forest. The rain forest was a seamless mesh of environmental and social constraints that could not be separated into mutually exclusive categories (Cleary 1991). But the notion of *ecología* was accepted and inserted as an essential component of their struggle. Chico Mendes was chosen as a representative of the tappers and, after the October meeting, he began to travel in this capacity, often accompanied or advised by Mary Allegretti, who had formed her own nongovernmental organization to work with rubber tappers in the research and development of viable alternatives to extractive reserves.

A parallel strategy burgeoned through the link with U.S. environmental groups. Its purpose was to target multilateral lending institutions and highlight the environmental and social repercussions of their development projects and policies. Steve Schwartzman, an anthropologist at the Environmental Defense Fund, incorporated the critiques made by rubber tappers into this larger project. He arranged for Mendes to meet with officials in these institutions and describe local responses and implications of their programs, essentially bringing a "human" face to the reports of devastation and disruption being wrought in the region. Throughout the 1980s, Schwartzman was closely affiliated with Mendes and often served as his interpreter; he continues to be involved with the National Council of Rubber Tappers.

Another outside connection was formed with Adrian Cowell, an independent British filmmaker. Cowell had begun filming a series of documentaries covering the "decade of destruction" of the Amazon. He met Chico Mendes and filmed him in one of his segments, forging an alliance that proved highly beneficial to the rubber tappers, as Cowell offered support and political advice over the years. Cowell's series, which aired in 1990, also helped publicize the destruction of the Amazon.

The Turning Point

After 1985, the Amazon region was marked by increased violence and confrontations with ranchers. As the rubber tappers became more organized in their opposition, the ranchers became more determined in their efforts to drive them off the land. Assassinations became common as union leaders and strong supporters were killed to intimidate others from joining the opposition efforts. A ranchers' organization was also formed to confront organized opposition by tappers. The *União Democrática Rural* (UDR), or Rural Democratic Union, is a conservative right-wing organization formed to further the interests of ranchers and large investors in the region and has been linked with increased violence in many rural areas. In Acre, the UDR gained control of one of the state's largest newspapers and subsequently refused to publish any news of rubber tappers' events.

The summer of 1988 marked a crisis point. Satellite photos of the Amazon identified thousands of fires burning in the forest—a sign of increased deforestation.[14] Fires are set after the forest is felled in order to clear the land of vegetation and to release the nutrients of the biomass into the soil. Worldwide phenomena such as droughts in the United States and southern Brazil and steadily climbing global temperature led to the conviction that climatic systems were being dramatically affected by increased deforestation. A cry went up all over the world to halt destructive land practices in the Amazon, and the rubber tappers were hailed as important protectors of the rain forest environment. The last few years' efforts of working with U.S. environmental groups paid off, as increased publicity led to global recognition of their existence and struggle in the forest.

In December, 1988, Chico Mendes—who by then was identified internationally as the spokesperson for rubber tappers in the Amazon—was assassinated, and his murder caused an international furor.[15] The ranchers responsible for his death were startled by the media attention, but they assumed that the commotion would subside soon. They were wrong. The death of Chico Mendes infused new energy and spurred the rubber tapper movement even further. International attention channeled new funds to the organizations working with rubber tappers, and a third meeting of the National Council of Rubber Tappers was held in March 1989. There, the Alliance of Forest Peoples was formally created. This alliance marked the first formal coalition of Indians, rubber tappers, and rural workers to fight against the common threat of encroachment on traditional lands.

The situation developed rapidly over the next two years. Rubber tappers are now at last formally recognized within the political system in the Amazon. Various rubber tappers entered the political arena and ran for state offices in the 1990 elections. A close affiliation with the Partido de Trabalhadores (Workers' Party) was formed. This marks the incorporation of the movement into a broader-based political struggle. Research has expanded in the region, and many people are currently examining strategies to strengthen forest products' ability to compete in markets and ways to diversify production possibilities within the forest.[16]

Although things are proceeding well, not all the problems within the movement have been resolved. After Chico Mendes's death, power struggles created some division in the group. Education and training have brought new leaders from the ranks of rubber tappers. More activity is occurring in other Amazonian states, as the National Council has coordinated meetings to organize local tappers in Rondonia and Amapá. The National Council has demanded a more powerful voice in matters and issues related to rubber tappers. Although no longer central to the movement, Mary Allegretti remains actively involved through the Institute for Amazonian Studies (IEA). She is an important consultant for the National Council of Rubber Tappers and provides political connections. The IEA has focused its research for the next two years on coordinating and organizing the implementation and creation of extractive reserves.

Conclusion

The rubber tapper movement demonstrates how a population that is traditionally disempowered through economic relations, physical isolation, illiteracy, and little or no social and political recognition can come to have a voice in national planning bureaucracies. Both locally and regionally, the rubber tappers have stepped out of the forest and into the political process. Their collective actions have first and foremost provided them with a collective voice. This voice can speak for the interests of rubber tappers and represent them in political forums, thus ensuring that their interests are at least recognized. This is a vital step, but it does not ensure that their interests will be incorporated into future development policies for the Brazilian Amazon. The tappers must continue to strengthen their organization and presence at all levels of the state and national bureaucracy. Having candidates run for political office is one method of accomplishing this purpose, along with continued efforts to organize forest peoples. Organization gains them a certain status both nationally and internationally and provides a central point from which assistance can flow in the form of information and funding. The National Council of Rubber Tappers now has representatives from each Amazonian state and is attempting to coordinate training and organizing among the forest peoples. The formation of the Coalition of Forest Peoples has identified a constituency for the entire Amazon region, which strengthens their ability to influence policy decisions and future policy directions. They have now become a force to contend within the region.

International attention to the plight of the rubber tappers also forced action on regional policies. Ex-President Sarney created a new program for Brazil called Nossa Natureza (Our Nature) as a direct response to international attention. In addition, before leaving office in 1989, Sarney created 30,000 square kilometers of protected extractive reserves in four Amazonian states. Incentives were temporarily halted for livestock raising, and licenses are now required for burning large areas of land. The tappers have been able to use these new laws in fighting deforestation of their lands. With legal precedent on their side, backed by state support, their efforts are beginning to have an effect on the region.

Brazil's most recent former president, Fernando Collor, showed a strong interest in environmental issues in the Amazon, as evidenced by his decision on gold miners in the Yanomami Indian territory and his appointment of José Lutzenberger, an outspoken environmentalist, as his Minister of the Environment.[17] Yet the Collor administration took no new action on extractive reserves. Collor is now out of office and facing impeachment. The new regime is led by interim president Itamar Franco (Collor's vice president). The new government is focusing on stabilizing the Brazilian economy, thereby giving environmental issues less attention.

Today, rubber tappers continue to be confident. Having gained sophistication in their dealings with the state, their leaders have matured in their political knowledge and are more aware of how to tap into avenues of power. Rubber tappers are intent on developing their concept of extractive reserves as a means of having the Brazilian and international community invest in the people of the forest in order to protect it. One of the major triumphs of the movement has been the acceptance of this concept by national planners. However, extractive reserves form only one element of a larger composite land use plan that will be modeled for the region. The actual structural elements and function of the extractive reserves within this plan are still to be determined. The underlying issue is the question of land tenure and property rights; other issues involve production relations, institutional design, and community arrangements. The concept of extractive reserves must continue to be debated as a promising alternative. It is far from being considered a triumph simply because it has been formally accepted.

The rubber tappers' movement encompasses an environmental component that links the culture and production of rain forest populations in the Brazilian Amazon to the outside world. Rubber tappers have been able to use "the environment" as a tool to raise their position in society and bring attention to their struggle. It is indeed surprising how rapidly and thoroughly the "environmental" language has been incorporated into the rhetoric and goals of the movement. The use of this language, however, does not necessarily imply complete acquiescence with the claims that U.S. and Western European environmental groups make regarding conservation and preservation. Today, justification for focusing on extractive populations is most strongly argued on the basis of their important role in protecting the resources of the Amazon. The "environment" brings a certain legitimacy to the tappers that has served to more fully incorporate them into a formal system of political change. Rubber tappers had little identity as a group with common interests prior to the movement. With the evolution of the movement and help from external agents, they have gained not only this identity but also the strength that comes from being organized into a constituency.

Once isolated, with little direct participation in or interaction with the state in any form, the rubber tappers in the Brazilian Amazon have gained a voice—a collective voice—that has catapulted them into politics and participation in regional development. It has opened up a space in the dialogue for their contributions and provided hope for a sustainable form of development based predominantly on their uses of the forest. The movement has empowered rubber tappers to step outside existing power relations and construct a place for themselves in the political scene (Hirschman 1986).

Notes

1. Extractive communities are populations of forest dwellers who extract nontimber forest products for sale and use as their main economic activity.
2. The Brazilian Civil Code acknowledges the right of occupancy (*direito de posse*) of a person living on a piece of land and who has made improvements (*benefeitorias*) on it. If a squatter has remained at least one year and one day, he or she has the right to legal protection and can be removed only through judicial action (Art. 508). After five years of uninterrupted and undisputed possession, the right of property can be granted (*direito de usurpação*).
3. Rubber plantations were tried in the Amazon; however, stands of rubber trees were susceptible to *microcyclus ulei*, or South American leaf blight. Thus, plantation-style cultivation was never successful.
4. During the brief period of World War II, however, tens of thousands of *soldados do borracha* (rubber soldiers) entered the forest. These rubber tappers were recruited under the aegis of patriotic support—they were told that their efforts were supplying rubber for the war machines and products of the Allies. Still an issue of contention today is the government's promise of a pension and retirement benefits for these rubber soldiers. This promise has not been honored.
5. This policy also reflected the close alliance that powerful rubber barons had with the federal government and their ability to ensure government support for rubber production.
6. Land booms have occurred throughout the Amazon at varying times. In Acre, the early 1960s marked the beginning of rising land values. Land speculation, however, follows infrastructure and depends on where roads and government projects are being built.
7. In some isolated areas, tappers remain indebted to rubber bosses and still pay rent for the use of forest rubber trails. However, these areas are fewer and fewer as dubious land titles are increasingly challenged. The rubber tapper movement has brought many of these cases to light and has presented the opportunity for many isolated tappers to verify land status and challenge illegal claims.

8. Rubber prices have been steadily falling over the years. During the week of 2 April 1991, seventy-five rubber tapper leaders staged an *empate* in Brasília to protest the falling prices (Environmental Defense Fund 1991). One of the demands of the tappers is to channel the funds collected from taxes on imported rubber to rubber tapping communities, thus providing a subsidy to these populations in much the same way that ranching and colonization has been subsidized in the past.

9. See Friedmann (1989) for a discussion of the role of external agents in social movements.

10. Chico Mendes was a key player in the rubber tapper movement. However, his story is not told here. There are several books about his life; see Revkin 1990; Shoumatoff 1990; Souza 1990.

11. Hecht and Cockburn (1989) make an interesting argument about the church's involvement. They suggest that the church's efforts tended to direct conflicts to legal channels, thus diffusing any threat to direct action and, indeed, preventing dramatic results.

12. The international programs of both the Environmental Defense Fund and the National Wildlife Federation are particularly active in providing support for the rubber tapper movement in Brazil.

13. There has been recent criticism of this "marriage of convenience" between what was essentially a rural workers' organization and U.S. environmental groups. Steve Schwartzman at the Environmental Defense Fund staunchly rejects this criticism. He claims that the groups shared a common goal of halting environmental destruction and that this sort of simplistic interpretation was mostly at the hands of the press in describing events that involved rubber tappers. Although the rubber tapper movement was cast in the most favorable environmental light, it never claimed to be solely about ecology. Larger implications of rubber tappers' proposals were simplistically discussed, yet never denied. Their proposals were not primarily focused on ecological preservation or species protection in tropical rain forest environments, but rather on the need to protect forest tracts for sustaining a viable economy based on the extraction of rubber and other forest products. Preservation strategies that emphasize, say, maintaining the Amazon forests as wilderness parks or as biosphere reserves would be of no direct benefit to the rubber tappers at all.

14. "Documento: A Amazônia Queimando," *Jornal da Tarde*, 25 August 1988, pp. 24–25.

15. He was shot at his home in Xapurí. He had received death threats from ranchers who were determined to deforest several extractive areas.

16. Cultural Survival Enterprises, a subgroup of Cultural Survival, a nongovernmental organization based in Cambridge, Massachusetts, is coordinating the marketing and research of extractive forest products. Ben and Jerry's Ice Cream and the Body Shop (a London-based cosmetics firm) already use forest products in their manufacturing processes.

17. Beginning in January 1990, the federal government began a series of efforts to dynamite airstrips that gold miners were using to enter the protected lands of the Yanomami Indians in the northern Amazonian territory of Roraima. Collor's administration created a lot of international publicity when the president, after visiting the region, publicly condemned the destruction that the gold miners were creating and

demanded that more airstrips be blown up. These efforts proved only temporarily useful; within two months, the airstrips were repaired and gold miners were returning to the area. José Lutzenberger resigned from his position in May 1992, in protest against the inaction of Collor's administration regarding environmental issues.

References

Allegretti, Mary Helena. 1987. "Reservas extrativistas: uma proposta de desenvolvimento da floresta Amazônica." Curitiba: Instituto de Estudos Amazônicos.

Allegretti, Mary, and Stephan Schwartzman. 1988. "Extractive Reserves: A Sustainable Development Alternative for Amazonia." *Report to World Wildlife Fund.* U.S. Project US-478.

Barbira-Scazzocchio, Françoise, ed. 1980. *Land, People and Planning in Contemporary Amazonia.* Cambridge: Cambridge University, Centre of Latin American Studies.

Branford, Sue, and Oriel Glock. 1985. *The Last Frontier: Fighting Over Land in the Amazon.* London: Zed Books.

Browder, John O., ed. 1989. *Fragile Lands of Latin America.* Boulder, Colo.: Westview Press.

Bunker, Stephen G. 1985. *Underdeveloping the Amazon.* Urbana: University of Illinois Press.

Cleary, David. 1991. "The Greening of the Amazon." In *Environment and Development in Latin America,* edited by David Goodman and Michael Redclift. Manchester: Manchester University Press.

Dean, Warren. 1987. *Brazil and the Struggle for Rubber.* Cambridge: Cambridge University Press.

Environmental Defense Fund. 1991. "Rubber Tappers Demonstrate in Brasilia." Press release. 2 April.

Friedmann, John. 1989. "The Latin American Barrio Movement as a Social Movement: Contribution to a Debate." *International Journal of Urban and Regional Research* 13(3): 501–10.

Gayley, John Homer. 1977. "The Politics of Development in the Brazilian Amazon, 1940–1950." Ph.D. dissertation, Stanford University.

Hecht, Susanna B. 1985. "Environment, Development and Politics: Capital Accumulation and the Livestock Sector in Eastern Amazonia." *World Development* 13(6): 663–84.

Hecht, Susanna. 1989. "Lands, Trees and Justice: Defenders of the Amazon." *The Nation.* 22 May, 695–702.

Hecht, Susanna, Anthony Anderson, and Peter May. 1988. "The Subsidy from Nature: Shifting Cultivation, Successional Palm Forests and Rural Development." *Human Organization* 47(1): 25–35.

Hecht, Susanna, and Alexander Cockburn. 1989. *Fate of the Forest: Developers, Destroyers and Defenders of the Amazon.* London: Verso.

Hecht, Susanna, and Stephan Schwartzman. 1988. "Income Formation in Acre: Rubber Tappers, Urban Dwellers and Regional Development Strategies." Unpublished.

Hemming, John, ed. 1985a. *Change in the Amazon Basin. Vol. 1: Man's Impact on Forests and Rivers*. Manchester: Manchester University Press.

Hemming, John, ed. 1985b. *Change in the Amazon Basin, Vol. 2: The Frontier after a Decade of Colonization*. Manchester: Manchester University Press.

Hirschman, Albert O. 1986. *The Political Economy of Latin American Development: Seven Exercises in Retrospection*. San Diego: University of California, Center for U.S.-Mexican Studies.

Kohlhepp, Gerd. 1982. "Regional Development Strategies and Economic Exploitation Policies in Amazonia." Paper presented at the Seminar on Regional Development Alternatives in the Third World, Belo Horizonte, Brazil, 8–13 August.

Lisansky, Judith. 1990. *Migrants to Amazonia*. Boulder, Colo.: Westview Press.

Melone, Michelle A. 1988. "Rubber Tappers and Extractive Reserves: A Development Alternative for the Amazon?" Master's thesis, University of California, Los Angeles.

Mendes, Chico. 1990. "A luta dos povos da floresta." In *Geografia: Pesquisa e pratica social*, edited by B. M. Fernandes. São Paulo: Marco Zero.

Revkin, Andrew. 1990. *The Burning Season*. Boston: Houghton Mifflin.

Salati, Eneas. 1987. "The Forest and the Hydrological Cycle." In *The Geophysiology of Amazonia*, edited by R. E. Dickinson. New York: John Wiley.

Schwartzman, Stephan. 1987a. "Entrevista com Chico Mendes em Washington." *EDF Information Bulletin*. Washington, D.C., 29 March.

Schwartzman, Stephan. 1987b. "Extractive Production in the Amazon and the Rubber Tappers' Movement." Paper presented at the Conference in World Environmental History, Duke University, Durham, 30 April.

Scott, James C. 1985. *Weapons of the Weak: Everyday Forms of Peasant Resistance*. New Haven: Yale University Press.

Shoumatoff, Alex. 1990. *The World is Burning*. Boston: Little, Brown.

Souza, Marcio. 1990. *O empate contra Chico Mendes*. São Paulo: Marco Zero.

Weinstein, Barbara. 1983. *The Amazon Rubber Boom: 1850–1920*. Stanford, Calif.: Stanford University Press.

Wilson, E. O., ed. 1988. *Biodiversity*. Washington, D.C.: National Academy Press.

FIVE

SUSTAINABLE LIVELIHOODS IN THE URBAN MILIEU

A Case Study from Mexico City

KEITH PEZZOLI

THIS IS A STORY ABOUT grassroots resistance and community-based environmental action in Mexico City's ecological zone. The focus is on the formation of Los Belvederes, a group of thirteen contiguous low-income settlements that were illegally formed in Ajusco, a highly contested mountainous and wooded area located on Mexico City's southwestern fringe. According to city plans, Ajusco lies within an ecological reserve that was to be maintained as a natural barrier against urban expansion. However, from the late 1970s to the present, the zone has been undergoing a rapid rural-to-urban transition. The legally designated urban limits have been extended outward three times since 1980 to accommodate urban encroachment inside Ajusco. Expansion of these limits has involved social unrest, ecological disruption, and violence.

During the early 1980s, the government planned to eradicate the thirteen irregular settlements of Los Belvederes.[1] The magnitude of the situation, however, made it practically impossible; several thousand families were involved, and community groups mobilized to resist the action. Herein lies the interesting part of the story—the innovative organized resistance. Besides well-worn strategies of marches and demonstrations, the grassroots movement generated bottom-up, proactive environmental action. Aided by technical assistance from external agents, grassroots activists in Los Belvederes began to promote innovative social ecology projects as a countervailing strategy to secure the presence of the families in the zone.

This chapter critically examines the grassroots environmental action and the role of external agents in the formation of Los Belvederes. Drawing on twenty months of research and fieldwork carried out between 1983 and 1991, the chapter outlines the social, political, and ecological background of the grassroots movement. Attention is drawn to the merits of a fundamental argument advanced by the ecological squatters: that the demand for land in the area renders it impossible to maintain the entire zone as a greenbelt for consumption (in the form of a national park or ecological reserve). Yet it is possible to develop a greenbelt for production, a place wherein grassroots social experimentation may be promoted to generate new forms of development that are resource sustainable and minimize ecological disruption.

Grassroots activists argue that their call for an experimental greenbelt for production sharply contrasts with the government's centralized sectoral approach to planning, which treats housing, economic, and ecological problems as separate issues. They point out that housing, economic, and ecological problems cannot be solved separately. Faced with chronic scarcities of income and resources, participants in the grassroots ecology movement see no alternative but to promote self-reliant forms of urbanization. Their proposals center on the development of appropriate technology that can reduce the cost of generating employment and recover capital investment through the rational use and reuse of resources. Some notable progress along these lines has been made. By drawing attention to Ajusco, this chapter aims to provide insight into the power relations and challenges facing grassroots groups that struggle to promote alternative technology and sustainable livelihoods.

Two challenges in particular stand out in the discussion that follows: (1) to fortify the barrio economy as a means of creating sustainable livelihoods, and (2) to strengthen the theory and practice of proactive, ecologically integrated planning. Meeting these challenges requires social learning and experimentation, which calls for creative and holistic ways of thinking about development, urbanization, economics, and ecology that can be translated into viable strategies and methods. People in the urban milieu face the enormous task of learning how to satisfy their basic needs for food, energy, housing, and meaningful employment, and they must learn to do this in ways that are ecologically sustainable. Social learning along these lines lies at the heart of the story that follows.

The Context

Mexico City is the world's largest metropolis with a total population of 20 million inhabitants that grows by 3.8 percent, or around 700,000 people, a year (Cornelius and Craig 1988, 52). Faced with chronic scarcities of income and resources, millions of Mexico City's inhabitants are forced to live under very difficult physical and social conditions (Garza 1987). Policies aimed at decentralizing development away from the capital city have been implemented, but with limited success (Rodriguez 1987). Despite mounting problems, Mexico City continues to attract both private investors and migrant workers (over 1,000 daily) from all over the country.

The metropolitan area of Mexico City (MAMC) continues to grow despite geographical factors that make it a poor host to megacity sprawl (Carabias and Herrera 1986). The MAMC is situated in the Central Mexican Basin, a high plateau—nearly 6,800 feet above sea level—surrounded by mountains. The contained ecosystem of the basin has become seriously degraded by urban and demographic growth, toxic emissions from industry and vehicles, extensive deforestation, the desiccation of its lakes, and the exploitation of materials for construction (Rivera 1987). The city is also prone to thermal inversions, a dynamic that compounds air pollution and its related illnesses.[2]

Owing to its altitude and subsoil conditions, Mexico City also has chronic problems of water supply. To meet growing demand, more and more wells have tapped into the valley's diminishing underground supplies. Consequently, the level of the water table has dropped, thereby exacerbating the sinking of the city's central areas. The ground level in some places has sunk as much as seven meters, causing rifts that provoke severe damage to pavement, buildings, and underground networks of water and drainage (Carabias and Herrera 1986, 63). At the same time, it is increasingly cost-prohibitive to pump water up into the valley from distant areas.[3]

It has also become increasingly difficult and expensive to supply water to parts of the city that have expanded up rocky mountainsides. For this reason, the government has enacted a ban against building higher than the 2,350-meter contour. The ban effectively outlaws the establishment of new urbanization on practically the entire western side of the Federal District (Connolly 1982). In low-income areas already established above this height, water gets delivered by truck and is stored in open fifty-gallon drums. This water is often heavily contaminated with parasites and other organisms that cause a high incidence of intestinal illness. Such is the case in the low-income settlements of Los Belvederes, which are above 2,600 meters in altitude.

Between 1940 and 1970, informal (self-help) production of low-income settlements in Mexico City—based largely on illegal and semi-legal means of access to land—alleviated an otherwise critical housing shortage (Dunkerley and Whitehead 1983). More recently, however, this traditional mode of access to land has been constrained by two sets of forces. First, after a generation of hyperurban growth, the available supply of unbuilt land in Mexico City has become more scarce and, as a consequence, more actively contested among potential users. Second, property development has become subject to more state control and more commercialized.[4] Compounding these constraints is the impact of the economic crisis and the politics of austerity programs (Ward, 1989).

Lacking viable alternatives, millions of Mexico City's inhabitants now live in low-income settlements occupying land that is unsuitable for urban development. Such settlements occupy the barren desiccated lake bed of Texcoco, hills that are unstable from mining, sites next to railway lines or factories that emit toxic waste, or, as in the case of Los Belvederes, zones designated for ecological conservation. As the supply of land becomes increasingly scarce and subject to more rigid controls, the contest for land heats up, as in the case of Ajusco.

On 31 July 1986, the General Program for the Urban Development of the Federal District (DDF) was presented to the public. It reclassified the entire Federal District into two zones: one for urban development (43 percent of the total land area), and one for ecological conservation and rural development (57 percent of the total land area). Although the thirteen settlements of Los Belvederes in Ajusco were incorporated into the legally designated urban area, all the area to the south of these settlements was zoned for ecological conservation and rural development. The program text explicitly spells out the politics of containment:

> The demarcation of the area for ecological conservation is one of the most urgent measures needed to contain horizontal urban growth. . . . In order to keep the ecological conservation area free from the pressures of urban expansion, its limits will be determined and marked by physical barriers. . . . The barriers may be natural, such as ravines or rivers, or man-made such as stone walls and concrete boundary markers. . . . Supporting the limits will be large signs, watchguard stations, and control offices—particularly at roadway access points where the pressures of urban expansion are very strong. . . . Also the special police force of ecology guards (ecoguardias) will protect the land. (DDF, 1986, 9, 67)

The politics of containment has given rise to an industry of destruction: a cycle of irregular settlement being formed, then eradicated, then formed again, in which certain public and private individuals reap huge profits through illicit land transactions. This cyclical process results in violent confrontations and losses. Beside all this, the politics of containment has simply not worked. Urbanization continues to press further and further into the ecological reserve. Clearly an alternative approach is needed, and this is where we may learn from the social experimentation at the grassroots.

The Case of Los Belvederes in Ajusco

Ajusco is a miniregion in the Tlalpan Ward of the Federal District, corresponding to the Sierra of Ajusco—a volcanic mountain range with forested foothills in the southwestern part of the metropolitan area. Although Ajusco itself is not a political entity (it does not have officially set boundaries), it is generally referred to as the area shown in Figure 5.1.

Given its great expanse and urban-rural mix, Ajusco is physically subdivided into lower, middle, and upper sections. Lower Ajusco (Ajusco Bajo) was initially settled and to a considerable extent consolidated prior to 1980. Middle Ajusco (Ajusco Medio) lies at the outermost edge of the officially designated urban area, which is rapidly changing from rural to urban land use. This is the part of Ajusco in transition, where newer settlements, including Los Belvederes, took hold and began to consolidate during the 1980s. Upper Ajusco (Ajusco Alto) refers to the southernmost rural area and undeveloped open spaces of the zone. It contains the volcanic peaks of the Sierra of Ajusco and three of the thirty-six rural settlements existing within the Federal District's ecological conservation area.

Up until the early 1970s, Ajusco was a sparsely populated rural area covering approximately twenty square miles with some forestry and agricultural activity. By 1988, around one-quarter of this land area was urbanized, with a population of over 250,000 people—the bulk of whom are low-income families living in self-built housing and without adequate public infrastructure and services.

Most of Ajusco is designated as an ecological reserve. Yet it is a highly contested terrain subject to intense pressures of urban expansion, where interests of the state, popular groups, *ejidatarios*,[5] and developers clash. Low-income people are not the only ones who have staked out land claims in Ajusco. The zone's abundant green space, clean air, and panoramic vistas have attracted real estate developers and higher-income groups interested in upper-class development. Historically, economically better off groups have concentrated in the southwestern part of the city and, in the case of Ajusco, the competition for land there is especially intense.

From the early 1970s to the present, the zone's rapid rural-urban transformation has involved fraudulent schemes by real estate developers, violence, mass eradication of incipient low-income settlements, popular resistance and opposition movements, widespread corruption, and deepening ecological disruption. For over a decade, it has been a priority on the city administration's agenda to gain greater control over Ajusco's development and land use conflicts.

This case study focuses on three of the thirteen settlements within Los Belvederes: Bosques del Pedregal (referred to as Bosques, for

Figure 5.1 Ajusco, 1988

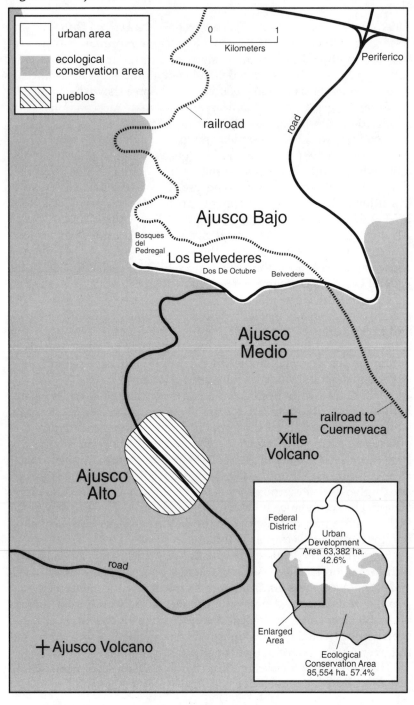

short), Dos de Octubre, and Belvedere. Together, the settlements of Los Belvederes cover 431 acres of land divided into 219 blocks containing 5,000 lots of approximately 200 square meters each. The population of Los Belvederes expanded rapidly from a few hundred in 1976 to roughly 50,000 by 1988.[6]

Prior to 1984, the irregular settlements of Los Belvederes were classified as illegal. They were situated in a restricted buffer zone between the areas marked for urban development and for ecological conservation. On numerous occasions the state moved to eradicate housing from the zone. However, due to the sheer magnitude of the population involved, the sophistication of popular resistance, and contradictory and inconsistent state action, plans to eradicate Los Belvederes were never realized. In 1985, Los Belvederes was incorporated into the legally designated urban area. State planners eliminated the buffer zone and for the third time since 1980 redrew the line that separates the area for urban use from the shrinking area for ecological conservation.

The rugged and steep volcanic terrain is one of the most striking features of Los Belvederes. The land juts up from the lower-lying part of Ajusco at inclines ranging from fifteen to more than forty-five degrees. More than half the settlements are situated on inclines thirty degrees or steeper. This has made access difficult, especially given the terrain's sharp, rocky surface. Significant portions of this land were used for agricultural production—predominately corn—until 1983, but it was soon subdivided for urban use. The resulting landscape reveals the stark contrast of the meeting of urban and rural space.

The average lot measures approximately 225 square meters and is occupied by about six residents—with an overall density of 150 inhabitants per hectare. Since 1983, the population density has increased substantially. The most common type of dwelling unit on these lots is a small room constructed with slabs of volcanic rock for walls, with branches, wood slats, and bituminized cardboard serving as roofing material.

Owing to the altitude and steep, rocky terrain of Los Belvederes, it has been clear from the beginning that introduction of normal infrastructure would be a problem. Potable water and drainage systems would be very expensive, if not impossible, to install. Water is delivered by special water trucks called *pipas* to water stations located at selected high points throughout the settlements. The water stations are level platforms holding dozens of fifty-gallon open-top metal drums. Each drum is linked to a household by garden hoses that carry the water downhill by gravity. The hoses can extend up to 300 meters in length, representing an enormous investment for each household. Although such a system may seem unsightly, the institutionalization of water delivery in 1983 marked a major step toward the consolidation of Los Belvederes.

A tour through Los Belvederes would not reveal many public services and facilities. There is a critical need for schools, medical clinics, and commercial and recreational facilities. These deficiencies, compounded by the insecurity stemming from lack of tenure, motivated the settlers to mobilize collectively to provide for some community facilities.

A Historical Sketch of State-Community Relations and Ecopolitics in Los Belvederes

Official measures to protect the Ajusco zone—to maintain ecological equilibrium—go back as far as the mid-1930s. In 1936, President Lazaro Cardenas issued an executive decree declaring the zone a national park (Parque Nacional Cumbres del Ajusco). Although President Cardenas called for a vast expropriation of land for the park, the decree was never implemented. In 1947, President Miguel Aleman limited the boundaries of this demarcated park and permitted a paper factory to exploit the zone's forest resources. Until the 1970s, very little effort had been made in the direction of ecological conservation. In August 1983, the state announced that "expert judgment" called for measures to eradicate Los Belvederes. The conclusion of that judgment can be paraphrased as follows: As a result of an investigation (done in consultation with the Subsecretariat of Ecology and the Ward of Tlalpan), which took into account the dictates of official plans and programs, it is concluded that there should not be any human settlements in the zone. The settlements of Los Belvederes do not comply with the intent of the buffer zone, which is to conserve the ecological equilibrium of Mexico City. Furthermore, given that the Sierra of Ajusco is one of the last remaining areas that oxygenates the air of the Federal District, its ongoing destruction is particularly alarming. The balance of the ecosystem is progressively disturbed and all inhabitants of the city are adversely affected. As if to prepare the public for a massive eradication of settlers from Los Belvederes, the press secretary of Tlalpan announced, on 19 March 1984, that the population of the zone would have to be relocated to other parts of the city. The reasons given were environmental problems, the impossibility of installing public services, and the fact that people could not display legal titles to the land (El Día, 20 March 1984).

In a partial reversal of this position, the Program for the Conservation of Ajusco—announced on 28 May 1984 by the mayor of the DDF, Ramon Aguirre Velazquez—declared that sections of Los Belvederes would be incorporated into the legally designated urban area. Although the program stated that there would be no massive eradication of families from the zone, it also indicated that residential use would now be restricted and densified through the relocation of families inside and outside the zone.

Settlers viewed the program with skepticism. They feared that demographic densification through relocation was a euphemism for eviction. Promises to regularize land tenure in some areas and not in others, on a case-by-case basis, were viewed as a divisive tactic to cause confrontations between settlements. The state's overtures to help people return to their points of origin was rejected as absurd: "[F]irst they will have to address the problems in the countryside that compelled people to migrate to the city," stated the newspaper *El Día* (8 June 1984).

The prospect of eviction mobilized the settlers of Los Belvederes to challenge government plans for the zone. As conflict intensified, activists argued that plans to eradicate their settlements were only partly derived from ecological concerns. They pointed to upper-class residential estates that continued to be built without any obstruction in the same reserve. Several popular groups—along with external agents—began to implement innovative social ecology projects as alternative strategies of urban development that would repudiate government plans to eradicate their settlements.

The settlers of Los Belvederes grouped to form a barrio-wide urban movement in January 1984, called the Popular Front for the Defense of the Settlements of Ajusco (hereafter referred to as the Front). The Front was spearheaded by popular groups from three settlements: Bosques del Pedregal, Dos de Octubre, and Belvedere. Citing the rights granted them under Article 24 of the Mexican Constitution, activists of the movement merged conventional demands for adequate housing and secure life space with more innovative arguments that proposed ecologically sensitive solutions. A pamphlet titled "The Settlements of Ajusco: In the Face of Repression" written by grassroots activists stated:

> Our Popular Front of Settlements, with Bosques, Dos de Octubre and Belvedere at the core, demands regularization by way of expropriation. But at the same time, we insist that the government take into account our work, cooperation and collective efforts—especially our technical proposals to create settlements of a new type: ecological spaces in which harmonious relations within civil society and between humankind and the natural environment are possible. (1984, 7)

Members of the Front proposed an integrated approach to urban development based on production that is "socially necessary, ecologically sound, and economically viable." This, they argued, was in sharp contrast to the government's centralized sectoral approach to planning, which treated housing, economic, and ecological problems as separate issues.

At the peak of popular resistance (1984–85), the alternative projects promoted by the Front in Los Belvederes were supported by many external agents, including university groups, newspaper reporters, independent research associations, a union of progressive lawyers, and political parties in opposition to the PRI (the political party in power).[7] There was even international support from groups in Austria, the United States, and Germany.

One of the first tasks faced by the Front was to challenge the ecological arguments of the "expert judgment" pronounced in 1983. Leaders of the movement—together with students activists from the Urban Sociology Department at UNAM (the National Autonomous University of Mexico)—argued that the judgment was a foregone conclusion that had little to do with the ecological realities of Ajusco. The settlers argued that they were being blamed for the extinction of certain species of flora and fauna that had long disappeared throughout the entire Sierra of Ajusco, even before the formation of Los Belvederes.

The ecology of Ajusco has been adversely affected for nearly three decades by the widespread deforestation and pollution caused by Peña Pobre, a paper-pulp factory, and by other industries in the area. Acid rain has been an additional factor. A glaring contributor to contamination in this zone has been the state itself, through the operation of an open-air waste dump site contiguous with Los Belvederes. As hundreds of tons of untreated wastes filled this dump site every day, the state accused settlers of being responsible for contamination of the supposedly pristine zone. The operation of the garbage dump was a blatant contradiction that underscored the lack of integrity in the state's ecological arguments about Los Belvederes. Even though this dump site was eventually closed, local settlers were convinced that the expert judgment was merely a pretext to justify eradication of their settlements. They refused to be singled out as the destroyers of the ecological equilibrium of the entire metropolitan area.[8]

The Front rallied against the agendas promoted by the state, using well-worn strategies including marches and protests, press releases, and open letters.[9] They also criticized the technocratic arguments advanced by the state and set forth alternative proposals that involved community participation in development decisions.

In August 1984, the settlers of Dos de Octubre and Belvedere, along with students from the Departments of Architecture and Biology at UNAM, submitted an urban and ecological project to the State's Special Commission on the Sierra of Ajusco.[10] Earlier in the year, a grassroots group from Belvedere published an open letter in the newspaper *UnoMasUno* to President de la Madrid, Mayor Ramon Aguirre Velazquez, and to "all democratic and revolutionary organizations" stating their legitimate claims over the settlement's land. The letter also responded to the language of government planning documents by stating that:

> Confronted with ecological constraints we have designed a settlement suitable to a zone of rural-urban transition, where inhabitants take into account and coexist with the natural environment. The designs include plans for organic waste recycling systems as a way to avoid the high costs of drainage while preventing black water filtration into the underground water supply. Also we will prevent deforestation of the zone and the circulation of automobiles will be limited. We will realize all these plans on the basis of collective work. (*UnoMasUno*, 9 March 1984)

At almost the same time, in August 1984, settlers from Bosques del Pedregal participated in a public hearing sponsored by the Coordinating Commission for Development Planning in the Federal District and the Special Commission for the Sierra of Ajusco. At the hearing titled "An Open Forum on the Ecology of the Southern Zone of Mexico City," grassroots leaders of Bosques presented a slide show of their settlement, along with proposals for turning the zone into a greenbelt for production as opposed to a greenbelt set aside for consumption. More specifically, they presented a proposal to transform their settlement into a productive ecological settlement, or *colonia ecológica productiva* (CEP).

The CEP was an ambitious attempt to integrate—within the territorial framework of the local community—the need for residential space, employment, food production, and cultural and political self-determination. Activists of Bosques stated the main objective of the project: "[T]o promote an ecologically valid, economically viable, and socially necessary solution aimed at resolving the problems in the Sierra of Ajusco, and more specifically in Bosques del Pedregal." The remainder of this chapter focuses on Bosques del Pedregal for three reasons: It was the first irregular settlement to be established in Los Belvederes; popular activists in Bosques provided barrio-wide leadership throughout Los Belvederes; and, finally, Bosques went furthest with its ecological projects and proactive community-based actions for developing the settlement.

Bosques del Pedregal and the CEP Campaign

The Council

The principal popular organization in Bosques del Pedregal that spearheaded the *colonia ecológica* campaign was the General Council of Representatives (hereafter referred to as the Council). The organizational structure of the Council (Table 5.1) was modeled on the Workers Union of UNAM (STUNAM), where grassroots Bosques activists had gained experience. Their objective was to create a form of legal representation that would encourage the maximum participation of people in matters pertaining to the settlement.

Table 5.1 Structure of the General Council of Representatives, Bosques del Pedregal

Body	Composition	Power/Function
General Assembly	All members	Maximum authority; ratifies decisions
Executive Committee	5 representatives elected during general assembly	Represents the settlement in all of negotiations
Assembly of Block Representatives	1 representative (plus 1 alternate) from each block (31 total)	Main decisionmaking body
Assembly of Sector Coordinators	1 representative from each sector (11 total) plus heads of any special commissions	Serves as check and balance against activities of Assembly of Block Representatives
Sector Assembly	All members of a sector*	Serves to mobilize people for political purposes or tasks requiring collective labor
Block Assembly	All members of a block+	Has the immediate authority to resolve problems internal to the block, subject to the rules of the association

*The settlement is divided into 11 sectors, each composed of 2, 4, or 5 blocks.
+The settlement is divided into 31 blocks, each composed of approximately 15 to 20 individual lots.

The Council functioned with a high degree of democratic participation. During 1983–84, I observed at each level of the organization. From what I could see, the decisionmaking process genuinely involved open discussion and debate. The Block Assembly was the most intimate meeting, where immediate neighbors gathered to discuss current events. The Assembly of Block Representatives was usually the most dynamic meeting. The General Assembly was usually well attended, often with over 1,000 participants. The Council's structure was not without faults. For instance, there was a bias against renters. There was also grossly unequal gender representation in leadership positions—the Executive Committee was composed entirely of men. Aside from these serious limitations, the organization was remarkable in its accomplishments.

The Council acted to a large extent as a government within a government. Given the failure of the judicial system to resolve conflicts over illicit land transactions (for example, a lot being sold twice), the Council provided both judicial and police functions and acted as the cooperative manager for land allocation and development. It also had a tremendous capacity to mobilize people and did so by bringing into action a sophisticated network of people, facilities for printing bulletins and newsletters, and strategically placed loudspeakers. People were mobilized to collectively organize basic infrastructure (streets, schools, meeting places, water and electric distribution) and to press their claims against the state.

The Council sought appropriate strategies in its attempt to ward off the relocations and densification called for by the Ajusco Conservation Program. In July 1984, leaders met and agreed to cooperate in the promoting the following:

- Combating the plagues infesting the trees in the settlement.
- Protecting all the trees with a ring of rocks around their base.
- Reforesting the zone by soliciting 20,000 fruit trees and 20,000 "oxygen" trees from the Tlalpan Ward (at the time this decision was made, 5,000 fruit trees had already been planted).
- Establishing two compost piles in Sector 1 of the settlement.
- Articulating with the Ajusco Cooperation Group to define an alternative approach to development that would transform Bosques into an ecologically productive settlement.

The Council promoted these measures as part of the barrio-wide effort led by the Front to develop a positive image of Los Belvederes. Popular groups in Belvedere and in Dos de Octubre promoted similar measures (but did not articulate with the Ajusco Cooperation Group) and worked most closely with investigators and university students from UNAM's Departments of Sciences and Architecture.

The Ajusco Cooperation Group

The Ajusco Cooperation Group was composed of five organizations. Two of these were popular groups from Bosques: the Council and the

Cooperative Society of Bosques del Pedregal in Struggle. The other three were external agents: the Alternative Technology Group (GTA), the Center for Biological Investigation, and Agro-Industry Integrated. The most influential of the external agents was the GTA. In view of the central role that the GTA played in the conceptualization and promotion of Bosques as a CEP, it is worthwhile to describe its agenda and the context out of which it emerged.

The Alternative Technology Group (GTA). GTA was founded in 1977 under the direction of Josefina Mena, a charismatic architect, and functions as a small multidisciplinary group of researchers committed to generating new technologies and promoting alternative development (Mena 1987). The group has a long history of working with low-income groups in both rural and urban settings.[11] One area of GTA's expertise is in developing alternative technologies for recycling organic household waste.

GTA views housing both as a factor of production and as a generator of resources that can be used to improve public health and the quality of life. Describing her group's work, Mena states, "[W]e aim at delimiting a school or scientific discipline that we have termed productive ecology" (1987, 547). The group's work aims at transforming household wastes into primary materials or inputs for ecologically sustainable development. It has devised wet and dry integrated systems for recycling organic wastes (sistema integrado de reciclamiento de desechos orgánicos; SIRDOs)[12] that treat effluent from human waste to be reused in irrigating urban agricultural plots and transform organic garbage—together with human waste—into high-grade, marketable fertilizer.

Initial contact between GTA and Bosques was made by Juan Barriga, a settler who was an active grassroots leader of the Cooperative Society of Bosques del Pedregal in Struggle. Barriga's training in civil engineering and service in the armed forces led him to recognize the SIRDO technology as a possible answer to the problems of underground water contamination in the zone. The system can be designed to serve from 20 to 1,000 families, and a larger system can serve a settlement radius of nearly two kilometers. There are two types of SIRDOs. The simpler of the two is a closed system that can best be described as an eco-outhouse. In 1985, three of these freestanding units were put into operation in Bosques.[13] Each unit is used by several families and is designed so that human and organic wastes[14] do not drain off or seep into the ground.[15] The final product emerges as a brown granular powder that can be used or sold as high-grade organic fertilizer.[16] The second type of SIRDO is a more complex system. Termed a SIRDO-*húmedo*, it is designed to recycle wastewater in addition to organic solids.[17] The SIRDO-*húmedo* also produces fertilizer, but it simultaneously recycles and treats sewage water as well as soapy water. The construction of a SIRDO-*húmedo* was begun in Bosques in 1985 with funding from a support group based in Europe[18]; it was designed for 120 families.[19]

Around the same time that Barriga and GTA got together, members of the Cooperative in Bosques met with Jim Conrad, an environmentalist visiting from the United States. Discussions with Conrad led to the idea of promoting Bosques as a CEP. The Cooperative decided to invite GTA into Bosques to help transform their settlement into a CEP. The Ajusco Cooperation Group was formed to define the project and determine appropriate strategies for its promotion and implementation.[20] Settlers of Bosques raised funds to cover necessary project expenses from a number of sources (for example, selling donated clothing and other items collected from upper-class neighborhoods).

The CEP *Document*

The Ajusco Cooperation Group produced a document titled *Colonia Ecológica Productiva*, which presented a tightly argued countervailing strategy backed by popular mobilization. The proposal is an excellent example of grassroots initiative in proactive ecologically integrated planning. The CEP document was presented by grassroots leaders to government officials in public hearings and planning sessions and to authorities in key administrative offices. The arguments and working hypotheses recorded in the document are summarized below.

1. The current population of Bosques is not marginal: It is productive and it can be an active agent in technological development. Furthermore, it is possible and necessary to conjoin productive development with ecological equilibrium and in this way generate a mode of urban development that does not provoke antagonism between these two factors.
2. The conservationist focus that the Tlalpan Ward has maintained conceives of Ajusco as a national park. But this conception dissociates the necessity of reforestation from the possibility of production. Given the demands on this space, it will be impossible to maintain it as a green belt for consumption. Instead it should be developed as a green belt for production.
3. Through community pilot projects—involving the operation and maintenance of appropriate technologies as well as the generation and distribution of resources—the auto-administrative capacity of the community can be elevated; so can its productive capacity. In terms of production, it is estimated that with an initial investment of 100 million pesos 340 jobs can be created.

4. Promoting social experimentation in Bosques to ameliorate the problems in Ajusco is in the national interest. If the CEP model is successful, it could benefit others by way of example.

5. The project coincides with the political intent of the Mexican Constitution and the government of the DDF. It fits within the guidelines of the Development Plan for the Metropolitan Zone of Mexico City and the Central Region, especially with regard to the lines of action: items 3.2, 3.3, and 3.5.

In addition to outlining these broad arguments and working hypotheses, the CEP document spelled out a wide range of specific proposals concerning urban land use and tenure, environmental control and ecological protection, human ecology and public health, and barrio-based pilot projects for production in the primary and secondary sectors of the economy. The SIRDO technology, described as an integral barrio-based approach to recycling liquid and solid wastes, served as the pivot of the plan.

Outcome of the CEP and Other Ecological Initiatives in Los Belvederes (1984–86)

The CEP project was used as a basis for popular mobilization and was actively promoted between 1984 and 1985. All those who strove to realize its objectives knew that it was an ambitious challenge. Despite the daunting scope of the task involved, there was optimism in Bosques. Josefina Mena, GTA's director, explained that

> [t]he social dynamic in Bosques del Pedregal has acquired a very different rhythm. This is reinforced by the CEP project—a project that expresses the distinct character of the settlers, including their priorities and their "productive ecology" consciousness. What is happening in Bosques represents a fundamental questioning of conventional planning concepts. Concepts of zoning, urban spatial categories, the conception of housing and the role of infrastructure have been transformed. (1987, 553–54)

At the same time, independent researchers enthusiastically supported the project. Martha Schteingart, a professor at the Colegio de México, argued that the CEP project "is an example of creativity and of the search for alternatives to improve the community, demonstrating at the same time, the importance of independent organization of the settlers and of their urban struggle to offer new solutions to the urban and ecological problematic" (1987, 30).

These observations were made at a time when the CEP project in Bosques—as well as similar initiatives in Belvedere and Dos de

Octubre—were well under way. The projects were supported by large numbers of settlers, and their initiatives received a great deal of positive press coverage.[21] Public protests, marches, and other forms of popular mobilization called for sustainable development, using ecological issues as their rallying point.

When the intensity of grassroots ecopolitics reached its peak in late 1984, the state responded by announcing that the provisions in the Ajusco Conservation Program calling for massive relocation of households would be revoked. The new official strategy stated that all of Los Belvederes would be included in the legally designated urban area, and every family would be given security of tenure on an individual basis.

The shift in state policy dramatically changed the terms of struggle. "Winning" the right to have their settlements incorporated into the legally designated urban area reduced the settlers' sense of insecurity and urgency. The "victory" was a result of political mediation and tended to remove the impetus for further mobilization. From the standpoint of popular mobilization, this pattern of development was typical and presented a major dilemma. The Movimiento Revolucionario del Pueblo wrote that, "[p]eriods of strong mobilization correspond to the struggle to satisfy permanent needs (access to legally secure land for housing, piped water supply, a school) or to unexpected crises such as transportation fare increases or compensation for grave accidents, but as soon as the critical juncture is passed, demands resume on general terms and organization disappears" (1983, 6).

Popular mobilization in Bosques and throughout Los Belvederes declined after mid-1985 but did not subside altogether. Winning the right to have their settlements incorporated into the legally designated urban area highlighted problems outside the realm of ecological discourse, thereby prioritizing other countervailing strategies. New battles had to be waged to secure the best terms for regularization and to resolve litigation regarding fraudulent land transactions and boundary disputes. To this end, settlements throughout the zone joined forces and created the Popular and Independent Coalition.

Although settlers no longer had to worry about forced evictions by the state, a new threat took its place for many households: the prospect of being displaced by economic forces. Many settlers on *ejido*[22] lands and private property feared that although they might have gained the legal right to (re)purchase their lots, they would not always have the finances to do so. They were also worried about the prospect of paying high taxes for services and infrastructure.

The rise of these new concerns and priorities was marked by a fall in concern with CEP and other ecological initiatives. For instance, in Belvedere, the grassroots organization Casa del Pueblo, working with university groups, bitterly denounced the state's support of "groups that instigate divisions in the community and hinder the projects to create an ecological settlement" (*El Día*, 31 March 1985). All through 1985, Belvedere was embroiled in violent conflicts stemming from disputes over land ownership; there were multiple deaths. In May 1985, university groups from UNAM announced that the profound conflicts in Belvedere "made it impossible to implement any new project" (*La Jornada*, 30 May 1985). Coordinators from the university announced that they had no alternative but to sever their relationship with Belvedere; projects that had been worked on over the past eighteen months would have to be aborted.

Yet in Bosques, the first eco-outhouse was put into operation during this period. Soon after, three similar units were installed and construction began on the SIRDO-*húmedo* system for 120 families. Although state support for these specific projects was promised, it never materialized, and funding was raised from external sources. Apart from early efforts at community fund-raising, most of the funding came from the MISEROR Foundation—a Catholic philanthropic agency based in Germany—and the Austrian Solidarity Network—a group of Austrian professionals sympathetic to the ecology movement. Due to galloping inflation during the late 1980s, the funds raised were barely enough to cover the cost of four eco-outhouses. Consequently, despite all the investment of community effort and resources, the SIRDO-*húmedo* technology lay incomplete and idle—creating the appearance that earlier efforts had been in vain.

Current Status of the CEP Campaign (1990–91)

Between 1987 and 1990, CEP initiatives in Bosques del Pedregal were essentially dead. In 1989, the GTA secured funding from the Canadian International Center of Investigation for Development to improve the design of the SIRDO-*húmedo* and to conduct further research on recycling inorganic wastes and the use of biofertilizers in urban agriculture. But by 1989, GTA no longer sustained a good working relationship with the community. The core SIRDO-*húmedo* plant was complete, but the tubing network necessary to connect the 120 families to the system had not yet been installed. The community had by then ceased to view the SIRDO project as a priority, their attention being focused on the processes and terms of land tenure regularization.

Official complaints regarding the contamination of Ajusco's aquifer revived suddenly, and the land tenure regularization process was interrupted once more. Attention reverted to the SIRDO-*húmedo* system. Settlers mobilized again in support of the SIRDO project. In December 1990, they were successful in getting the *Delegado* (elected representative) of Tlalpan to commit funds for the purchase of materials needed to connect the SIRDO to 120 families, provided the citizens donated their labor. In January 1991, construction of the sewage-pipe network began.

Although the SIRDO-*húmedo* project is now almost complete, the relationship between GTA and the Council continues to be strained. GTA faults the leadership of Bosques for allowing the government to define the terms of crisis in the zone. It argues that in 1984 the leadership was proactive in its approach, proposing alternatives and demanding space for social experimentation. Yet now, GTA claims, the leaders of Bosques employ tactics that are out of step with the current political realities in Mexico:

> During the past sexenio [six-year presidential term], the form of struggle employed through demonstrations and pressures from the base had political impact. In the present sexenio, given the politics of modernization pursued by the new President of the country, these pressures from the base do not have the same impact, nor do they serve as an instrument of negotiation as they did before. Despite this, the leaders of Bosques have their interests centered in exercising pressure through political acts, such as demonstrations, sit-ins, and other populist actions, in order to secure land tenure regularization. (GTA 1990)

The Council faults GTA for raising expectations that could not be fulfilled. The SIRDO-*húmedo* and other ecological initiatives lay dormant between 1985 and 1990. The leadership of Bosques argues that CEP lost its relevance as a political rallying point: Although it sounded good in principle, in reality it proved immensely difficult to translate into action.

The coming years may mark a new beginning in the settlement, with GTA and the Council making mutual efforts to resolve their differences. Meanwhile, GTA is working closely with the families who will directly benefit from the SIRDO-*húmedo* once they are connected to the system. Concurrently, there will be a period of social experimentation funded by a two-year research grant—received by GTA from the Canadian International Center of Investigation for Development—to design and monitor methods for the community operation of the SIRDO-*húmedo*. "The primary objective of the investigation is to determine the technical, social, and economic conditions that will enable the autonomous operation of the SIRDO" (GTA 1990). Although the technology is fairly simple, its success will depend on people transforming their patterns of household behavior and consumption. At the time of this writing, a five-week pilot project was under way with thirty households involved in sorting and measuring their organic and inorganic wastes.

Conclusion

Since the late 1980s, the Mexican government has stated its policy to definitively eradicate all illegal settlements occurring within the ecological reserve. Despite all the measures adopted—miles of chain-link fencing that marks the urban-ecological perimeter, billboards warning against trespassing and illegal land transactions, tighter government controls over land use and construction permits for all projects in rural areas, and repeated eradication of incipient settlements—the urban sprawl continues with a slow, yet relentless momentum.

The trend toward the concentration of urban populations in megacities raises grave concern regarding the future of such metropolitan regions and their hinterlands. Addressing the future of cities of Pacific Rim countries—including Mexico City—Douglass observes: "[e]nvironmental degradation and loss of arable land on a global scale are everywhere *calling for innovative efforts* to sustain the material and ecological bases for the expansion of human agglomerations which no longer produce food and are consuming energy and producing wastes at exponential rates" (1989, 9; emphasis mine). Although the call for such innovative efforts is largely concerned with alternative approaches to development outside the urban realm (studies on agroecology, social forestry, environmental protection and conservation), this conclusion attempts to focus on prospects for creating sustainable livelihoods within the urban milieu.

In view of the hyperurbanization taking place in Mexico City, it must be noted that rural development and support for traditional livelihoods continue to be extremely important. Any plan that aims to engender sustainable livelihoods in the Central Mexican Basin would be futile unless serious efforts are simultaneously made to promote rural development and decentralization. In short, without effective decentralization policies and rural development strategies, urban sprawl and ecological disruption in the MAMC will continue—irrespective of the most ingenious grassroots initiatives or, for that matter, the worst forms of quasi-militarist politics of containment.

Getting to the root of irregular settlements and related ecological problems in Mexico City ultimately requires fundamental changes in the institutions that control land allocation and prices and those that set priorities for national and municipal development goals (Peattie 1982; Friedmann and Weaver 1979). The issue here, as Friedmann suggests, is "the creation of an alternative social order which necessarily involves a restructuring of basic relations of power" (1987, 400).

The two preceding arguments make abundantly clear the complexity of the challenges facing the people in Los Belvederes. Indeed, given this complexity, one could argue that the CEP campaign had little chance of being anything more than a "reactive utopia," in that it lacked the capacity to put forward a historically feasible alternative to mainstream development (Castells 1983, 327–31). But to end on such a note would be to miss a great deal. Important lessons were learned by the people who participated in the CEP campaign. As Ramírez Saiz points out with regard to contemporary urban movements throughout Mexico:

> [t]he literature on the different social movements has stressed their reactive and disruptive character more than their ability to take constructive initiatives. This is a valid characterization, but in the case of the MUP [Popular Urban Movements] it should include recognition of their ability to use the government's legal and technical language to propose viable alternatives corresponding to their demands. It is true that this has only been possible at the level of neighborhoods or locally targeted plans, and not for entire cities of regions, nor for the country as a whole. Nonetheless, it does represent an advance in the forms of the urban movements' struggle. (1990, 234)

My aim in these concluding comments is to draw lessons from the proactive experience around the CEP project in Los Belvederes, both for Mexico City and for other cities in Latin America. More specifically, the discussion returns to the two challenges raised at the outset of this chapter: (1) to fortify the barrio economy as a means of creating sustainable livelihoods, and (2) to strengthen the theory and practice of proactive, ecologically integrated planning.

Fortifying the Barrio Economy

Urban land and ecological problems are inextricably bound and share common roots in that each can be related to the inadequate creation of livelihood opportunities. This crisis, measured by rising levels of joblessness and underemployment and the failure of the formal sector to generate enough jobs or to provide adequate living wages, has resulted in the proliferation of informal economic activities. Consequently, "the survival strategies of the poor have coalesced in many countries into significant aggregate contributions to their economies, and the informal sector continues to offer the only employment hope for many people" (Reilly 1991, 3).

There are no technical fixes for these problems. To a greater extent than ever, solutions depend on effective social organization and on collective self-provisioning at the grassroots level. What is needed, therefore, is a concerted effort "to create the conditions for an effectively working democracy that consists of strong representative institutions and the collective empowerment of ordinary citizens in their own communities and, beyond these boundaries, in mass-based social movements and political parties" (Friedmann 1986, 22).

What would this mean in practical terms? Here Friedmann provides a guiding perspective: Planning at the local level would aim at transforming the barrio into "a combined housing-production-living unit involving new relations of power" (Friedmann 1986, 27). In the case of Los Belvederes, one could argue that this was the aim of the CEP campaign. At its zenith, the CEP campaign had thousands of families rallying under its "productive ecology" banner. At the same time, the movement had networked across the urban-rural divide and had successfully articulated multiclass alliances with independent researchers, university students, newspaper columnists, international agencies, and *campesinos* both locally and from the northern part of the country. Yet once the land tenure regularization program began in 1985, these connections eroded. Herein lies one of the most significant lessons of the case.

Effective community-based environmental action promoted by the CEP activists requires more than good planning and motivation; it requires continuity and cohesion in terms of social organization. This may still not be enough. Social organization was highly cohesive throughout Los Belvederes in the early stages of its development, but it rapidly eroded when political and economic conditions changed. Given the harsh conditions and lack of services at the beginning, settlers had many reasons to cooperate and work together. For instance, they had to set up and conduct classes for their children, clear streets, lay down provisional infrastructure for electricity and water, and, generally speaking, look out for one another. Households engaged in joint decisionmaking on a daily basis; out of necessity, they collectively produced their own livelihoods (Díaz Barriga 1991). In this context, each household could be described as a proactive unit linked to other households through productive relationships in a larger household economy (Friedmann 1988, 41). However, as Los Belvederes became established over the years with more services secured from the state, there was less urgency for settlers to act collectively. The waning of collective action has to be understood within the national political context, where the provision of urban services by the state in Mexico "has been one of the most powerful and subtle mechanisms of social and institutional control of everyday life" (Castells in Ramírez Saiz 1990, 235).

One way to describe this widely documented outcome is what Max Weber referred to as the expropriation of the means of administration, which results in communities losing their capacity for collective organization and control over local development decisions. But collective organization is essential for creating jobs in the informal or cooperative survival economy. At the same time, it engenders *social power*—a dynamic force essential for motivating the social experimentation and practice necessary to create sustainable livelihoods.

Conversely, a decrease in social power undermines the opportunity for low-income groups to generate wealth. This point was acknowledged by activists in Los Belvederes who wanted to create sustainable livelihoods through a "productive ecology." They urged the state to expropriate the land and to establish a collective tenure arrangement, as opposed to regularization on an individual basis. The reason for this was, above all, political. As Castells has observed for similar situations, the settlers feared that standard regularization would individualize the problem—"dividing the land would create a specific relationship between each squatter and the administration" (Castells 1983, 198). Activists were concerned that their movement could be fragmented and lose its internal solidarity, and this is precisely what happened. Although the state adamantly refused to consider establishing collective tenure as an alternative route to legalization, some members of the movement continued to press the case. Meanwhile, others began negotiating contracts to (re)purchase their individual lots from a cabal of developers backed by the government. This drove a wedge into the movement and seriously undermined its collective strength.

In the future, popular groups will have to become more astute in their negotiation of the legal and institutional terrain. In Los Belvederes, groups cited their constitutional rights in novel arguments that effectively exposed the shortcomings of official plans for the area (Ramírez Saiz 1990, 242). In the case of the CEP campaign, its close link to the land question may well have been its undoing. When ecological arguments are so closely linked to the struggle for land, the land question takes precedence. And once the threat of forced eviction passes, the ecological initiatives lose currency. Energy may have been more effectively concentrated on getting financial and technical support—whether from receptive city officials, businesspeople, research institutions, or charitable organizations—for cottage industries and entrepreneurial ecological initiatives. Indeed, at one point, the state promised funding for the proposed eco-projects. When officials did not follow through on this promise, the settlers mobilized to demand accountability.[23] Yet this was a side show—the main drama continued to center on land tenure. These developments suggest that grassroots groups have to define long-term strategies to ensure that ecological initiatives do not fall prey to political expediency. It is in this respect that progress on the SIRDO technology is so important—not just for its value as a sound ecological system, but also for its capacity to change patterns of behavior, to create new meanings (garbage as resource), and to generate jobs.

Proactive Ecologically Integrated Planning

The state's politics of containment and its sectoral approach to irregular settlements and ecological problems in Ajusco have clearly been inadequate. Does this mean that all pretense of maintaining an ecological reserve should be abandoned, and that all fetters on urban expansion, either legal or illegal, should be removed? Obviously not. The question is one of control over resources. But by whom? Although state intervention in Ajusco is not completely devoid of good intention, I have already noted the dubious context within which planning takes place. There seems to be a strong argument for vesting control of land allocation and management decisions in local communities. Although there are no automatic guarantees, community control over land use may enhance social power and the prospects for a more holistic approach to the urban-ecological crisis. The point here is to create space for grassroots initiatives and social learning. There are no easy solutions for a genuine proactive ecologically integrated approach to planning. They must be worked out in practice and learned from experience. Such approaches cannot be prescribed by policymakers and planners at the national level, but require social experimentation and involvement at local levels.

In conclusion, Mexico City is now facing ecological, social, economic, and political problems of unprecedented proportions. At the same time, it is one of the world's most exciting cities, where social experimentation with new approaches to solving these problems is under way. In its search for legitimacy as well as for solutions, the state would do well to support the forms of social experimentation and struggles to create sustainable livelihoods that are integral to the CEP initiative. The recent decision by officials in the Tlalpan Ward to fund the completion of the SIRDO-*humédo* is a promising development. As the government's paternal approach to land allocation and management becomes less viable, one can at least hope that there will be greater incentive for politicians to break out of old patterns and support innovative grassroots initiatives.

Notes

Fieldwork underlying this essay was made possible by a doctoral dissertation fellowship from the Inter-American Foundation. Much of the case study described in this article has already been published in a volume edited by David Goodman and Michael Redclift titled *Environment and Development in Latin America: The Politics of Sustainability* (New York: Manchester University Press, 1991).

1. The settlements are termed "irregular" because occupants do not hold legal property titles to the land they inhabit.
2. By some estimates, hundreds of thousands, if not millions, of people suffer pollution-related illnesses in Mexico City (for example, emphysema, pneumonia, bronchitis, asthma, cardiovascular complications, conjunctivitis, sinusitis, laryngitis, allergies, and bloody noses) (*Los Angeles Times*, 21 April 1991, M1). In some areas of the city, breast-fed infants are ingesting toxic levels of once-airborne lead that has become concentrated in their mothers' milk. The high concentration of lead found in newborns has been shown to be related to low birth weights and developmental problems such as altered reflexes and learning disorders. Other studies indicate that the dangerous amount of fecal dust suspended in the atmosphere (from open-air defecation) is causing many people to suffer respiratory infections (*La Jornada*, 22 April 1991, 15). More generally, although no one knows the pollution-linked cancer rate, some experts estimate the number of pollution-triggered deaths at 5,000 annually (*Los Angeles Times*, 21 April 1991, M1).
3. As Brown and Jacobson point out, water must be lifted into Mexico City from progressively lower catchments, which entails enormous energy costs:

   In 1982, Mexico City began pumping water from Cutzamala, a site 100 kilometers away and 1,000 meters lower than the city. British geographer Ian Douglas reports that "the augmentation of the Mexico City supply in the 1990s will be from Tecolutla, which is some 200 kilometers away and 2,000 meters lower." Pumping water this far will require some 125 trillion kilojoules of electrical energy annually, the output of six 1,000–megawatt power plants. Construction of these plants would cost at least $6 billion, an amount roughly equal to half the annual interest payments on Mexico's external debt. The city is thus faced with three rising cost curves in water procurement—increasing distance of water transport, increasing height of water lift, and, over the long term, rising energy prices. (1987, 36)

4. The Mexican government recently launched an Urban Saturation Program that aims to account for and utilize every nook and cranny within the Federal District (*UnoMasUno*, 3 April 1991).
5. *Ejidatarios* are farmers. They occupy *ejidos*, rural land that was distributed to landless peasants through agrarian reform after the Mexican Revolution. The term *ejido* refers to the legal corporation, composed of *ejidatarios*, which owns the land under important limitations (for example, it cannot be sold, rented, or mortgaged).
6. Estimate from Subdirectorate of Ajusco, Tlalpan.
7. Actually, the role of political parties such as Partido Socialista Unificado de Mexico (PSUM) and Coordinadora Nacional del Movimiento Urbano Popular (CONAMUP) was very limited. To some extent there was a connection to PSUM through affiliation with CONAMUP. But for the most part, the groups had little to do with electoral politics or political campaigns.
8. In January 1984, a group of biologists from UNAM, the Interdisciplinary Group for Agrobiological Studies, wrote up the results of a technical-ecological study. The biologists, in support of the zone's settlers, concluded

that "the population of these settlements causes little harm to the environment, given that it has already been contaminated by industry, automobiles, and by the excessive falling of trees—without reforestation—by companies which exploit the forest in a way concerned only with profit in order to produce paper or furniture." Many of the arguments of the settlers and sociology students against the judgment drew from the biologists' report.

9. For instance, the march and demonstration that concluded in front of the offices of CENCOS, the Center of Social Communications, on 7 June 1984 (see *El Día*, 8 June 1984); the press line-up in front of the Superior Court of Justice of the DDF on 16 October 1984 (see *La Jornada*, 16 October 1094); and the grievance letter addressed to President Miguel de la Madrid and to public opinion, printed in *UnoMasUno* and signed by leaders of the Front on 14 August 1984.

10. See *El Día*, 16 August 1984; *La Jornada*, 23–24 September 1984.

11. As Redclift (1987, 164) points out, there are two environmental movements in Mexico. The first is composed mainly of middle-class urban people. The second "is made up of poor people, both urban and rural, whose attempts to improve their livelihood are linked, increasingly, to sustainable practices." GTA has worked closely with groups in the second movement.

12. Description of these technologies comes from my own observations and from Mena 1987. For a short publication specifically about the history and function of the SIRDO technology, see Schmink 1984.

13. GTA improved the design and operation of this technology based on experiences in rural areas including Quintana Roo, Yucatan, Compeche, and Chiapas. It also gained experience in Merida and other parts of Mexico City.

14. Inputs—besides human waste—may include vegetable husks and peelings, discarded food, weeds, and paper products. Inputs may even include dead pets. Soon after Bosques put its first eco-outhouse into operation, a pet dog died giving birth. The pet belonged to Hipolito Barriga, a dedicated community leader who placed the dog into the SIRDO after cutting her up (to facilitate decomposition). Hipolito did this to make a point. When the SIRDO was shown to local authorities or to possible funding agencies, settlers were quick to point out that not only did the unit turn garbage into a resource, it was also odorless; if it could handle a rotting dog, it could handle anything. The dog ended up as fertilizer used to feed the Barriga family's lemon tree and garden.

15. Each eco-outhouse contains one toilet with two holding bins beneath it. The first bin to be put into use is prepared with start-up materials including some foliage and lime; when it is filled to capacity it is sealed off. The second bin is then prepared and used while the first bin is emptied.

16. These observations are substantiated, according to Mena (1987, 552), by studies carried out by investigators in the UAM-Iztapalapa under the direction of Dr. David Muñoz and by LANFI (*Laboratorios Nacionales de Fomento Industrial*), Depto. de Bio-tecnología, under the direction of Dr. Gustavo Viniegra Gonzalez.

17. There are SIRDO-*húmedos* functioning in the states of Mexico, Yucatan, Morelos, and in the DF (Federal District) El Molino.

18. I am referring to a solidarity group that was started by Dr. Peter Baumgartner specifically to support projects in Bosques. I introduced Dr. Baumgartner to the Bosques community in 1983. Between 1983 and 1985, he managed to raise thousands of dollars in Austria for CEP initiatives.
19. Each housing unit linked to the system is connected to the SIRDO-*húmedo* plant by two tubes: one for black water and the other for grey water. Through the tube for grey water, discharge is conducted away from each house to a filtering device that enables 70 percent of the water to be recycled for irrigating vegetables, fruits, and all types of cultivations. The black water is conducted to a sedimentation tank in which anaerobic digestion takes place. The sludge from this initial process is then passed into another holding tank. In this tank the sludge is mixed with other solid organic household waste (deposited on a daily basis), and the contents undergoes aerobiosis decomposition.
20. One of the unique aspects of this group is that the relationship between GTA and Bosques was expanded to include other research agencies.
21. See "Intentan crear la primera colónia ecológica de México en el Ajusco," *El Día*, 27 April 1984; "Surge la primera colónia ecológica en el país," *El Nacional*, 30 June 1984; "La hermosa gente: Bosques del Pedregal," *Ovaciones*, 28 June 1984; "Piden que el DDF tome en cuenta los asentamientos en el Ajusco," *El Día*, 31 August 1984; "La ecológia como arma política," *La Jornada*, 2 December 1984.
22. See note 5 above.
23. On 15 November 1985, approximately 1,500 settlers of Bosques took over the administration offices of the Tlalpan Ward for one hour. They protested the lack of support and demanded to know what happened to the supposed 1,700 million pesos that were promised for financing services and ecological projects (*El Día*, 16 November 1985).

References

Brown, Lester R., and Jodi L. Jacobsen. 1987. *The Future of Urbanization: Facing the Ecological Constraints*. World Watch Paper 77. Washington, D.C.: World Watch Institute.

Carabias, J., and A. Herrera. 1986. "La ciudad y su ambiente." *Cuadernos Politicos* 45(January-March): 56–69.

Castells, M. 1983. *The City and the Grassroots*. Berkeley and Los Angeles: University of California Press.

Connolly, P. 1982. "Uncontrolled Settlements and Self-Build: What Kind of Solution? The Mexico City Case." In *Self-Help Housing: A Critique*, edited by Peter Ward, London: Mansell.

Cornelius, W., and A. Craig. 1988. *Politics in Mexico: An Introduction and Overview*. Reprint series 1, 2d ed. San Diego: University of California, Center for U.S.-Mexican Studies.

DDF. 1986. "Programa de integración social del território: Tlalpan, Belvederes."

Díaz Barriga, M. 1991. "Urban Politics in the Valley of Mexico: A Case Study of Urban Movements in the Ajusco Region of Mexico City, 1970 to 1987." Ph.D. dissertation, Stanford University.

Douglass, Mike. 1989. "The Future of Cities on the Pacific Rim." In *Pacific Rim Cities in the World Economy,* edited by Michael Peter Smith, New Brunswick, N.J.: Transaction Books.

Dunkerley, H., and C. Whitehead, eds. 1983. *Urban Land Policy: Issues and Opportunities.* Washington, D.C.: World Bank.

Friedmann, John. 1986. *Life Space and Economic Space: Essays in Third World Planning.* New Brunswick, N.J.: Transaction Books.

———. 1987. *Planning in the Public Domain: From Knowledge to Action.* Princeton, N.J.: Princeton University Press.

———. 1988. "The Latin American *Barrio* Movement as a Social Movement: Contribution to a Debate." *International Journal of Urban and Regional Research* 13(3): 501–10.

Friedmann, John, and Clyde Weaver. 1979. *Territory and Function: The Evolution of Regional Planning.* London: Edward Arnold.

Garza, G., ed. 1987. *Atlas de la Ciudad de México.* Mexico DF: DDF and Colégio de México.

GTA. 1990. "Proyecto Bosques, Ajusco." Mexico DF: GTA.

Mena, Josephina. 1987. "Technología alternativa, transformación de desechos y desarrollo urbano." *Estudios Demográficos y Urbanos* 2(3): 545–55.

Movimiento Revolucionario del Pueblo. 1983. "Elementos de una Linea política para el movimiento urbano popular." México DF: mimeo.

Peattie, Lisa. 1982. "Some Second Thoughts on Sites and Services." *Habitat International* 6: 131–39.

Popular Front for the Defense of the Settlements of Ajusco. 1984.

Ramírez Saiz, J. M. 1990. "Urban Struggles and their Political Consequences." In *Popular Movements and Political Change in Mexico,* edited by J. Foweraker and A. Craig. Boulder, Colo.: Lynne Rienner.

Redclift, Michael. 1987. *Sustainable Development: Exploring the Contradictions.* New York: Methuen.

Reilly, Charles 1991. "When Do Environmental Problems Become Issues? Whose Issues? And Who Manages Them Best?" Paper based on remarks at the UNRISD Workshop on Sustainable Development through People's Participation in Resource Management, Geneva, May 1990. Rosslyn, Va.: Inter-American Foundation.

Rivera, M. 1987. "La transformación del suelo ejidal en suelo urbano: el caso del ejido de San Nicolas Totolapán." Tesis de Licenciado en Sociología, Universidad Nacional Autónoma de México, México, D.F.

Rodriguez, V. 1987. "The Politics of Decentralization in Mexico: Divergent Outcomes of Policy Implementation." Ph.D. dissertation, University of California, Berkeley.

Schmink, Marianne. 1984. "Administración comunitária del reciclamiento de desechos: El Sirdo." Monograph #8. New York: Seeds Publications.

Schteingart, Martha. 1987. "Expansión urbana, conflictos sociales y deterioro ambiental en la Ciudad de Mexico: El caso del Ajusco." *Estudios Demográficos y Urbanos* 2(3): 477–499.

Ward, Peter. 1989. "Political Mediation and Illegal Settlement in Mexico City." In *Housing and Land in Urban Mexico,* edited by A. Gilbert. Monograph Series no. 31. San Diego: UCSD Center for U.S.-Mexican Studies.

SIX

ROMANCING THE ENVIRONMENT

Popular Environmental Action in the Garhwal Himalayas

HARIPRIYA RANGAN

WHY DO WORDS LIKE *environment* and *ecology* make so many people living in the Garhwal Himalayas see red? Why do so many of them make derisive comments when the Chipko movement figures in any discussion? Why is it that in most parts of Garhwal today, local populations are angry and resentful of being held hostage by Chipko, an environmental movement of their own making?

It is very rare for national newspapers in India to carry much news of the Garhwal region, unless of course, some major natural disaster occurs in the area—an earthquake, a flood, or an avalanche in the interior ranges—and a number of people die as a result. Regional newspapers, however, routinely report protests against the Forest Conservation Act, complaints against the red-tapism of the Central Ministry of Forests and the Environment, and criticism of the leaders of Chipko for jeopardizing development in the region (see for instance, a news item titled "Bahuguna's Statements Criticized" [translation] in *Amar Ujala*, February 8, 1991). Indian readers are advised to look up the page covering Uttarakhand in *Amar Ujala* (a Hindi newspaper read widely in western and northwestern Uttar Pradesh) and go over the *shikayatnama* or complaint section that appears at least twice each week, describing the problems faced by various villages and blocks in the hill districts of Garhwal and Kumaon. Thus when Agarwal and Narain write in the national business daily, *The Economic Times* (March 31, 1991), on the growing resentment in Garhwal towards the constraints imposed by new environmental laws, and the Central Ministry of Environment, it represents an important step toward recognizing the issues confronted by communities of a region where, according to the stories popularized by the movement's spokespeople, life after Chipko has been suspended in the realm of "happily every after."

As I conducted my field research over eighteen months on issues related to forestry and regional development in the Garhwal Himalayas, it was impossible to ignore the criticism and resentment that emerged from diverse quarters against environmentalists, new environmental laws, and the rhetoric used by Chipko's leaders to publicize the movement beyond Garhwal. Locally elected block officials, village communities that vigorously defend development of the region, and forest officers who have borne the brunt of environmentalists' criticism are all angry at the paralysis that has occurred as a result of laws such as the Tree Protection Act of 1976 and the Forest Conservation Act of 1985 and its 1988 amendment. Despite populist exhortations for greater community control and local management of forest resources, environmentalists rigorously support these laws which require regulation and intervention by the Central Ministry of Forests and the Environment. But before I go into the details of how popular environmental action has played out in Garhwal, it is necessary that I begin by recounting the romantic story of Chikpo, a tale that has gladdened the heart of many an earnest environmentalist around the globe.

Chipko's compelling narrative begins nearly thirty years ago (Dogra 1983; Shiva and Bandyopadhyay 1986a, 1986b, 1987; Weber 1988; Guha 1989). Soon after the Indo-Chinese War in 1962, the people of Garhwal encountered an Indian government determined to establish firm control of the regions along its international borders. Garhwal—which lay across the mountain range from Tibet—was one such region. Control was manifest through rapid deployment of security and resource development projects—roads were built through the area, army bases were established, mining and hydroelectric projects were planned—so that the region of Garhwal would be integrated into the mainstream of India's national development.

All these activities opened the region to increased movement of people and goods. The forests in Garhwal were the first to face the full force of this activity, as they were rapidly exploited to meet commercial and local demand. By the early 1970s, the activity began to affect village communities. The region reeled under the devastation caused by a succession of natural disasters. Torrential downpours during the monsoons eroded mountainsides and caused floods that swept people, land, and cattle away. Entire villages and small towns were wiped out of existence. Each attempt at rehabilitation brought growing awareness among the local communities that the rapid depletion of the forests was directly linked to the disasters in their region. Discussions between community activists and villagers led to a resolve to protest further extensive felling or clearing of forests in Garhwal.

Yet life had to go on. Several village cooperatives that had been established in the late 1960s depended on forest resources, and people also depended on tree and grazing rights granted to them by the State Forest Department. Competing interests heightened the awareness that trees would have to be cut, but in a more selective and judicious manner. Thus, when the Dasholi Village Cooperative Society asked to be granted three ash trees to make agricultural implements, the Forest Department denied the appeal. The Forest Department claimed that it had already auctioned the trees to a sporting goods company. Members of the village cooperative were angered by the department's stance and decided to prevent the ash trees from being felled at all. The strategy of prevention was to be nonviolent; when the timber contractors arrived on site with their labor, groups of people from the nearby village urged them not to cut the trees. When verbal persuasion failed, the villagers threw their arms around the trees, and the contractors were compelled to leave empty-handed. Chipko—which in the Garhwali language means "to adhere"—had come into being as a strategy of resistance, symbolized by tree hugging.

In the years that followed, the Chipko strategy was adopted by other village cooperatives and communities in Garhwal as an effective means of drawing the government's attention to the social and economic problems faced by people in the region. Men, women, children, the elderly—almost everyone was eager to prevent large-scale commercial felling in the state-controlled forests adjoining their villages. Communities argued that if fellings continued in the forests, their land, cattle, and livelihood would be in danger of destruction by landslides and erosion during the rains. It was in this manner that Chipko came to be identified as a popular movement to save the environment, the resources, and the livelihoods of people in the Garhwal Himalayas.

As the Chipko strategy was adopted by other communities in Garhwal, it fired the enthusiasm and imagination of people. Chipko's emergent leaders found support among students, activists, and intellectuals with strong environmental concerns. Together, they launched campaigns against timber businesses. Soon Chipko began to be represented as a movement that sought to protect the Himalayan environment. Denouncing national and state governments for jettisoning environmental and ecological issues for short-term gains, "deep ecologists" argued that India's security and prosperity lay in protecting Himalayan forests from any kind of commercial exploitation.

The state finally seemed to give in to the demands made by leaders of the movement. Timber businesses were banned from felling forests; a state government enterprise was created to take their place and work the forests in a more judicious manner. The National Forest Policy praised the Chipko movement, stating:

> [t]hough the main demand of the Chipko movement in 1973 was an end to the contract system of forest exploration [sic] and allotment of raw materials for local, forest-based industrial units on concessional rates, since then there has been a basic change in the objective of the movement. It has developed into an ecological movement of permanent economy from a movement of short-term exploitative economy. The movement is striving to get the scientific truth accepted that the main products of the forest are oxygen, water and soil.[1] (Lok Sabha Secretariat 1985, 70)

By the time Chipko gained recognition as a popular environmental movement to influence state policies, the issues of sustaining viable livelihoods for local communities in Garhwal had been submerged under the polemic and rhetoric raised over deforestation and ecology. Chipko became the movement to save the Himalayas and India's environment at large, but few of its spokespeople seemed concerned about how localities were to survive and prosper under the bleak economic conditions prevailing in Garhwal.

The Chipko movement exists today as a fairy tale, a myth sustained and propagated by a few self-appointed spokespeople through conferences, books, and journal articles that eulogize it as a social movement, peasant movement (Guha 1986), environmental movement (Shiva and Bandyopadhyay 1989), women's movement (Jain 1984), Gandhian movement (Weber 1988)—in short, an all-encompassing movement, beyond compare. In this way Chipko has joined the host of Indian myths that weave the fabric of reality symbolizing the Himalayas.

To a large portion of Indians, the Himalayan region is a single, homogenous symbol, a reality created out of the fabric of myths and legends. For almost all people, except those who live within it, the Himalayan region is the container of an ascriptive—rather than a geographical, social, and cultural—reality. Such propensity for symbolism is seen in the statement made by a famous Indian philosopher, who declared:

> [e]xistentialism says that potentiality is more important than actuality. This is true: the Himalayas of the *rishis* and *yogis* [hermits and sages], is more important as an ideal to use than are the actual rocks and the miserable huts of the people there. (Bharati 1978, 78)

This sort of symbolism also infuses the visions of environmental activists and intellectuals who champion the Chipko movement's cause. They argue that the essence of this popular movement has been a concern for the Himalayan environment in its own right—the "deeply ecological" content of Chipko.[2] "Deep ecology" advocates assert that forests of the Himalayas bear soil, water, and pure air rather than any economic value—a provocative argument in environmental debates, but not a view likely to be expounded by the people who live and labor within this landscape.[3] Yet it is precisely this symbolic representation of Chipko that the state chooses to identify as the movement's essence. Perhaps this is why many communities in Garhwal today are resentful of being held hostage by the movement and its ideologues. If we wish to understand the processes that have led to the growing disaffection with Chipko, we must begin by looking through the veils of narratives and myths that enshroud the social and economic realities of the Garhwal region and its people.

The Myths of Margins

Garhwal, with its spectacular mountains and forests, is usually categorized as a "marginal region" based on two axioms. The first is that mountain-forest areas in the Himalayas are vast repositories of natural, geological, and energy resources that have not been exploited to their fullest potential due to their geographical remoteness and relative isolation. The second axiom is that because of the region's mountainous terrain, infertile soils, and lack of irrigation, productive agricultural labor cannot increase without enormous investments of capital. Almost all the literature available on the socioeconomic problems of Garhwal is based on these axioms, although there may be different theoretical perspectives. For purposes of explanation, the body of literature on Garhwal can be classified into three categories: the "official" Malthusian stance, the "antimodernization" perspective, and the "national political economy" approach.

The Ignorant Peasant

The Malthusian stance is found in most state-initiated regional planning and rural development programs addressing hill regions in India. The reasoning advanced by this perspective is that because of the existing constraints in mountain-forest environments, limited amounts of agricultural lands are available, and possibilities of expanding cultivation are extremely limited for local populations. Demographic growth increases pressure on agriculture and rapidly exceeds the "carrying capacity" of land, forcing young and able men to migrate to the plains and cities in search of employment. The allure of urban amenities and modern consumption further accelerates the immigration of young men to the plains, leaving women, children, and the aged behind in the hills. The reasoning continues: Because the people left behind lack adequate strength and skills to engage in cultivation, the productivity of land further dwindles, and these people becoming increasingly dependent on remittances of emigrated household members for subsistence. Thus people living in mountain-forest regions are viewed as being caught in, and contributing to, a perpetual cycle of backwardness.[4]

These dimensions of the economic backwardness and social ignorance of hill populations are then extended to explain deforestation and the environmental degradation of Himalayan regions. Human and livestock population growth increases pressure on the scarce amounts of productive land, forcing peasants to desperately seek subsistence by encroaching upon forest areas to bring more land under cultivation or pasture. Thus village forests and pastures are overexploited and result in substantial deforestation and soil erosion of mountainous slopes. Constant encroachment upon forests for fuelwood, grazing, and cultivation accelerates land degradation to the extent that during the monsoons, heavy downpours cause enormous landslides, which destroy terraced slopes and transport vast quantities of silt downstream. This, in turn, causes floods and destroys the stability of lowland cultivation. Such natural and ecological disasters further erode the subsistence economy of hill peasants and force their migration to cities in the plains.

The peasants, therefore, are the root cause of the socioeconomic and environmental problems in the Himalayas. The Malthusian stance points its finger firmly at the ignorance and shortsightedness of peasants, seeing them as the prime agents perpetuating the processes of environmental degradation and economic backwardness in hill areas (Khan and Tripathy 1976; National Forest Policy 1985; Bora 1987; Dobhal 1987).[5]

Modernization and the Noble Peasant

This perspective accuses the modernization strategies adopted by the state of causing environmental problems in the Himalayan region. Environmental activists and intellectuals often espouse the view that forests—previously remote and inaccessible to urban areas—provided the basic needs for local communities that, in turn, respected and maintained the delicate balance of the mountain-forest ecosystem through time-honored traditions. But the pursuit of rapid economic growth by the modernizing state destabilizes the equilibrium of this ecosystem. The state constructs roads into these areas and brings them within easy reach of urban capitalists who ruthlessly exploit forests for commercial profits. The combination of extensive commercial felling and unsound silvicultural practices promoted by the government to cater primarily to industrial and urban demand prevents rural households from meeting their basic needs from forests (Shiva and Bandyopadhyay 1986a, 1986b). Since fuel, fodder, fruits, fiber, and fertilizers can no longer be obtained entirely from small community forests, rural households are forced to seek these domestic needs beyond their villages. All these factors combine to result in the rapid deterioration of the mountain-forest ecosystem. Heavy monsoons batter deforested mountain slopes, causing landslides, destroying cultivated terraces, and carrying vast amounts of fertile soil down the rivers (Dogra 1983).

Rural households in the hill regions are affected by these processes in two ways: Men are forced to migrate to the plains looking for work; those who remain spend more time and effort to obtain the essentials of survival. Deforestation around the villages causes water springs to dry up, forcing women and children to walk longer distances to collect water and fuelwood (Berreman 1989).

From this perspective, problems in hill regions are caused primarily by commercial exploiters who ruthlessly destroy mountain-forest ecosystems, profiting from the modernization strategies promoted by the state. Commercial exploitation of forests denies local populations their traditional right to meet basic needs (Shiva and Bandyopadhyay 1987, 1989; Weber 1988).

Peasants against the State

The political economy approach traces the history of the appropriation of and control over the Himalayan region and its resources and reveals how these political and economic processes have consistently served the interests of dominant classes in India. Forest policies of colonial and postcolonial governments are clearly biased in favor of the nation's industrial and commercial elite. As the basic needs of local populations are ignored, poor peasants engage in an unequal struggle against the state and national elite in an attempt to regain control over access to forest resources (Guha 1983, 1985, 1986, 1989; Guha and Gadgil 1989; Somanathan 1991).

Problems of Oversight

Although each of these perspectives provides different causal explanations for problems of ecological degradation and economic backwardness in the Himalayas, they share common assumptions regarding the subsistence nature of peasant economies and the homogeneous character of communities within the region.[6] State planners perpetuate the Malthusian myth of overpopulation that supposedly drives ignorant peasants toward the destruction of natural resources and subsequently jeopardizes national economic development. Their analysis conveniently ignores how state forest policies and management practices have affected local economies in Garhwal.

For the antimodernizers, the peasants of Garhwal are recent victims of modernization's relentless onslaught, the mythical "noble savages" who fight a losing battle for their basic needs against rapacious urban capitalists.[7] Obsessed with images of self-contained village communities living in harmonious ecological utopias, activists espousing this vision overlook the fact that most communities in Garhwal have been involved in a well-established economy based on commercial extraction of forest resources, agriculture, livestock rearing, and regional trade for more than two centuries.

By focusing on the opposition between local populations and the state, the political economy perspective comes closest to providing a realistic explanation of the economic and environmental problems in Garhwal. Yet this perspective fails to examine the regional economy in any detail to see why peasant conflicts in Garhwal have persisted over forest resources rather than over issues of agrarian reform. Because of a romanticized view of peasant struggles, the political economy approach ignores the importance of forest-based activities in household income formation and the processes of social and economic differentiation occurring within communities in the region.[8]

The major facts overlooked in the myths generated by each of these perspectives is that households and communities in Garhwal have traditionally relied on diverse activities such as petty extraction and trade of forest commodities, wage labor in forests and plantations, and labor exchange for access to grazing rights in state-owned forests as important sources of income. Rather than being supplemental to agriculture, these forest-related activities have often been central to shaping household and community relations, local labor processes, and social, cultural, and political institutions. These dimensions of household and local economies have been ignored largely because of the presumption that most people living in "marginal" regions like Garhwal are solely dependent on agriculture for their subsistence. Census handbooks reinforce this presumption through their method of classifying rural occupations.[9] In addition, most of the literature on settled rural communities tends to ignore subsistence or market activities generated outside the agricultural field, even though these may be far more important in contributing to household incomes.[10] State-sponsored rural development programs follow a sectoral approach that is predominantly focused on increasing productivity in agriculture through capital investments in irrigation, technological inputs, and energy supply. For a region such as the Garhwal Himalayas, this approach is usually ineffective because financial outlays are pitifully small for the implementation of such grand schemes. More importantly, these approaches fail to consider the nonagricultural economic activities of households and local communities in the region.

Beginning from the early nineteenth century and perhaps even earlier, forestry as a formalized economic activity penetrated almost every forested region that fell under control of the British colonial government. Garhwal was one such region. Forestry provided new legal and economic definitions of forests in terms of land use, tenure, and economic value. Resources in other spheres of activity such as agriculture, hunting, fishing, and livestock rearing were simultaneously redefined for local households and village communities. Local economic activities were transformed through the new relations established around land and forest tenure, these relations altered not only the rural landscape but also the nature of work in villages and towns within the region. It is necessary to understand the social and economic processes emerging from state forestry and forest-based activities that have affected the environment and given it new meanings in the Garhwal Himalayas.

Forestry and the Regional Economy

Garhwal falls within the geographical area broadly termed Uttarakhand, which comprises the eight hill districts of the state of Uttar Pradesh (Figure 6.1). The region can be defined roughly as the area that contains the watersheds of three major tributaries of the Ganges —the Yamuna, the Bhagirathi, and the Alakananda. Extending from the sub-Himalayan tracts called the *terai* and *bhabhar* to the trans-Himalayan regions bordering Tibet, Garhwal is, despite its uniformly rugged topography, extremely varied in its natural resource attributes and cultures. Local communities scattered across the mountains speak different languages and dialects, are culturally distinct from one another, and have diverse social and economic organizations. Nearly two-thirds of this terrain is classified as forest area (U.P. Forest Department 1983).

Trans-Himalayan trade played an integral role in sustaining the household economies of local populations for a long time—from pre-British times (before 1816) to as late as the mid-twentieth century.[11] In addition, pilgrimage sites in the Garhwal Himalayas have always provided an important seasonal economic activity. During the early years of colonial control in Garhwal, the geopolitical importance of controlling a territory that shared its boundaries with Tibet was greater than the economic value represented by its forests. Garhwal provided a strategic location for watching over the exchanges and transactions between Imperial Russia and Tibet, as well as vantage control of thriving trans-Himalayan trade routes and mountain passes into central Asia. The prospects of expanding colonial trade into the interior of Imperial

Figure 6.1 Northern India, Northwestern Uttar Pradesh: Garhwal Region

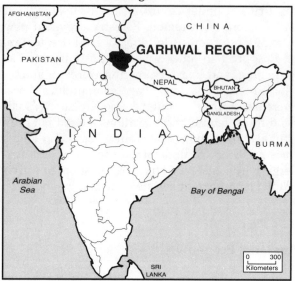

China and gaining control of the vast mineral wealth in Tibet held overwhelming allure for merchants, manufacturers, and colonial administrators of the British East India Company.[12] After the company's war with Nepalese rulers and settlement of boundary disputes in 1815, administering control over this vast mountainous region represented an additional burden on state revenues. Thus the areas of geopolitical importance were retained under British control, and the remainder was returned to native rulers (Stebbing 1922; Saklani 1986). During this period, Garhwal's forests were seen as a barrier to increased revenues for the colonial government. Referring to earlier policies that were overwhelmingly concerned with deriving revenue from agriculture, Berthold Ribbentrop, Inspector-General of Forests in India between 1867 and 1900, wrote:

> [N]o apprehension was felt that the supply of forest produce would ever fall short of demand, and forests were considered an obstruction to agriculture rather than otherwise, and consequently a bar to the prosperity of the Empire. It was the watchword of the time to bring everywhere more extensive areas into cultivation, and the whole policy tended in that direction. (Ribbentrop 1900, 60)

In the attempt to expand state revenues and consolidate British rule in the region, extensive forest areas in Garhwal and the neighboring hill division of Kumaon were felled (Tucker 1988), and the land was given in permanent settlement to proprietors and cultivators.[13]

As the government expanded its administration and control over different economic spheres ranging from tea plantations to the establishment of hill resorts, forests were rapidly cleared and their timber used for construction. Following the Indian Mutiny in 1857, the colonial government found it necessary to expand railroad networks for quick movement of merchandise and troops, so as to extend control over its more remote territories. The construction of railways required steady supplies of hardy timber species. During the early years of railway building, wooden ties were imported from Norway to meet these needs, since the colonial government was reluctant to use valuable teak forests for this purpose and did not have any clear assessment of the extent and nature of forests within its territories (Ribbentrop 1900; Stebbing 1922). Forest surveyors and botanists explored the Himalayan forests for substitutable species[14] and in due course they found appropriate varieties in the northwestern region and foothills (Smythies 1925; Troup 1976).

As extensive forest areas were brought under its control, the colonial administration faced the problem of resolving the conflicting demands on forest resources made by various economic enterprises. The confusion over how forests should be defined and whose needs they should serve continued well into the 1930s, as the Forest Department was shuffled between the Public Works, Revenue, and Home departments (Ribbentrop 1900; Stebbing 1922; Rawat 1983).[15] By 1868, four years after the colonial Forest Administration was established in Garhwal, forests were placed under the control of a Forest Conservator as well as a District Commissioner who controlled the revenue and judicial administration of the region.[16] Three categories of forests emerged from the enactment of forest laws: (1) reserved forests, owned and controlled solely by the State Forest Department, which could extend the rights of use to local communities at its pleasure; (2) protected and civil forests, owned by the State Revenue Department, but accessible to local communities through legal rights, both prescriptive and granted; and (3) village forests, which, although broadly regulated by the Revenue Department, were managed by village institutions (Ribbentrop 1900, 98–108). Today, reserved forests constitute nearly 80 percent of the designated forest area in Garhwal. Private ownership is almost nonexistent, and village forests have dwindled to less than 6 percent of the total area classified under forests (U.P. Forest Department 1983).

Monopoly control over reserved forests presented a set of contradictory responsibilities to the Forest Department. On the one hand, forestry laws stated that government control of forests was intended primarily to conserve natural resources and prevent environmental degradation in the interests and welfare of its subjects. On the other hand, the Forest Department was expected to manage its reserves so that a sustained supply of timber and other raw materials for public works and industry was provided at low cost, in addition to increasing revenue and profits for the state.[17] The latter objectives were often stressed over the former, and the Forest Department was mainly preoccupied with organizing extraction of commercially valuable species of timber and forest commodities in profitable ways.[18] In Garhwal, for example, the Forest Department was able to reap large profits by auctioning tracts of marked trees to the highest bidders, who would harvest the timber with hired labor. Resin, tanning dyes, and other raw materials useful for industry were extracted by temporary labor hired by the Forest Department, so that it retained its monopoly over market supply. Households were required to pay fees (depending on the market value) for extracting "minor" products such as medicinal herbs, fruits, and grasses from reserved forests. Villages were granted collective rights for gathering fuelwood, grazing cattle, and extracting a limited quota of trees for repairing or building houses, on the condition that they would, in exchange, provide labor for maintenance work and fire protection of reserved forests (Ribbentrop 1900, 218–19).

This diverse array of contracts and regulations around different forest commodities allowed the Forest Department to realize substantial profits from the areas under its control. Most of the financial risks in extractive activities were borne by private contractors and subcontractors (both British and native businesspeople) and by local households engaged in petty extraction and trade of forest commodities. Simultaneously, the work force required for routine maintenance and fire protection of forests was secured at little or no cost through the prescriptive and granted rights institutionalized by forest laws.

The redefinition and transformation of household and local economic activities by the colonial state became progressively clearer after 1878, following the enactment of forest laws in Garhwal. Although the forest laws were represented as mutually beneficial to local communities and the state, they were, in essence, the avenues through which government extended its control over both the resources and the social organization of extractive activities. State regulation through the Forest Departmant was exercised even over village forests in Garhwal to such an extent that the legal control vested in communities proved, in fact, to be illusory.[19]

With almost every extractive activity being regulated by taxes, levies, and contracts, many households found themselves being pushed out of what had been viable forest-based economic activities. Although some households belonging to upper castes and classes benefited from contracts with the Forest Department and grew wealthier, most others were compelled to extract the only "free" resources available to them—fuelwood and fodder. Colonial forest officers noted that ownership of flocks and herds multiplied rapidly "on account of the security afforded under a settled Government, and in consequence of the higher prices that could be realized for cattle" (Ribbentrop 1900, 61). Fuelwood collection became a valuable source of household income, since it could be sold to pilgrims, settlers at hill stations, and army cantonments.

But even fuelwood and fodder collection did not remain "free" for very long. The Forest Department regulated fuelwood extraction through contracting systems to meet the spiraling demand for fuel generated by industry, the railways (Guha 1983), and urban energy consumption. Village communities were forbidden from collecting firewood for sale and allowed to extract only specific amounts from state forests for household consumption. Grazing and fodder collection were regulated in several ways: collecting annual taxes on the heads of livestock held by each household; levying fees on the number of cattle grazed within reserved forests; controlling fodder collection through contractors, who would collect fees from households or sell the fodder at market prices. To ensure labor contributions for the maintenance and protection of its forests, the Forest Department established cattle pens within the reserves. Households were allowed to shelter their cattle in these pens during the grazing season and were leased an acre of land nearby for growing short-term commodity crops such as potatoes and seasonal vegetables (Ribbentrop 1900, 218–19; Rawat 1983, 51–105). As revenues from fodder collection and grazing grew, the Forest Department found it profitable to allow the Gujjars—nomadic communities— to graze their large herds in its forests. The Gujjars paid a fee upfront for grazing rights for certain dates; additional fines were imposed if they stayed late. The Gujjars' migration from the plains to the hills was seasonal and could be regulated more effectively than the locals' use of grazing land for their small herds.[20]

By the first half of the twentieth century, there were dramatic changes in the working landscape, social relations, and distribution of economic activities both within and among communities in Garhwal. The full force of colonial forest policy was revealed in the dwindling incomes of many households that, due to lack of alternatives, were being restricted to subsistence cultivation for their livelihoods. Men began working as wage laborers for businesspeople—both local and from outside Garhwal—who purchased contracts for timber extraction from the Forest Department. Women and children, who in the past had largely controlled the extraction of minor forest produce, were now restricted to collecting fuelwood and fodder for household consumption and tending the agricultural plots. In addition to seeking work as wage laborers, men continued to provide labor corveés for maintaining reserved forests so they could retain the grazing rights and leases to small plots granted to them by the Forest Department (Berreman 1972; Rawat 1983, 100).

As I noted earlier, subsistence cultivation has rarely been adequate to meet household needs for communities in Garhwal. The income from extraction and sale of forest commodities, participation in the seasonal pilgrimage economy, and the thriving trans-Himalayan trade allowed a majority of households in the region to meet their consumption needs from subsistence agriculture as well as the market. Prosperity from these activities further allowed expansion of cultivation of cash crops such as tobacco, opium, potatoes, ginger, turmeric, and amaranth (Atkinson 1882; Walton 1910). But with numerous regulations on forest extraction, coupled with the waning importance of trans-Himalayan trade in the regional economy, very few households could find alternative avenues of income generation within their localities.

Conflicts over access to and extraction of forest products erupted regularly in different parts of Garhwal well into the time of India's independence from colonial rule. In 1915, forest laws were revised in response to local communities' vigorous protests of excessive restriction and regulation of forest extraction (U.P. Forest Department 1958).

In 1921, a Forest Grievance Committee was formed to demand deregulation of reserved forests and their subsequent conversion to civil forests. In 1922, a local political leader involved in the national independence movement published a booklet on problems relating to forests in the region (Pant 1922). Labor corveés for the Forest Department were challenged, and forest laws were amended when several nationalist leaders joined in protest with local communities and transformed them into noncooperation movements against the British Raj (Dogra 1983; Guha 1989; Rawat 1983). Households asserted their right to fire the forest floor annually for healthy growth of fodder grasses, and forest officials lamented the destruction and damage to regeneration, soil, and water conditions in the region. A large number of these conflicts were recorded as "crimes and offenses" in government documents and continued well into the 1960s (Berreman 1972; Saklani 1986).

Freedom from colonial rule brought very little change to forest management practices in Garhwal. If anything, colonial forest policies were implemented with greater zeal by the Indian state. The National Forest Policy adopted in 1952 clearly revealed its position by claiming that forests were "national resources" requiring protection and scientific management by the state and could not be left to the reckless exploitation by ignorant peasants living near the forest areas. State control over forests was also justified as being in the "national interest" of fostering social stability and economic progress (Ministry of Agriculture and Irrigation 1976).

Soon after India's war with China in 1962, the regions along the Chinese border became the object of national security concerns. The geopolitical strategies followed by the Indian government were strongly reminiscent of the policies adopted by the colonial administration after the Indian Mutiny. Trans-Himalayan trade came to an end, army bases were established, and road construction, hydroelectricity, and mining projects were vigorously pursued in the region. Large tracts of Forest Department lands were acquired and cleared for these projects, and access to reserved forests was further restricted for local communities. During the 1950s and 1960s, the region's economy underwent rapid transformation as young men belonging to particular castes and communities began enlisting in the army.[21] Others with formal education sought employment in the plains and cities. Women and children, now restricted to maintaining subsistence plots, remained behind in the villages, their work no longer regarded as important in contributing to household income. Some households made sharecropping arrangements on parts of their land with lower-caste peasants or migrant peasants from western Nepal, as the men left the village to seek work elsewhere.

The idea of a postcolonial state working toward national development, stability, and progress had considerable popular appeal in the

1950s and 1960s. This may have been the reason that there was no opposition against the numerous activities of the state in Garhwal. Yet toward the end of the 1960s and in the early 1970s, when local communities—faced with a series of natural disasters and dwindling economic opportunities—found little help coming from national or state-level administrations, the stirrings of discontent began. In addition, conflict seemed imminent when local forest contractors who had formed village-level labor cooperatives for forest extraction and cottage industries found themselves unable to compete with timber businesses from outside the region for Forest Department contracts. In 1973, when the Forest Department refused to grant the Dasholi Village Industry Association's request for three ash trees to make agricultural implements, the conflict erupted in the form of Chipko. The Chipko strategy was adopted by several villages in Garhwal and the neighboring hill region of Kumaon, serving as a vehicle for other issues within local communities. Although Chipko came to be known as an environmental movement, it was also involved in protests against the sale of alcohol in hill regions as well as the plight of women, who felt increasingly marginalized within their households and communities (Jain 1984; Shiva and Bandyopadhyay 1986a, 1987). Student activists demanded the creation of a state separate from the rest of Uttar Pradesh and were seen as joining the broader needs of the region with Chipko's environmental concerns (Guha 1986; Berreman 1989).

Chipko's subsequent fame as a popular environmental movement emerged through astute political lobbying by its emergent leaders, who made connections with nascent environmental groups based in larger cities of northern India. An erstwhile forest contractor in Garhwal rapidly gained recognition as the prominent leader of the movement when he demanded an end to all commercial extraction of timber, so as to save the Himalayan ecology from further destruction. Other local leaders found their demands for local industrial development and employment being submerged by the environmental rhetoric that demanded the preservation of the Himalayas in its own right.

Despite its representation as a popular environmental movement, Chipko did not have a universal base among village communities in Garhwal. The movement was concentrated around district centers and nearby villages in Tehri, Pauri, and Chamoli, where some of its charismatic leaders established their base, and in towns in both Garhwal and Kumaon, where college students were actively demanding the creation of a separate state.[22] Most other village communities within the region remained isolated from the movement, although they depended no less on extractive activities. Households living in the northwestern areas bordering Himachal Pradesh and in villages closer to the Tibetan border were, in many ways, economically worse off than people living near roads and towns.[23] The problems of lower-caste peasants

and Nepalese migrants in the region—eking out their marginal livelihoods as sharecroppers and wage laborers, with almost no rights to
forest access—were completely absent from the graphic portraits of
village communities painted by Chipko's leaders for the world outside Garhwal.

Regional Transformation in the Post-Chipko Years

The latter half of the 1970s was a good time for Chipko, when the
movement gained national and international recognition. As people
outside Garhwal came to hear its story, it was far too appealing and
romantic to be ignored. For students, activists, and intellectuals it represented a near-perfect model of grassroots environmental action—a
movement that had grown out of a remote little village in the periphery, spread across the Himalayan region, and was inspiring similar
movements in other parts of India. It was a tale—with apologies
to Shakespeare—full of sound and poetry, signifying some hope for
the environment.

How then do we reconcile this image with the resentment and
anger of many local communities in Garhwal toward the Chipko
movement? To follow our story through the wake of Chipko's success,
we must begin with a swift glance at the broader canons of India's
political economy around the early years of the movement.

A quick examination of popular myths held by the Indian intelli-
gentsia during the Chipko era reveals remarkable consonance with the
views propounded by traditional development theory. Aggregate
planning by the state was believed to be far superior than the market
in determining investment allocation and achieving economies of
coordination. The state itself was perceived as a benevolent institution
with no selfish interests, functioning as a prime mover in guiding the
country on the path of economic growth and progress. These popular
beliefs led to a blanket endorsement of indiscriminate state intervention and public-sector expansion during the late 1960s and early 1970s
in India (Bardhan 1991). Populist rhetoric backing such action held
that the state would play a more socially responsible and efficient
role—against the greed and narrow, self-serving vision of the private
sector—in managing the country's resources and increasing productivity in all the major economic sectors.[24]

Against the broad context of national policy and the general eupho-
ria surrounding state takeovers, the growing opposition against private
forest contractors in Garhwal was sufficient excuse to justify the
creation of the Uttar Pradesh (U.P.) Forest Corporation in 1975. The
corporation was to function independently from the Forest Department
as a public-sector firm, replacing the private contractors who had until

then been extracting timber from tracts auctioned annually by the state's Forest Department. The rationale behind this action was that illicit cutting of timber would cease if private contractors were banned from working the forests. Felling operations would be conducted with greater care and efficiency, and the state's revenues would profit substantially from monopoly of timber supply to wholesale and retail traders. Forests were henceforth to be worked either by the corporation or by a network of labor cooperatives. Between 1975 and 1980, the U.P. Forest Corporation expanded its operations in phases across the entire state, and by the beginning of the 1980s it had begun working the forests of Garhwal.

Looking back at one of the earliest recorded protests, popular resentment against private contractors and the Forest Department was primarily over the issue that although forest resources were being extracted and sold at great profit in the market, there was no spin-off, no local trickle-down effect, from this highly lucrative economic activity. The people also resented the fact that the Forest Department always seemed to favor private businesspeople over local cooperatives or cottage industries in awarding contracts. The advent of the U.P. Forest Corporation may have partially assuaged the fears, even raised the hopes, of most communities living near forest areas in Garhwal. Since one of the stated aims of the corporation was to work forests with the aid of labor cooperatives, there was hope that men from local communities could be organized into labor groups and be gainfully employed for six to eight months of the year.

There are no registered forest-labor cooperatives in existence today in Garhwal—they were doomed from their very birth. During the transitional period between the formation of the Forest Corporation and its actual functioning in the hill districts, private contractors continued to hire their own labor for felling operations. Given the antagonism between contractors and local communities, it was understandable that they would not recruit labor from the newly formed cooperatives. Cooperatives that were given tracts to work by the Forest Department often ran into difficulties, either because they lacked adequate felling and conversion skills or because political and social rivalries within local communities created deep divisions in their management. Thus, by the time the Forest Corporation began its operations in Garhwal, most labor cooperatives had either disbanded or were working in extremely limited areas.

The labor regime adopted by the corporation was identical to the practices established by its predecessors, the private contractors. Labor for felling is supplied by "mates"—agents who control a band of workmen and move from one demarcated tract to another until the end of the felling season. Almost all mates are migrants to the Garhwal region—a large proportion come from western districts of Nepal, and a smaller number come from the neighboring state of Himachal Pradesh. Mates invariably organize their labor gangs at their places of origin after having settled an entire season's contract with the corporation. Nepalese labor is to be found everywhere in Garhwal, ranging from hill towns and district headquarters to the most far-flung villages in the region. They bear the popular reputation of being skilled, hardworking, and reliable, and most agencies like the Forest Department or the Forest Corporation point to these reasons for preferring migrant Nepalese labor over local workers.[25] Thus despite the banishment of private contractors and creation of the State Forest Corporation, there was little improvement in the economic opportunities available to local communities in Garhwal.

With environmentalists espousing the cause of Chipko and garnering substantial attention from the media, forests had become fairly controversial entities by the mid-1970s. Attention centered primarily on problems of deforestation and rapid loss of forest cover across India. Ironically, this time blame was assigned not to avaricious forest contractors or corrupt forest officers, but to state-level administrations. Environmental activists were quick to point out that between 1950 and 1980, 4.3 million hectares of designated forestlands had been converted to nonforest purposes. Forestlands lay entirely under the control of state departments, which—in their eagerness to promote industrial growth and reap quick profits—had diverted large forest areas for developmental purposes. Such irresponsible acts of state governments, it was pointed out, could be checked only by the higher authority of the central government. In 1976, therefore, the Indian Constitution was amended to include forests among the list of subjects about which state governments had to confer with the central government before embarking on any development projects.

In the years that followed, there was a spate of forest-related legislation: In Uttar Pradesh, the Tree Protection Act of 1976 prevents individuals from felling marketable species of trees for timber (classified as protected species by the Forest Department) on their own lands without obtaining permission from Forest Department officials; in 1980, the Indian government passed the Forest Conservation Act, which makes it mandatory for state governments to seek prior permission to transfer even one acre of forestland for nonforest purposes (Agarwal and Narain 1991); again in 1980, a fifteen-year ban on all green felling was imposed on areas falling above the 1,000-meter altitude in the Himalayas. The latest amendment to the Forest Conservation Act in 1988 deems it illegal for any agency, other than the state government, to engage in afforestation projects without permission from the central government.

For a hill region like the Garhwal, the concerted impact of all these laws has had overwhelming consequences. With more than two-thirds of its lands designated as forests, almost every developmental activity has been affected. People of the area offer numerous examples of projects held up for years before receiving permission from the central government: nine years for sanctioning a stretch of road construction, one kilometer of which passes through a reserved forest; traditional irrigation channels that are unfinished because certain sections would have to pass through designated forestlands; electric transmission lines not installed because the Ministry of Environment opines that far too many trees would have to be destroyed for the purpose. The list goes on. Although the Ministry of Environment moves to its own defense by arguing that cases requiring less than nine hectares of land are processed fairly quickly, the fact remains that smaller appeals for forestland are rarely accompanied by the kind of political pressure that big projects carry and are therefore more likely to be shelved indefinitely. As Agarwal and Narain (1991) point out, projects like the Tehri and Narmada dams have powerful lobbies in the states. These lobbies push relentlessly until their projects are cleared by the central ministries.

It should come as no surprise that this excessive centralization has antagonized local communities in Garhwal. Demands for a separate state of Uttarakhand—comprising the eight hill districts of Uttar Pradesh—is seen as the only logical means of regaining some measure of local control over the region's development (*Himachal Times* 1990c). Once part of a social and environmental movement that called for the protection of trees and the ecology of the Himalayas, several communities in Garhwal may now be willing to start a movement that calls for chopping down the forests in the region. In fact, political groups such as the Uttarakhand Revolutionary Front (UKD) have gone on record, volunteering to clear forest areas required for any development project promoted by local communities.

Conclusion

Nearly twenty years ago, the Chipko strategy raised several issues that confronted local communities in Garhwal: the need to ensure the availability and continuity of resources that many households depended on for their livelihood; the need to enhance the quality of their environment; and the need to give voice, to cry out a version of their lives to a larger world that was either indifferent or threatened to undermine their attempts at self-definition. Their voices cried out partly for the semblance of prosperity they had already lost, but they also seemed to say, we "cry to affirm ourselves, to say, here I am, I matter too, you're going to have to reckon with me" (Rushdie 1991, 99).

Yet when the time came for the communities in Garhwal to be heard by the larger world, their voice in the Chipko movement had all but ceased to exist. The brief love affair between Chipko's activists and the state had resulted in the romantic ideal that the Himalayan environment by itself mattered more than the people who eked out their existence within it. If some of the communities in Garhwal are ready to brandish their axes today (Agarwal and Narain 1991), it must be seen as yet another attempt to affirm themselves and give voice to the difficulties of sustaining livelihoods within their localities.

The social, environmental, and economic processes occurring in Garhwal can be interpreted very differently when forestry and forest-based extractive activities are incorporated into the concept of the region. Any state policy or theoretical framework that claims to address the problems of deforestation and environmental degradation in the Himalayas by focusing purely on subsistence agriculture or the basic needs of peasant households—while ignoring the importance of forest-based activities—will be extremely limited in its approach and mostly detrimental to local communities. Neither the causal relationship expounded by government planners nor the environmentalists' repeated invocations of the hoary and harmonious village traditions of forest use has much relevance in altering the complex processes of marginalization occurring today in Garhwal.[26]

Ecological degradation in Garhwal has arisen from conflicts over increasing state control of forest territory, control of forest labor, extraction of forest products, and the appropriation and distribution of profits derived from forest-based economic activities. Equally important has been the battle over definitions. The forests of Garhwal continue to serve as political and economic battlefields for different actors—from the state to individuals within the households of local communities—where sylvan margins are challenged, contested, defined, and redefined. It would be naive to presume that these battles ended with the Chipko movement.

There are no simple solutions for the households and local communities of Garhwal. The demand for a separate state within the Indian Union has very little meaning if the Center does not reduce its pernicious control over how local resources are used. Threats to cut down trees will win very few environmental activists or intellectuals over to their side and will only reinforce the state's view that ignorant hill peasants are the root cause of ecological degradation in the Garhwal Himalayas.

Some positive change would occur if the state, as well as activists and intellectuals, could be persuaded to reexamine their own roles, their underlying ideologies and intentions that define the environmental policies currently enforced in the Himalayas (*Indian Express* 1990; *Himachal Times* 1990a, 1990b). This would be helpful in amending the later versions of forest laws that currently restrict almost any kind of profitable forest resource extraction by local communities in Garhwal.

It may also allow local and regional economies to develop resource-based activities beyond subsistence agriculture and revive the modest desires of communities to remain and prosper within their localities.

Notes

Major funding for field research was provided under the Junior Fellowship Program of the American Institute of Indian Studies. The author is grateful to Sylvie Chesneau, Jenna Dixon, John Friedmann, Michelle A. Melone, Falguni Sarkar, and Professor James Wescoat, Jr., for useful criticisms of and suggestions for earlier drafts. Responsibility for the final version rests solely with the author.

1. The document also refers to the suspension of commercial fellings in forests beyond the 1,000-meter altitude in the Himalayan districts of Uttar Pradesh in 1983, noting that this action was taken in response to the demands made by the leaders of the Chipko movement. It claims that suspension of timber felling by the government along with consciousness-raising efforts by Chipko "slowed down, if not totally stopped the process of deforestation in the Uttarakhand region and other hill areas of U.P."
2. See various articles by Shiva and Bandyopadhyay (1986b, 1987, 1989) and Berreman (1978, 1989), who set forth this argument.
3. The countryside is hardly ever a landscape for those who work the land (Williams 1973, 120–21).
4. Levels of backwardness are also determined according to existing physical, geographical, and infrastructural conditions, such as accessibility by road, availability of piped water supply and irrigation, land-person ratio, number of industries, and many other factors. Since most hill regions fare poorly according to these criteria, they are additionally characterized as being functionally backward.
5. The Malthusian stance also allows the Indian government on occasion to conveniently shift the blame across political borders, by stating that a small number of peasants in Nepal and the Indian Himalayas wreak havoc on the environmental and economic stability of the enormous populations living in the plains. See Ives and Messerli (1989) for a systematic critique of this politically expedient explanation.
6. Some researchers have questioned the very basis of the cause-effect relationships of deforestation asserted by each of these perspectives (Thompson and Warburton 1988, 1–53).
7. The emphasis on "basic needs" has also been challenged through studies of the changing utilization of forest resources among rural households in Garhwal. Richards argues that "[a]fter the early 1900s illicit cutting [of wood] has grown progressively, with a rapid increase after 1947, to the effect that by 1980, for many peasants, *subsistence*, rather than merely supplemental, income may be at stake in the forests" (Richards 1987, 299–304; emphasis added).
8. Even Ram Guha, who has written extensively on the history of social and ecological struggles in the Garhwal and Kumaon Himalayas from a political economy perspective, fails to question the basic-needs assumptions underlying the accounts of peasant struggles in the region.

9. According to the 1981 census of India, occupational categories in rural areas are the following: cultivators, agricultural laborers, household industry, and other workers. A cultivator is defined as one who has "engaged in cultivation as a single or family worker of land owned or held from the government, held from private persons or institutions for payment in money, kind or share. Cultivation includes supervision or direction of cultivation." The category "other workers" is said to comprise all workers who are not cultivators, agricultural laborers, or engaged in household industry. This category covers "factory and plantation workers, government employees, teachers, priests, entertainment artists, workers engaged in trade, commerce, business, transport, mining, construction, etc." (Director, U.P. Census Operations 1982, xxix).

10. This conceptual problem seems to persist in most state-initiated rural development programs and projects that concentrate mainly on increasing crop production and strengthening market ties by emphasizing technological change and reorganization of the production process in agriculture. See Hecht, Anderson, and May (1988) for a critique.

11. In the early years of colonial administration in Garhwal, a British settlement officer remarked, "Tibetan trade offered employment to thousands in the most sterile parts of the Garhwal and provided a market for produce in the same region, thus encouraging agriculture." The principal imports from Tibet were gold, borax, salt, and wool; Garhwal exported woollen cloth, grain, herbs and spices, butter, and beet sugar. The colonial government received revenue from trade in both forest-based produce and agriculture, just as previous rulers of Garhwal had done, but it attempted to maintain a lenient relationship with local and trans-Himalayan traders in the hope that British merchants and manufacturers might one day gain entry through them into Tibet (Turner 1800; Moorcraft and Trebeck 1841; Landon 1906; Rawat 1983).

12. Rennel (1788), Turner (1800), Moorcraft and Trebeck (1841), Webber (1902), and Landon (1906) provide graphic descriptions of the difficulties of entering the closely guarded and impenetrable boundaries of Tibet; the vast estimates of mineral reserves such as gold, tin, and borax; and the wasteful forms of extraction employed by natives. Appointed in 1864 by the colonial government to survey the forest wealth of the North-West Provinces, Thomas Webber used this opportunity to adventure unofficially into Tibet to satisfy his curiosity and gauge the wealth of this forbidden land.

13. Stokes (1959) provides a more extensive discussion on the ideology of land reform and British expectations from permanent settlement of property in colonial India.

14. Teak forests in southern India and Burma were managed primarily to meet the needs of the Imperial Navy. Native species of timber used for railway ties were sal (*shorea robusta*), chir (*pinus roxburghii*), and deodar (*cedrus deodara*). Sal, deodar, and chir were found in abundance in the Garhwal, Kumaon, and the northern provinces of British Punjab. In addition, forests under the control of native princes were leased for extraction of valuable species of timber (Ribbentrop 1900; Stebbing 1922; Smythies 1925; Troup 1976).

15. The rationale for bringing extensive tracts of forests under state control was eloquently argued by Ribbentrop, who stated, "our Indian forests were thus exposed at the same time to the legitimate demands of a rapidly spreading modern civilization and the waste which accompanies

a more primitive state of society" (1900, 61–62). His entire line of reasoning is mirrored by the Malthusian arguments advanced by contemporary government officials in India.

16. This is also reflected in the numerous revisions of the Forest Acts made in 1878, 1911, 1927, and 1940. The 1927 Act reclassified the forests in such a way that one category of forests was controlled by the Revenue Department and the other was worked and controlled by the Forest Department to meet the construction requirements of public works, railways, and industrial production (Ribbentrop 1900; Stebbing 1922; Rawat 1983).

17. Peluso (1988) observes that the colonial administration in the Dutch East Indies was faced with a similar dilemma.

18. In contrast to mining, which organizes its activities around the extraction of a nonrenewable resource, forestry requires its activities to be organized around a renewable resource. When contrasted with industry and even agriculture, the production time for commercially valuable species within forests can be extraordinarily long, and substantial amounts of time must be spent before profits can be realized (Mann and Dickinson 1978). Attempts to improve the efficiency of forest resource production through monocultural plantations offer a different set of problems and constraints (see Troup 1976; Hecht and Cockburn 1989). Yet forests can be worked profitably through an array of social relations around extraction such as contract farming, corveé labor, tenancy, and sharecropping (Mooney 1983).

19. That local households were fully aware of this illusion was evident in the laments of forest officers who claimed that village communities, not without reason, kept their village forests poorly maintained lest the Forest Department move in to appropriate the well-preserved and improved resources. See the communications between the Superintendent of Forests, Dehra Dun, and the District Commissioner of Meerut Division, 1897, quoted in Guha (1983).

20. This practice continues to the present day and is intensely disliked by local communities (Dogra 1983), who regard migrant herders as opportunists who not only benefit from the prime grazing areas within the forests but also allow their cattle to stray into village lands and ruin the standing crops.

21. This tradition was established a few years after the Mutiny when Garhwali and Gorkha recruits to the British army were promised a share of the Kumaon treasury for their loyalty. The identification of "martial races" by the colonial government was a policy followed after the Mutiny to ensure the loyalty of particular groups that were recruited to serve its armies (Stokes 1959). In 1879, the Garhwal Regiment was formed and annually recruited a number of men from the region (Rawat 1983). Service in the army is seen not only as a stable source of income but also as matter of great pride and status among households.

22. Interviews with elected block representatives, Gopeshwar, 1991.

23. Interviews with village elders, Konain, Pargana Jaunsar-Bawar, 1991.

24. Each act of nationalization or state takeover, if one looks beyond controls and regulations, has largely been used to expand the job prospects and security of professionals and white-collar workers (Bardhan 1984, 58).

25. More to the point, of course, is that migrant laborers from Nepal are willing to work for lower wages and can be controlled more efficiently by

"mates." Most social science research on Garhwal focuses primarily on outmigration from the hills to the plains, but I have yet to come across any study that focuses on migration into hill regions (excluding studies of transhumance communities). Migrant laborers from western Nepal, for instance, form a very visible part of the social and economic landscape in Garhwal. They often stay on for a year or two before returning to their villages; mates often make annual trips lasting three to four months to recruit men from their homelands. Nepalese form a rather amorphous and ambiguous community, and they are not all necessarily migrants to the region. Some households have lived in Garhwal for decades, although they continue to be perceived as outsiders. In most of the areas I visited, Nepali households rarely own land. They often lease or depend on sharecropping arrangements with land-owning households.

26. The excessive emphasis on "deep ecology" and environmental preservation by some Chipko activists is remarkably similar to the ideologies of conservation advanced by colonial and postcolonial administrators, even though their arguments are stated differently.

References

Agarwal, Anil, and Sunita Narain. 1991. "Chipko People Driven to *Jungle Kato* [Cut the Forests] Stir." *Economic Times*, 31 March.

Amar Ujala. 1991. "Bahuguna's Statements Criticized." February 8.

Atkinson, Edwin T. 1882. *The Himalayan Gazetteer*. Vol. III, Part I. Reprinted 1981. New Delhi: Cosmo.

Bardhan, Pranab. 1984. *Political Economy of Indian Development*. New Delhi: Oxford University Press.

———. 1991. "State and Dynamic Comparative Advantages." *Economic Times*, 19–20 March, New Delhi.

Berreman, Gerald. 1972. *Hindus of the Himalayas: Ethnography and Change*. Berkeley and Los Angeles: University of California Press.

———. 1978. "*Himachal: Science, People and "Progress*." Copenhagen: IWGIA.

———. 1989. "Chipko: A Movement to Save the Himalayan Environment and People." In *Contemporary Indian Tradition: Voices on Culture, Nature, and the Challenge of Change*, edited by C. M. Borden, Washington, D.C.: Smithsonian.

Bharati, A. 1978. "Actual and Ideal Himalayas: Hindu Views of the Mountains." In *Himalayan Anthropology: The Indo-Tibetan Interface*, edited by J. F. Fischer, The Hague: Mouton.

Bora, R. S. 1987. "Extent and Causes of Migration from the Hill Regions of Uttar Pradesh." In *Migrant Labour and Related Issues*, edited by Vidyut Joshi, New Delhi: Oxford IBH.

Director, U.P. Census Operations. 1982. *District Census Handbook, District Tehri Garhwal: Series-22, Uttar Pradesh, Village and Town Directory Part XIII-A*.

Dobhal, G. L. 1987. *Development of the Hill Areas: A Case Study of Pauri Garhwal District*. New Delhi: Concept.

Dogra, Bharat. 1983. *Forests and People: A Report on the Himalayas*. Unpublished.

Guha, Ramachandra. 1983. "Forestry in British and Post-British India: A Historical Analysis." *Economic and Political Weekly* 18(45): 1882–1896 and 18(46): 1940–1947.

———. 1985. "Forestry and Social Protest in British Kumaun, c. 1893–1921." In *Subaltern Studies, Volume 4*, edited by Ranajit Guha, New Delhi: Oxford University Press.

———. 1986. "Commercial Forestry and Social Conflict in the Indian Himalaya." *Forestry for Development Lecture Series.* University of California, Berkeley: Department of Forestry.

———. 1989. *The Unquiet Woods: Ecological Change and Peasant Resistance in the Himalaya.* New Delhi: Oxford University Press.

Guha, Ramachandra, and Madhav Gadgil. 1989. "State Forestry and Social Conflict in British India." *Past and Present* 123 (May): 141–177.

Hecht, Susanna B., Anthony B. Anderson, and Peter May. 1988. "The Subsidy from Nature: Shifting Cultivation, Successional Palm Forests, and Rural Development." *Human Organization* 47(1): 25–35.

Hecht, Susanna, and Alexander Cockburn. 1989. *Fate of the Forest: Developers, Destroyers and Defenders of the Amazon.* London: Verso.

Himachal Times. 1990a. "Amendment of Forest Act for Developing Hill Areas." 2 April, Dehra Dun.

———. 1990b. "Consolidation of Hill Land Holdings Soon." 1 June, Dehra Dun.

———. 1990c. "Uttaranchal Demanded: Economic and Political Passions Aroused." 11 April, Dehra Dun.

Indian Express. 1990. "U.P. to Amend Tree Protection Act." 28 March, New Delhi.

Ives, J. D., and Bruno Messerli. 1989. *The Himalayan Dilemma: Reconciling Development and Conservation.* London: Routledge.

Jain, S. 1984. "Women and People's Ecological Movement: A Case Study of Women's Role in the Chipko Movement in Uttar Pradesh." *Economic and Political Weekly* 19(41): 1788–94.

Khan, Waheeduddin, and R. N. Tripathy. 1976. *Plan for Integrated Rural Development in Pauri Garhwal.* Hyderabad: National Institute of Community Development.

Landon, Percival. 1906. *The Opening of Tibet.* New York: Doubleday.

Lok Sabha Secretariat. 1985. *National Forest Policy.* New Delhi: Government of India.

Mann, Susan A., and J. M. Dickinson. 1978. "Obstacles to the Development of Capitalist Agriculture." *Journal of Peasant Studies* 5(2): 466–81.

Ministry of Agriculture and Irrigation. 1976. *Report of the National Commission on Agriculture (Part IX—Forestry).* New Delhi: Government of India.

Mooney, Patrick. 1983. "Towards a Class Analysis of Midwestern Agriculture." *Rural Sociology* 48(4): 563–84.

Moorcroft, William, and George Trebeck. 1841. *Travels in the Himalayan Provinces of Hindustan and the Panjab from 1819 to 1825.* Vol. I. London: John Murray.

Pant, Gobind Ballabh. 1922. *The Forest Problem in Kumaon.* Allahabad: Government Press.

Peluso, Nancy Lee. 1988. "Rich Forests, Poor People, and Development: Forest Access Control and Resistence in Java." Ph.D. dissertation, Cornell University.

Rawat, Ajay S. 1983. *Garhwal Himalayas: A Historical Survey: The Political and Administrative History of Garhwal 1815–1947.* Delhi: Eastern Book Linkers.

Rennell, Sir James. 1788. *Memoirs of the Map of Hindoostan.* London: Royal Society.

Ribbentrop, Berthold. 1900. *Forestry in British India.* Calcutta: Government Press.

Richards, J. F. 1987. "Environmental Changes in Dehra Dun Valley, India: 1880–1980." *Mountain Research and Development* 7(3): 299–304.

Rushdie, Salman. 1991. "Outside the Whale." *Imaginary Homelands: Essays and Criticism 1981–1991.* London: Granta Books.

Saklani, Atul. 1987. *The History of a Himalayan Princely State: Change, Conflicts and Awakening: An Interpretive History of the Princely State of Tehri Garhwal 1811–1949.* New Delhi: Durga Publications.

Shiva, Vandana, and J. Bandyopadhyay. 1986a. *Chipko: India's Civilisational Response to the Forest Crisis.* New Delhi: Intach.

———. 1986b. "Environmental Conflicts and Public Interest Science." *Economic and Political Weekly* 21(2): 84–90.

———. 1987. "Chipko: Rekindling India's Forest Culture." *The Ecologist* 17(1): 26–34.

———. 1989. "The Political Economy of Ecology Movements." *IFDA Dossier*, no. 71. (May–June): 37–60.

Smythies, E. A. 1925. *India's Forest Wealth.* London: Oxford University Press.

Somanathan, E. 1991. "Deforestation, Property Rights and Incentives in Central Himalaya." *Economic and Political Weekly* 26(4): 37–46.

Stebbing, E. P. 1922. *The Forests of India.* Vols. I and II. London: Bodley Head.

Stokes, Eric. 1959. *English Utilitarians and India.* Cambridge: Cambridge University Press.

Thompson, M, and M. Warburton. 1988. "Uncertainty on a Himalayan Scale." In *Deforestation: Social Dynamics in Watersheds and Mountain Ecosystems*, edited by J. D. Ives and D. C. Pitt. London: Routledge.

Troup. R. S. 1976. *Silviculture of Indian Trees.* Vols. I, II, and III (1915–1919). Dehra Dun: Forest Research Institute.

Tucker, Richard. 1988. "The Depletion of India's Forests under British Imperialism: Planters, Foresters, and Peasants in Assam and Kerala." In *The Ends of the Earth: Perspectives on Modern Environmental History*, edited by Donald Worster. Cambridge: Cambridge University Press.

Turner, Capt. S. 1800. *An Account of an Embassy to the Court of Teshoo Lama in Tibet.* London: Blumer and Row.

U.P. Forest Department. 1958. *Annual Progress Report of Forest Administration in Uttar Pradesh 1954–55.* Allahabad.

———. 1983. *Forest Statistics of Uttar Pradesh.* Lucknow.

Walton, H. G. 1910. *British Garhwal: A Gazetteer, being Volume XXXVI of the District Gazetteers of the United Provinces of Agra and Oudh.* Reprinted 1989. Dehra Dun: Natraj.

Webber, Thomas. 1902. *Forests of Upper India and Their Inhabitants.* London: Edward Arnold.

Weber, Thomas. 1988. *Hugging the Trees: The Story of the Chipko Movement.* New Delhi: Viking (Penguin India).

Williams, Raymond. 1973. *The Country and the City.* London: Oxford University Press.

SEVEN

PEOPLE VERSUS THE STATE?

Social Forestry in Kolar, India

SHIVSHARAN SOMESHWAR

IN THIS CHAPTER, I examine the debate concerning a govern-
ment-initiated social forestry program in Kolar district, Karnataka
State, India. The purpose is to explore the limits of state action and
village-level participation in programs for biomass production
and distribution in rural areas of the Third World.

The farm forestry component of the social forestry program in
Kolar has been a tremendous success, but the community forestry
projects have not fared as well. As a result, although quantities of
biomass are available in the market, mainly for urban and industrial users, biomass availability has not markedly improved for the
poorer sections of the rural population.[1] The state forest department attributes the failure to nonparticipation of villagers, mainly
due to the inability of the "community" to come together. Sensi-
tized by outside criticism, community forestry programs now
involve local villagers—but mainly in the program implementation
phase. Critics of the program maintain that the failure of community forestry can be attributed to the lack of villager participation
in *all* the phases. They plead for complete decentralization of projects to the village level, outside the purview of the state, and argue
that current forestry practice must be replaced with strategies of
local community management of biomass resources, detached from
the forest department.

Based on research in Kolar, India, in 1989, I find that both the official views and their critics have some merit. However, the solutions
presented on either side are unlikely to alleviate the biomass shortage
of the rural poor. The difficulty lies in the way that community
forestry has been focused on issues of empowering poorer sections of
the rural population and the role of the state in facilitating such

empowerment. Involving villagers is crucial to the community forestry programs, and decentralization is necessary to some degree, but I argue that such actions will not yield the desired results. Given the skewed distribution of social, economic, and political power among rural households, complete decentralization of forest management to the village level would probably work against the interests of the poorer sections of the population. Participation of villagers has to be achieved by building social institutions that will mediate power relations between the largely powerless poorer sections of the population and the dominant forces at the local level. Further, such mediating institutions have to be based on existing social networks within the subaltern sections of the population.

Kolar: Land, Biomass, and People

Kolar district is located in the southern *maidan* (plains) region of Karnataka state and is its easternmost district (Figure 7.1). It is bounded by the districts of Bangalore and Tumkur on the west and on all the other sides by the districts of the adjoining states of Andhra Pradesh and Tamil Nadu. Kolar is one of the most densely populated districts in the state. With a density of 232 persons per square kilometer, the total per capita availability of land in 1981 was 0.43 hectares. If only the cultivated area is taken into account, the per capita availability of land is only 0.17 hectares. According to the 1981 census, the extent of land under agriculture is just over 55 percent, with less than 20 percent being irrigated. Forests account for less than 14 percent of the total land use. Dry farming is the predominant agricultural mode. The rivers of the district are small and seasonal. The district has thousands of ancient irrigation tanks, many of which are now silted. The average annual rainfall of the district is 730 millimeters. However, according to the District Handbook, the rainfall is often meager and erratic, rendering agriculture a gamble.[2]

The amount of forest area in the district is low compared to the national standard (under 14 percent versus 23 percent). The actual forest area may be even lower, as the figure refers to the land area officially designated as forest, not necessarily to the actual condition of the vegetation. Most of the forest areas, revenue lands, and village commons are confined to hilly tracts; the intervening plains have been ploughed. In these tracts, the soil is rocky, gravelly, or very shallow and is not very productive. Low rainfall combined with high biomass demand—for livestock and fuel—has seriously degraded these areas. The vegetation is mostly of the thorny scrub type, typical of the *maidan* tracts of the state.

Figure 7.1 Kolar District, Karnataka State, Southern India

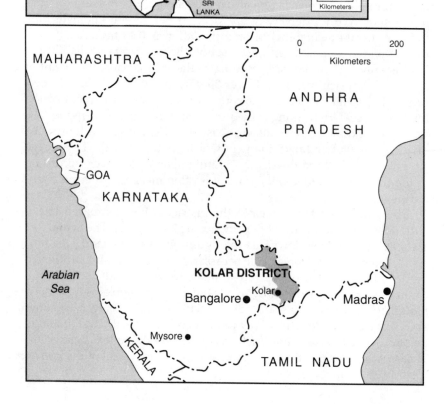

With agriculture forming its economic backbone, the district has been described as "somewhat backward" in industry (*District Census Handbook* 1984). The proportion of main workers[3] to the total population is about 36 percent, lower than the state average. Over 50 percent of the main workers are classified as cultivators, much higher than the state average of 38 percent. Agricultural laborers account for slightly over 23 percent of the main workers, with the rest being engaged in household industry and other work.

As in other parts of Karnataka, Kolar's rural population is highly stratified (Table 7.1). At the top of the rural hierarchy is the landlord class that operates large farms. Cultivation on these farms is carried out by a combination of wage labor and smallholder tenants. Most of the private investment in rural areas comes from the landlord class, which also forms a major source of loans—without collateral—taken by cultivators and landless laborers. Next are the categories of large, medium, and small farmers who not only cultivate their own land but also lease land from the landlord class. Small farmers tend to cultivate land wholly with their own labor and, on occasion, hire themselves and their family members out as wage labor to landlords or large and medium farmers. At the very bottom of the socioeconomic hierarchy are the landless households that are entirely dependent on wage labor.

Table 7.1 Size Distribution of Operational Holdings in Rural Kolar

Social Class (Size of Holdings)	Households (%)	Percentage of Land Held
Marginal and small peasants (< 2 ha)	73.5	37.0
Medium farmers (2–4 ha)	16.9	25.6
Large farmers (4–10 ha)	8.2	25.5
Landlords	1.4	11.9

Source: Derived from *District Census Handbook: Kolar District* (Bangalore: Karnataka Government Press, 1984).

There is an overlap between socioeconomic class and caste in rural Kolar. The strata of landlord and large and medium farmer usually belong to the four or five socially dominant castes. Within these castes, further stratification follows lineages. Following Bhagwan and Giriappa (1986) and comparing landholding assets and income levels, four broad rural social classes can be differentiated: (1) an upper class consisting of the landlords; (2) a middle class of large and medium farmers and small entrepreneurs; (3) a small peasantry consisting of small peasants and artisans; and (4) wage labor made up of marginal peasants, landless laborers, and bonded servants.

Ragi (*Cynosurus corocanus*) is the major food crop in dry farming. Sugar cane and paddy are other major crops. Manufacture of jaggery (unprocessed sugar) from sugar cane is an important cottage industry. In recent years, mulberry has been cultivated for rearing silkworms, a cottage industry that provides employment to a large number of people. Vegetables have been exported out of the state since historical times (Rice 1897). A recent phenomenon is the growth in tomato cultivation (with borewell irrigation) for urban markets outside the district. The productivity of dry farming, the major agricultural activity, is low. For example, the yield rate of ragi in 1980–81 was 820 kilograms per hectare and would fetch less than $150 (rupees 1,230).[4]

The term *biomass*, as it is used here, includes only fuelwood, lops and tops (branches and twigs used as firewood), timber poles, and fodder. A rural household in Kolar can obtain biomass in three ways:

1. Production on private property for self-consumption.
2. Purchase for cash or in kind. The former generally applies to fuelwood and fodder in the rural market. The latter involves an exchange for labor, either field or domestic, and generally applies to lops and tops as well as fodder from private lands.
3. Collection from village commons, revenue lands, and the state forests.

The relative combinations and proportions of these three methods of satisfying a household's energy demands depend on the amount of labor (time) and cash income required, the terms and conditions of tenancy, and the magnitude of labor committed in place of cash to work off debt. As can be seen in Table 7.2, there are large differences in levels of biomass consumption in the rural areas.[5] Households in the wage labor category generally consume only one-third the amount used by the average middle farmer households, and half that of the small peasant households. The two upper classes purchase roughly half of all the fuel they consume and gather the rest; the wage labor class (marginal peasant, landless labor, and bonded servants) gathers all the fuel required for consumption.

The nonfirewood component of fuel demand—dry and green twigs and branches from bushes and trees, dry leaves, mill wastes, and field harvest residues—of all four classes is gathered outside of any organized market. These better-off classes largely produce most of the nonfirewood biomass on their own lands and may depend on the market to meet 10 to 20 percent of their needs. For the wage labor

Table 7.2 Annual per Capita Consumption of Traditional Fuel

Class (1)	Firewood (2)			Nonfirewood Biomass (3)			(2) as % of Total Consumption (4)	Cattle Dung (5)		
	Kg	% Purchased	% Self-Produced	Kg	% Purchased	% Self-Produced		Kg	% Purchased	% Self-Produced
Middle class (includes landlords)	530	60	40	350	20	80	60	0	—	—
Small peasantry	305	50	50	240	15	85	52	45	0	100
Wage labor	135	7	93	310	0	100	28	40	0	100

Source: Derived from M. R. Bhagwan and S. Giriappa, "Class Character of Rural Energy Crisis: The Case of Karnataka," *Economic and Political Weekly* 21(30): 1317–21 (1986).

class, however, the amount of nonfirewood fuel used is almost 2.5 times larger than its firewood consumption. Wage laborers usually gather all the nonfirewood biomass they need for consumption and also sell some to other classes in rural areas. Wage laborers are entirely dependent on village commons, revenue lands, and state forests for their supply. In Kolar, fuels such as kerosene and electricity constitute only a small portion of total fuel consumption for all the classes and are not considered here.

There is also a wide range in the fodder requirements for different classes. The rural middle class owns between seven and eight heads of cattle per household, which is four times that owned by small peasants or wage laborers. Exceptions to this occur in communities that traditionally practice livestock rearing. Such families in Kolar may own several hundred heads of livestock, mainly goats. Small peasants and wage laborers rely exclusively on village grazing lands (*gomals*), revenue lands, and state forests for fodder. Stall feeding is rare, and livestock is usually driven out to pasture.

Since public lands are the major source of biomass in Kolar, there is intense pressure for fuel and fodder from rising human and livestock populations. Yet the total extent of such lands is shrinking because of increased conversion to agriculture and urban uses. In addition, demand for fuel in the urban areas has led to large-scale extraction from rural public lands, resulting in serious ecological degradation of this semiarid landscape. Shortages of fuelwood, fodder, construction timber, and pulpwood for industries, along with increasing pressures on the remaining tree cover, have led to a number of state-sponsored afforestation programs. The most important of these is the social forestry program promoted by the Karnataka State Forest Department.

The Karnataka Social Forestry Program

In Karnataka and elsewhere in India, the existing classification of forests is the legacy of the Indian Forest Act of 1865. Forests are broadly classified as (1) reserved forests or state forests, (2) community privilege areas, and (3) pasturelands (*gomals*).

Reserved forest areas were specifically set aside for meeting ecological needs, national infrastructure (for example, railways) and defense needs, and firewood requirements of urban areas. The areas excluded from reservation—wastelands, district forests, civil forests—had to satisfy rural needs for firewood, small timber, fencing material, fodder, and mulch. In reserve forests, specific acts allowed for rights of way, waterways, and right to water use. Certain privileges, such as collection of dead fuel and fallen leaves and grazing rights, were also conceded under specific orders. Community privilege areas such as civil and district forests, minor forests, and *paramboks* (forests along watercourses) were specifically set aside for use by rural populations, chiefly to meet local needs for small timber, bamboo, thorns, firewood, and fodder. Yet their classification remained ambiguous in that they were also viewed as lands potentially useful for agriculture. In contrast, the pasturelands were specifically meant for cattle grazing and could not be converted to agriculture.

Since the middle of the nineteenth century—when forest management and land use policy began—to the present, the population has multiplied threefold, and the number of cattle has increased two and a half times. Between 1947 (the year of India's independence from British rule) and 1970, the national government's prime concern was meeting the food requirements of its population and fostering rapid industrial growth. During this period, therefore, large tracts of civil forests, community privilege areas, and *gomals* were released to promote agriculture and other developmental activities. Between 1951 and 1976, agricultural land increased by 43 million hectares, most of it at the expense of nonreserve forests that were supplying rural people with firewood, fodder, and small timber (Shyam Sunder and Parameshwarappa 1987).

With the emphasis on rapid industrialization, a number of forest-based industries producing paper and plywood were established in the 1960s and 1970s. The combined needs of urban and rural populations and industries outstripped the capacity of reserved forest areas set aside for this purpose. In Karnataka state alone, annual firewood consumption ranges between 8 and 11 million tons, with a deficit estimated at 4 million tons (Shyam Sunder and Parameshwarappa 1987). In rural areas the deficit is met by wresting biomass from adjacent forests, irrespective of their classification.

Concerned with the serious shortage of firewood and fodder, the government of India undertook a number of rural afforestation projects under a "social forestry" program,[6] through its National Rural Employment Program and the Drought Prone Area Program. The primary objective of the Social Forestry Project was to increase supplies of fuelwood to rural and semiurban areas through the establishment of 150,000 hectares of plantations located throughout the state (Gaonkar 1989). The secondary objective was to provide small timber, fodder for livestock, fruit, bamboo, and other minor products. Between 1979–80 and 1982–83, social forestry programs of the Karnataka State Forest Department afforested 18,000 hectares of public land—primarily revenue lands—and distributed 211 million seedlings to farmers (World Bank 1983). External funding was solicited to further strengthen the programs, first from the World Bank/International Bank for Reconstruction and Development (the hard-loan section; IBRD) and then in

1982 from World Bank/International Development Association (the concessional-loan section; IDA) and Overseas Development Administration (ODA 1988). As a result, the Karnataka Social Forestry Project was able to continue for another five years, from 1983–84 to 1988–89 (Arnold et al. 1989).[7] The two major components of the afforestation program were:

1. *Community forestry*, in which timber and fodder species were to be planted on government-owned pasturelands and agriculturally unproductive (C and D class) public wastelands, banks and edges of irrigation tanks, along roadsides, canal banks, and in village commons.
2. *Farm forestry*, in which tree planting was promoted on private farms through the development of nurseries, distribution of seedlings, and provision of advisory services.

The program envisaged that community forestry plantations would be maintained by the Forest Department for the first two years, after which the responsibility would rest with *mandal panchayats* (bodies composed of both elected representatives from a group of villages in a district and district-level bureaucrats from the agriculture, irrigation, and banking sectors).

During these five years, the physical achievements of the program—in terms of hectares planted and number of beneficiaries reached—was impressive. For example, between 1983–84 and 1988–89, 386 million seedlings were raised in Karnataka state, and "an impressive amount of new tree planting has been accomplished over the first five years—28,516 hectares of block plantations [by the Forest Department], and the equivalent of probably about 90,000 hectares of planting under farm forestry [by farmers on private lands]" (Arnold et al. 1989). Simultaneously, however, the social forestry program has been increasingly criticized on a number of fronts: the failure of community forestry, the success of farm forestry at the expense of poor households, and the ecological deterioration caused by inappropriate species "foisted" onto farmers. In the following section, I review these criticisms and evaluate the social forestry program with specific reference to its impact on the rural poor residing in the Malur *taluk* (sub-district) of Kolar district, Karnataka.[8]

The Effects of Social Forestry Programs in Kolar

As explained in the previous section, farm forestry production is primarily for sale, and biomass from the community forestry component is intended for consumption by the villagers. With nearly 90,000 hectares being planted through the farm forestry component, its physical achievement has far outstripped the community forestry component, which has afforested only about 28,000 hectares. Thus, contrary to its prime objective of alleviating rural biomass shortage, the Karnataka social forestry program has resulted primarily in timber production for the market.

Market Production Bias

Since the initiation of the program, Malur *taluk* in Kolar district has experienced huge increases in the trade of timber produce from private farms. Between 1977 and 1987, annual exports of firewood and pulpwood to markets outside the district rose from 1,758 tons to 4,902 tons, and the export of poles rose from almost none to 946,312 in number. These figures refer only to the timber products exported and do not take into account the production and supply kept within the district itself. The records also do not include produce utilized by households or any transactions outside the market system. The success of the farm forestry component has also resulted in several tile and brick kilns being set up in Malur *taluk*, entirely independent of subsidies from the Forest Department. Over thirty of the forty-three kilns functioning in 1989 were set up after 1970. An estimated 23,000 tons of firewood per year is used by these kilns and is supplied exclusively by the farm forestry component of the program (Venugopal 1989).

It is more difficult to assess the performance of the community forestry program in terms of its impact on biomass consumption of the rural poor because they collect and utilize biomass from reserved forests, village commons, revenue lands, and private lands. Extraction and consumption of biomass from these lands are unrecorded and are outside the purview of any regulatory mechanism.

Land Conversion to Tree Farming

Relation to Agricultural Land Use. A number of researchers have suggested that strong market signals from industrial and urban sectors have promoted tree farming on lands previously used to grow subsistence crops (Shiva, Sharatchandra, and Bandyopadhyay 1981). A study published in 1987 states that:

> The districts of Kolar (and Bangalore) have been traditionally the largest ragi-growing areas in the state. Pulses and oilseeds together with ragi are inter-cropped on the same fields. By the end of 1982–83 itself, 63.3 percent of agricultural lands originally cultivating these food crops have been covered under eucalyptus. . . . What the World

Bank and Overseas Development Authority have done is to support a program of conversion of farmers' lands into massive tree-farming. The fact must be recognized that lands that had been traditionally under food cultivation are no longer available for such purposes, as a direct consequence of "farm forestry." (Chandrashekar, Krishnamurthy, and Ramaswamy 1987, p. 937)

Under the auspices of the farm forestry component, tree planting was undertaken with great vigor on private farm lands in Malur *taluk*. This led to a sharp increase in the land under private tree plantations: from 1,660 hectares in 1975–76 to 21,070 hectares in 1985–86, the latest records available—an increase of over 1,200 percent (Table 7.3).

Table 7.3 Land Used for Agriculture and Tree Farming in Malur *Taluk*

Year (1)	Land under Agriculture (ha) (2)	Change in (2) (ha) (3)	Land under Trees (ha) (4)	Change in (4) (ha) (5)	Total Land (ha) (2+4) (6)
1975–76	35,766	—	1,660	—	37,426
1976–77	30,390	-5,376	1,930	+270	32,320
1979–80	32,632	+2,242	1,930	0	34,562
1983–84	27,850	-4,782	8,587	+6,657	36,437
1984–85	22,265	-5,585	16,437	+7,850	38,702
1985–86	23,048	+783	21,070	+4,633	44,118
Total change		-12,718		+19,410	

Source: Derived from S. Venugopal, *Forest Plantations: A Boon to the Rural Economy* (Bangalore: Government of Karnataka, 1989).

A large proportion of land previously under cultivation has been converted to tree farming, with the rest remaining fallow. It is difficult, however, to establish from these figures alone that the farm forestry program is the principal cause for the steady decline of land under agriculture. For example, between 1975–76 and 1976–77, land under tree farming increased by 270 hectares, and land under agriculture fell by 5,376 hectares. Only ten years later, in 1984–85, the total extent of land under agriculture and tree farming exceeded the area existing in 1975–76. It is pertinent to note that urban demand for biomass has played a major role in enticing farmers to grow trees on croplands. In Malur *taluk*, lands converted to tree cropping had an average annual yield of 0.45 tons per hectare, compared with 0.56 tons per hectare on unconverted lands.

Relation to Availability of "Free" Biomass. Conversion of private lands to tree farming can have negative effects on poor households that depend on such lands to meet part of their biomass requirements. Two types of land conversions take place: Lower-quality agricultural land formerly under food crops is converted to tree farming, and private lands that were formerly unused are converted to plantation forestry. As I noted earlier, the landless and marginal sections of the rural population in Kolar depend on community privilege areas, state lands, and private lands for their biomass requirements. They obtain agricultural residues following the harvests from private lands as well as a variety of biomass, including grass, leaves, and twigs, from fallow plots. Thus private farmlands are an important biomass resource base for the rural poor. When these lands are converted to tree farming, they cease to "produce" free biomass, and community privilege areas are subjected to increased extraction.

Predominance of Eucalyptus Species in Social Forestry

The controversy over eucalyptus plantations has three interrelated arguments within the larger debate on social forestry. First, rural people find eucalyptus less useful than other native species for their biomass needs; second, the Forest Department has encouraged eucalyptus at the cost of native fast-growing species; and third, large-scale planting of eucalyptus has led to ecological devastation in rural Kolar, resulting in lower aquifer levels and a general loss of soil fertility.

The first contention is valid for Malur *taluk* in the Kolar district. Rural people tend to find eucalyptus of less use when compared with local species such as mango and jackfruit. Eucalyptus species—including its 450 subspecies—are not browsed by livestock. Relative to other local species, eucalyptus burns at a much faster rate and at higher temperatures, thus requiring larger amounts of fuelwood collection for traditional cooking. Due to the acute biomass shortage, poorer rural households use larger quantities of eucalyptus biomass to prepare their meals.

Critics of social forestry programs contend that eucalyptus species have been chosen primarily for their use in the rayon and paper industry (Samaja Parivartana Samudaya 1988). Citing a study carried out by the Karnataka Bureau of Economics and Statistics, they note that 97 percent of all eucalyptus species grown in Kolar is sold to industries. Species with much faster growth rates and of greater use to local populations have been ignored (Bandyopadhyay and Shiva 1985).

In another study, Guha accuses the farm forestry program of being in league with industrial interests:

[T]he industry encouraged private farmers to plant eucalyptus, offering them advances. . . . However, the eucalyptus epidemic on farmland has also relied heavily on government subsidies. Thus farmers have been

> supplied free seedlings, technical help, and soft loans, all under a most
> inappropriately named "social forestry" program which benefits only
> industry and commercial farmers, while the rural poor, worse hit by
> the biomass shortages, are left out in the cold. (Guha 1988, 25)

This is valid criticism of earlier phases of the program. At present,
however, eucalyptus accounts for less than 25 percent of all species in
community plantations managed by the Forest Department, with *Acacia auriculiformis*, *Dalbergia sissoo*, and *Acacia nilotica* forming the major
species. Eucalyptus continues to be in high demand within the farm
forestry component for two reasons: Eucalyptus is a hardy and fast-
growing species well suited to the semiarid conditions of Kolar, and
industrial demand for eucalyptus ensures secure markets and safe
returns on investment. Above all, it is not browsed by livestock and
requires minimal protection and maintenance. Hence eucalyptus is
"naturally" selected as the favored species by farmers in Malur *taluk*.

The ecological controversy over eucalyptus plantations, however,
rages on. According to a study by Chandrashekar and his colleagues:

> [T]he roots of eucalyptus spread laterally, sucking all the shallow
> water resources and soil nutrients. This has the effect of depriving the
> water resources and soil nutrients of the adjoining fields that are
> under food cultivation, with pronounced adverse effects on the crop-
> yields. . . . The consequence is a sharp reduction from the already low
> levels of crop-yields causing severe hardship to these small and mar-
> ginal farmers. In this situation of despair, farmers who had lost all
> interest in cultivating food crops and who had no interest in Eucalyp-
> tus are driven to abandon raising food grains and let the Eucalyptus
> vector spread on their fields as well. (Chandrashekar, Krishnamurthy,
> and Ramaswamy 1987, 939)

This statement has been contested by others in several scientific forums
and conferences. A research project devoted to the study of fast-growing
species has been undertaken to investigate variations in growth rates,
water use, and nutrient requirements for eucalyptus, acacia, and other
tree species, along with agricultural crops such as rice and ragi.
According to farmers interviewed in Kolar, there has been no percep-
tible decline in the aquifer levels as a direct result of eucalyptus plantations. They also claim that alternating eucalyptus with food crops
has not resulted in any marked reduction in food production.

Effects of Tree Farming on Labor Displacement

Critics maintain that because trees require less care than food crops,
planting trees on farmlands has diminished employment opportunities for the rural poor:

[F]or the landless laborer, what little employment was available to him through the production of food crops, disappears as the farmland goes under eucalyptus. [In Kolar] the most significant crop has traditionally been ragi, with a mixed cropping of pulses like cow-pea. These crops are planted in rotation with horse-gram, bengal-gram etc., oilseeds, groundnut, etc. These food crops, besides generating employment through sowing and harvesting, also require labor for manuring the fields, thinning, weeding, threshing, winnowing, etc. The annual labor requirement for the traditional rainfed cropping patterns is of the order of 100 man-days per acre. The eucalyptus on the other hand, after the initial planting requires absolutely no labor for maintenance, since it is not browsed, and generates negligible employment till it is ready for harvesting. (Shiva, Sharatchandra, and Bandyopadhyay 1981, 55–56)

During my interviews in Malur, farmers constantly referred to labor shortages as the primary reason for converting agricultural land to tree farming. Landed farmers explained that local labor was scarcely available, given the increased opportunities for employment in nearby cities of Kolar and Bangalore. As a result, average day wages had risen from seven rupees—the rate for male labor over the past few years—to twelve rupees at present, leading farmers to opt for less labor-intensive tree farming. Day-wage laborers, however, confirmed the arguments made by critics of social forestry programs. When interviewed, laborers claimed that conversion of agricultural land to tree cropping meant a reduction in opportunities for wage employment, leading them to migrate to urban areas to look for work.

Small Farmers' Lack of Involvement in Farm Forestry

The farm forestry component has often been criticized for not involving marginal and small farmers. It is argued that only large landholders take advantage of the free distribution of seedlings and derive economic benefits, because small and marginal farmers must cultivate for subsistence and cannot convert their limited landholdings to tree farming.

Empirical studies conducted in Kolar do not support this criticism. Of the 3,189 farmers supplied with 2.4 million seedlings in Kolar during 1987–88, 523 (16.5 percent) were marginal farmers, 2,362 (74 percent) were small farmers, and only 304 (9.5 percent) were large farmers. The program does not have an inherent bias toward large farmers. It is interesting to note, however, that large and medium farmers engaged in extensive plantations, but marginal and small farmers planted seedlings along their field boundaries and near water holes, thereby using land more intensively.

Lack of Popular Participation in Community Forestry

One of the major problems faced by the community forestry program in Kolar is the high prevalence of "illegal" extraction by villagers from community plantations. Although intended to meet household consumption needs, community forest plantations in Kolar have become the resource base for village people who extract biomass for sale in the market. This has led to the denudation and degradation of community forestlands. Officers of the Forest Department explain this process of degradation as a result of the inherent inability of the villagers to take care of their own land. In contrast to this position, I believe that the roots of the problem are in the very structure of the community forestry program. The two areas that create and sustain the problem of lack of collective responsibility involve management and distribution policies.

Problems Inherent in Management Structure. The Forest Department assumes the initial responsibility of afforestation and management of community forestry plantations in village commons and state lands. After two years, the plantations are handed over to the *mandal panchayats* for management and distribution of benefits. In this process, the community forestry component is identified as a technical-silvicultural experiment conducted by the Forest Department, with the village people regarded as passive beneficiaries. Following are some examples that illustrate this dimension of the program.

- Local people are generally not consulted regarding selection of tree species or the process of planting on community lands. There is no evidence from earlier plantations that any process of consultation was gone through, or indeed the department staff thought there should be any. Consultation was seen as a process which would be held with the village authorities when they were elected, not with the villagers themselves (Arnold et al. 1989). In Malur, the species mix in the community forestry component is regarded as a technical matter better handled by the Forest Department staff, thereby leaving unresolved the issue of the compatibility of community forestry species with local preferences for biomass use.

- In the earlier phases of the program, the Forest Department would plant the entire village commons and then fence the area to prevent browsing by livestock or trampling by humans. This resulted in immediate shortages of biomass for the village community, since no part of the commons could be utilized for the next two years. On a number of occasions, this led villagers to protest against community forestry projects in their commons.

Over the years, the Forest Department has modified its approach in Malur by planting and fencing smaller blocks within the commons, maintaining access for biomass collection in the remaining areas.

- The argument that rural people will not plant trees themselves or take care of trees planted by others is not well-founded. In the absence of guaranteed tenure or usufruct rights, however, people are often unwilling to spend their resources, time, and energy on a project whose direct benefits remain unclear or insecure (Fortmann and Bruce 1988). Hence the villagers feel estranged from the community forestry plantations. Several villages in Kolar regard the plantations as belonging to the government rather than as part of their own commons. Lack of clarity in defining both use and responsibility has thus led to the "free-rider" problem, with village households extracting resources from community plantations to increase their incomes. This has resulted in indiscriminate biomass extraction and contributed to the degradation of community forestry lands.

- In many cases—even after the plantation is handed over to the *mandal panchayat*—community participation has remained low. The primary reason behind this lack of involvement is how the *panchayat* functions as an institution. *Mandal panchayats* are identified as the institutions that should manage community forestry plantations on the assumption that—being a democratically elected body—they represent the interests of their village communities. This then leads to the assumption that such *mandal panchayats* will manage community forests in the interest of those who elected them, especially the rural poor, who depend on the commons for their biomass needs. Village people in Kolar feel quite differently about such assumptions. Poorer households are skeptical of *panchayats* and regard them as institutions that are controlled by and serve the interests of rural elites. Many landless and marginal farmers in Kolar stated that they rarely participated in local *gram sabha* (the village-level governing body), let alone *mandal panchayat* meetings. A poor farmer said, "We are at the mercy of the rich and the powerful. It is best not to meddle in their dealings. . . . I am noticed the moment I step into the meeting [hall]. God help me if I say something that may displease my [master]! . . . I am a marked man. Why should I risk my neck?" This matter-of-fact statement reveals the silent "violence" that exists in rural societies and brings into question whether the interests of all segments are represented by a democratically elected body.

- Some *panchayats* in Kolar have sold biomass produced in the village commons and used the funds to pay outstanding telephone bills. In other *panchayats,* some members have refused to accept community plantations from the Forest Department. One *panchayat* member explained the reason for refusing the projects: "Look," he said, "the amount of trees, leaves, and grass from community forestry plantations is extremely limited when compared to local demand. I can't distribute the produce only to my supporters and friends, because the entire village would know instantly. My opponent—belonging to the opposition party—would promptly try to incriminate me and use it to his advantage. . . . Why go through all this for the sake of some trees and grass? . . . I tell my people, if you need anything, come to me. I'll try getting it from the government."

Thus, for a variety of reasons, many *panchayats* have failed to carry out the objectives of the community forestry program. With institutional structures ill-suited for effective management, they have only heightened the sense of alienation among village populations.

Problems Regarding Distribution of Biomass Resources. The most important aspect of the community forestry program, from the villagers' perspective, is the distribution of the benefits. Because of the lack of clear policies, confusion over this part of the program prevails among villagers as well as concerned officials. My interviews with Forest Department officials revealed several issues that remained unclear: for instance, whether the Forest Department had control over 50 percent of forest produce (particularly timber) or none at all; whether forest produce would be controlled by *mandal panchayats* (which cover a number of villages) or only by *panchayats* of villages contiguous to community forest plantations.

Even five years following the initiation of this program, my interviews revealed that there are divergent views regarding distribution, among both the "managers" and the "beneficiaries." Some felt that if the biomass produce were distributed regionally by the *mandal panchayat,* particular villages would almost certainly be favored over others; others felt that distribution should occur at the level of the *mandal,* since the poor quality of community forests contiguous to their own villages would result in shortages of biomass. A few members of the *mandal panchayat* said that the produce should be sold in the market and the money invested in *mandal*-level infrastructure, such as schools and community services. Other members stated that the produce should be distributed equally among the *mandal* population, and a minority suggested that the biomass be distributed free of charge only to the poorer households. All these differing opinions reflect the lack of any clear guidelines regarding distribution of produce from community forest plantations, thus creating a heightened sense of insecurity and uncertainty among the rural poor.

Unclear policies of distribution also reinforce the absence of community interest in the program. Amidst the confusion over distribution of biomass produce, poor households utilize the resources to the maximum possible extent—extraction both for household use and for sale in the market—thereby causing what is popularly termed the "tragedy of the commons."

In summary, the effects of the social forestry program in rural Kolar have been both positive and negative. Industrial and urban demand for biomass has made the farm forestry component of the program a relative success. The products of farm forestry are, for the most part, sold in the market. Kolar has gone from being a firewood importing district in the early 1970s to exporting firewood. Success in farm forestry production has given rise to other economic activities in the district, including a large number of firewood-consuming industries. On the negative side, however, land conversion to tree farming has meant a decline in the availability of biomass to poor households from private lands.

The management structure of the community forestry component has resulted in the estrangement of poor villagers—the majority—from the program, and confusion over distributional policies has heightened the problem. With little effort made toward generating community interest in the forestry program, intensive extraction of biomass for both household use and sale in the market has led to unsustainable practices and degradation of community forestry lands.

Alternative Proposals for Social Forestry: Greening the Commons

Critics of the social forestry program have put forward a number of alternative proposals for social afforestation (Shiva, Sharatchandra, and Bandyopadhyay 1981; Gadgil and Hegde 1988; Guha, Mahale, and Dandavatimath 1988; Agarwal and Narain 1989; Gadgil and Guha 1989). Based on the failures resulting from state management practices and the functioning of the biomass market, they advocate management of biomass resources by rural communities at the village level. All the alternatives are conceptually similar, in that they advocate redirection of social forestry efforts away from market solutions.

Based on the social forestry experience in Karnataka, Gadgil and Guha (1989) have put forth a detailed alternative proposal. The main points of their normative model are summarized below.

The majority of poor households in rural areas collect, rather than purchase, most of their biomass needs from the commons. Unfortunately, such lands are under pressure everywhere—partly from growth in population, but primarily because of overexploitation by the state in the interest of urban and industrial sectors.

> Barely a century ago, there did exist a widespread network of village forests, with well-knit local communities guarding and managing these resources quite effectively. But at that time these communities had the right to exclude outsiders from their community lands and to punish any of their own erring members. The British, by emphasizing state monopoly over forest production and protection, took away such authority, grudgingly replacing it with some privileges. This divorce between use of and control over resources has had disastrous consequences, with the open access resources subjected to continual over exploitation. (Gadgil and Guha 1989, 9)

They contend that since local officials are either without adequate powers or participants in shortsighted exploitation, state management of community forestry will prove ineffective. They argue that transferring the control of the commons to private hands is not the solution, as this would "ultimately end up benefitting a small class of richer landowners at the cost of the bulk of the rural population" (Gadgil and Guha 1989, 9). Gadgil and Guha argue:

> [T]he only ecologically sustainable and socially just option, especially in the long run, is to design an effective system of community management resting on local control. . . . To ensure the effective protection to and equitable distribution of forest produce, the organizational unit for the management of common lands should be the *village*, not larger and more heterogenous units such as revenue village or mandal panchayat. The control of such land should not be with the revenue or forest departments or any other government agency. . . . [The system proposed here] calls for an entirely new legal framework transferring effective control over common lands to relatively small and homogeneous local communities. (Gadgil and Guha 1989, 10)

The authors argue for a special role for the poor and landless families, artisans, and women, all of whom are more dependent on common lands and less politically powerful in village communities. They contend that the commons can remain dedicated to meeting subsistence needs of the population "only . . . if their production is not allowed to enter the open market, otherwise the urban-industrial sector with its vastly greater purchasing power would quickly appropriate all produce" (Gadgil and Guha 1989, 30).

Along with transfer of effective control of common lands to the villagers, Gadgil and Guha call for a halt on state subsidies that promote biomass production on these lands. They argue for "access to the produce of common lands only at a price adequate to ensure its protection and regeneration," with three exceptions: The weaker sections of the population should pay for the produce they need in the form of labor contributions; the government should provide limited financial subsidies to the landless and to marginal families; and nomads and artisans should be allowed customary use of biomass resources on common lands under careful regulation. Concerning industrial demand, the authors insist that "there must be no unsustainable demand of non-essential industries on the forest resources" (Gadgil and Guha 1989, 30).

Consistent with their criticisms, their proposal turns away from the market and rejects all forms of "external" control, including that of elected political representatives. The rhetoric of their solutions leads one to believe that it is fairly easy to separate rural biomass production from the demands of both rural and urban society. On closer examination, however, a number of questions remain unanswered:

- If the village is the unit of organization, what kinds of management institutions should be devised for villages that, like most villages in Kolar, have a high degree of socioeconomic differentiation?
- Collective effort arises when the user population lives close to the resource base and is more or less equally dependent on the commons and, hence, equally interested in maintaining its quality (Ostrom 1985). But in many villages, proximity to the commons is not synonymous with dependence. In Kolar, for example, only the landless and marginal farmers depend exclusively for their biomass resources on lands to which they do not have tenurial rights (see Table 7.2). Other sections of the rural population depend on common resources—including revenue and state lands—to varying degrees. Thus, in an unequal rural society with different classes having disparate levels of dependence on the commons, what is the organizational mechanism required to overcome the "free-rider" problem posed by Hardin (1968)? How is "collective adoption" or cooperation between poor and rich to be achieved (West 1983), given that the poor are less likely to join organizations, are very sensitive to equity considerations, and are unlikely to comply voluntarily with schemes they regard as inherently unfair?
- Trees planted on commons for household or communal subsistence use have a commercial value and may develop private rights (Fortmann and Bruce 1988). Were this to happen, what would be the method of equitable distribution?

- Given the need for collective effort in community management, what are appropriate incentives for promoting such effort? Should collective effort be based on the self-interest of each village household in meeting its biomass needs from the commons, or on some notion of a "village community"? If collective interest is posited, is the commons sustainable in areas that have no tradition of collective effort?
- What is the mechanism of protecting rural biomass from the market? What incentives must those who are less dependent on the commons receive so that they continue to support collective effort?
- If all the villages in a region adopted such a solution, how would poor households in urban areas meet their needs for fuelwood, which is currently provided by rural areas?
- What is the role of the state? On the one hand, having transferred effective control of the common lands to the villagers, the state is not expected to continue investing in biomass production on village commons. On the other hand, the special arrangements that would have to be made to supply villages without adequate commons and the urban poor would imply the need for continued state involvement.

Gadgil and Guha correctly identify empowerment of the local population as key to an equitable management of natural resources. However, their solution of complete decentralization is inappropriate. They mistakenly identify state management as the raison d'être for the problems of the community forestry program and equate decentralization with equitable participation in resource management and decisionmaking processes. The authors are indeed accurate in identifying excessive state involvement in community forestry as being inimical to local participation. They rightly criticize the bureaucracy's token attention to popular participation. Their call for complete decentralization of the forestry program may be a calculated attempt to shock the bureaucracy into action, and perhaps it should be taken in that spirit. Setting aside the shock value of the proposal temporarily, it is necessary, as I have indicated earlier, that community-oriented social forestry programs be reexamined on a number of fundamental issues. In a society with unequal distribution of resources, forcing collective participation by *all its members* to ensure successful management of the commons may be a difficult task. Thus "collective adoption" may not be as voluntary as we might imagine. Cernea points out that:

[In a socially heterogenous local rural society] the interests of community members often differ to such an extent that unified action is impossible. The "commons syndrome" is particularly intractable since it runs contrary to the need for community members to cooperate in establishing woodlot, in abstaining from premature cuttings, and in protecting against animals. What is advantageous for one subgroup is not necessarily advantageous for another or for individuals. (Cernea 1985, 281)

Within a democratic political system, and given the high biomass demand in both the urban and rural areas, there are few workable options to prevent farmers from selling their biomass in the market. Urban and industrial demands, as the critics point out, threaten sustainable management of the commons, providing individuals incentives to "free ride" and exploit. The normative model of Gadgil and Guha, however, does not deal with the question of incentives to prevent *all* rural households from opting out of the system.

The solution outlined by the authors calls for major changes in the existing structure of rural-urban linkages. Their proposal requires the poor to "confront" the rest of society by standing against the interests of urban populations and industries dependent on biomass and by seeking to circumvent the existing (elected) power structure in rural areas.

Any solution that requires separation of village commons from the larger biomass market actually implies greater state responsibility. It becomes the responsibility of the state to supply biomass to villages with inadequate commons, special groups within villages, urban areas, and industries. This means greater pressure on state-managed forestlands.

The idea of rural self-sufficiency expressed in the model implies socioeconomic stability or stagnation, which is viable only in a society with stable cultural demands and stable demography. As Bergmann points out in another context, this perpetuates economic dualism between city and country through the "coexistence of technically modern, commercialized enclaves oriented towards economic exchange, with intensive energy input on the one hand, and ecologically stable regions with traditional economy and low energy input on the other" (Bergmann 1989, 22).

The main drawback of Gadgil and Guha's approach lies in the contradictory roles they prescribe for the state. Decentralization to the village level on the one hand would mean minimal state involvement in resource development decisions. The state is expected, on the other hand, to take care of the demands of the urban industrial sectors as well as "special" population groups in the rural areas. Gadgil and Guha view biomass needs in simple terms of urban rich versus rural poor, government versus villagers, urban and industrial consumption versus rural subsistence demand, and they promote a view of the village as a self-sufficient, homogeneous, organic *community*. This perspective has little in common with the rural reality in Kolar or else-where in India.

Participation, Mediating Institutions, and Social Forestry

The failure of the community forestry component of the Kolar social forestry program is mainly due to lack of genuine participation of vil-lagers in the management structure of the program. Following Mont-gomery (1987), I use the term *participation* in a specific sense to mean the involvement of significant numbers of persons in situations or actions that enhance their well-being—income, security, and self-esteem. A management approach that treats villagers as passive recipi-ents of program benefits heightens their estrangement by entrusting the program to the inappropriate social institution of the *panchayat*. In the absence of any mechanism that includes their interests, the poor households resort to exploitation of the commons for personal gain. The proposal for greening the commons fails on two accounts. On the one hand, its weakness lies in assuming the voluntary collective adop-tion of the program by the entire village population, albeit differenti-ated by class and caste; on the other hand, its weakness lies in its attempt to carry out natural resource management outside of, and apart from, the state apparatus. Attempts to isolate the community bio-mass from the market may prove futile and give rise to free-rider prob-lems that signal the end of any collective action related to the program.

In an unequal society, decentralization of decisionmaking does not necessarily result in decisionmaking by all sections of the population. More than likely, the disempowered groups would continue to be out-side any such process. In such a situation, social institutions that give voice to the disempowered must be actively promoted. Although such institutions need to function independently from the state, the state has to play an active role in facilitating their formation. Contrary to current perceptions regarding the role of the state, management of natural resources cannot and should not be completely divorced from the state. Institutions that regulate resource production and distribution need to maintain a dialectical relationship with the state. In other words, social institutions that mediate on behalf of the powerless need to confront as well as seek help from the structures of the state. The key to a just distri-bution of natural resources is the mediation of social institutions.

The failure of community forestry is related to the general failure to integrate rural and particularly impoverished households with the management of the program. The absence of institutions that support the livelihood strategies of individual households proves detrimental to the entire community and indicates the need to organize rural communities through participatory social institutions that work toward common goals.

Community forest management requires institutional arrangements with a long time horizon and sustained commitment (Uphoff 1986). As we have observed, people need to be involved in all the stages of the cooperative effort. It is unfeasible to implant community forestry organizations from outside and expect local people to manage existing plantations efficiently on behalf of the collective interest of the village.

In Kolar, the need for a participatory institution in the community forestry program did not automatically result in its creation. As Bergmann observes:

> The formation or emergence of such [institutions] is a problem . . . tied to the immanent self-affirmation of the traditional rural power structure. To be efficient, the [institutions] must be free from their opponents. But this freedom or independence from the established ruling strata implies a challenge to . . . society; it questions and attacks its foundations. (Bergmann 1989, 22)

In Kolar, in the absence of an "inclusive" institution, the community interest in the program suffered to the disadvantage of poor households. However, "[m]uch has been written about 'popular participation,' and it could go the way of other buzz words—a paragraph in a report stating its necessity and very little follow-up—a cosmetic process" (Noronha and Spears 1985, 254).

Participatory institutions are rarely reflexive and unadministered. The problems associated with the formation and development of such institutions preclude spontaneity. Some of the general problems are the need to trade off economic efficiency versus social equity, strong charismatic leadership versus member participation, achievement versus process, high-intensity interaction through face-to-face relationships in small organizations versus the advantages of economies of scale made possible by large size, and the need for professional help versus self-management.

Usually, participation takes the form of organized action (Montgomery 1987). Given the contentious nature of community forestry, these problems require the mediation of existing institutions. Mediating institutions are those that stand between the private life of households and institutions in the public realm—capitalist enterprises, organized labor unions, cooperatives, and so forth. Because they are familiar to participants, these institutions can mediate between households and megastructures of society (Berger and Neuhaus 1977).[9] Mediating institutions can help create sustainable structures by utilizing local resources and leadership skills to facilitate cooperative forestry management.

Thus the problems of natural resource management in Kolar, and elsewhere in the Third World, are to be found in both the state and civil society. Paradoxically, the solutions include both protagonists. We cannot dispense with either the state or civil society. What I wish to stress is that to produce and manage natural resources in the Third World, we need to build institutions rooted *in* society that have an identity separate from the state. Yet we also need the state to be an active partner in building and mediating between such social institutions.

Notes

1. I use the term *biomass* in a restricted sense to include only household requirements of fuel and fodder.
2. Quoting the Kolar *District Census Handbook:* "at the end of the eighteenth century the district suffered from a dreadful famine. Again during the invasion of Lord Cornwallis (1791), many died of starvation. The decade following 1851 was one of misery as scarcity conditions followed year after year. The great famine of 1875–76 and 1876–77 proved most calamitous. In 1899 the rainfall was very scanty. During the 20th century also, scarcity conditions from failure of rains have occurred now and then" (*District Census Handbook* 1984, 13).
3. Workers are classified in the Indian census as follows: *Main workers* are those who have worked for at least 183 days of the preceding year, even though they may be not be continuous; *marginal workers* are those who have worked for less than 183 days during the entire period. The category of agricultural workers is as follows: *Cultivator* is a person engaged as employer, single worker, or family worker in the cultivation of land owned or held from the government or held from private persons or institutions for payment in money, kind, or share; *agricultural laborer* is a person who works on another person's land for wages in money, kind, or share and has no right of lease or contract on the land.
4. The yield rate was obtained from the Kolar *District Census Handbook* (1984) and the rate for ragi from Shyam Sunder and Parameshwarappa (1987).
5. This discussion is based on the seminal work of Bhagwan and Giriappa (1986) on the rural energy crisis in Karnataka. I have contextualized their findings by fieldwork in Kolar in 1989.
6. *Social forestry* is a term used by the National Commission on Agriculture, India, in 1976, to denote tree-raising programs to supply firewood, small timber, and minor forest produce to rural populations.
7. Subsequently the second phase of the project, to cover a period of three years from 1989–90 to 1991–92, was approved (Gaonkar 1989).
8. The discussion is based partly on a field survey I conducted in the summer of 1989 in Kolar district. Extending over five weeks, it included interviews with villagers—landed and landless, rich and poor; timber merchants; local leaders, including members of the *panchayats* and *zilla parishads;* and local staff of the Forest Department. I also met with a number of environmentalists, nongovernmental organizations, and officials of the Forest Department and the World Bank involved in Karnataka social forestry in Bangalore and

Delhi. For formal evaluation of project finance, and silviculture management, refer to World Bank (1983), ODA (1988), and Gaonkar (1989).
9. "The modern phenomena of private life," write Berger and Neuhaus (1977,
5), "where an individual must carry on a bewildering variety of activities
with fragile institutional support, requires access to mediating institu-
tions/structures."

References

Agarwal, A., and Sunita Narain. 1989. "The Greening of India." *Illustrated
Weekly of India* 4 June, 30–35.
Arnold, J. E. M., P. Howland, P. J. Robinson, and G. Shepherd. 1989. *Evalua-
tion of the Social Forestry Project in Karnataka, India.* London: Overseas
Development Administration.
Bandyopadhyay, J., and Vandana Shiva. 1985. "Eucalyptus in Rainfed Farm
Forestry: Prescription for Desertification." *Economic and Political Weekly*
20(40): 1687–88.
Berger, Peter L., and Richard Neuhaus. 1977. "To Empower People: Mediating
Structures and the Dilemmas of the Welfare State." In *To Empower People:
The Role of Mediating Structures in Public Policy,* edited by Peter L. Berger
and Richard Neuhaus. Washington, D.C.: American Enterprise Institute.
Bergmann, T. 1989. "Participation of the Local Society in Development."
Regional Development Dialogue 10(2): 3–23.
Bhagwan, M. R., and S. Giriappa. 1986. "Class Character of Rural Energy Cri-
sis: The Case of Karnataka." *Economic and Political Weekly* 21(30): 1317–21.
Bruce, Judith, and Louise Fortmann. 1988. "Why Land Tenure and Tree
Tenure Matter: Some Fuel for Thought." In *Whose Trees? Proprietary
Dimensions of Forestry,* edited by Louise Fortmann and Judith Bruce. Boul-
der, Colo.: Westview Press.
Centre for Science and Environment. 1985. *The State of India's Environment
1984–85. The Second Citizens' Report.* New Delhi: CSE.
Cernea, Michael M. 1985. "Alternative Units of Social Organization: Sustain-
ing Afforestation Strategies." In *Putting People First: Sociological Variables in
Rural Development,* edited by Michael M. Cernea. New York: Oxford Uni-
versity Press.
Chandrashekar, D. M., B. V. Krishnamurthy, and S. R. Ramaswamy. 1987.
"Social Forestry in Karnataka. An Impact Analysis." *Economic and Political
Weekly* 22(24): 935–941.
District Census Handbook: Kolar District. 1984. Parts XIII A and B. Series 9. Ban-
galore: Karnataka Government Press.
Fortmann, Louise, and Judith Bruce, eds. 1988. *Whose Trees? Proprietary Dimen-
sions of Forestry.* Boulder, Colo.: Westview Press.
Gadgil, M., and Ramachandra Guha. 1989. "Greening the Commons." *Main-
stream,* 21 January.
Gadgil, M., and K. M. Hegde. 1988. "Greening the Commons in Karnataka."
Deccan Herald, 12 June, Bangalore.
Gaonkar, P. D. 1989. *Report on the World Bank/Overseas Development Administration-
aided Karnataka Social Forestry Project, 1983–88.* Bangalore: Government
of Karnataka.

Guha, Ramachandra. 1988. "Commercial Forestry: Defending the Indefensible." *Deccan Herald*, 19 June, Bangalore.

Guha, Ramachandra, P. D. Mahale, and P. G. Dandavatimath. 1988. "Common Lands and the Rural Poor: A Case Study of Karnataka." Mimeo.

Hardin, G. 1968. "The Tragedy of the Commons." *Science* 162: 1243–48.

Montgomery, John D. 1987. *Bureaucrats and People: Grass Roots Participation in Third World Development*. Baltimore: Johns Hopkins Press.

Noronha, R., and J. S. Spears. 1985. "Sociological Variables in Forestry Project Design." In *Putting People First: Sociological Variables in Rural Development*, edited by Michael M. Cernea. New York: Oxford University Press.

Olson, M. 1965. *The Logic of Collective Action: Public Goods and the Theory of Groups*. Boston: Harvard University Press.

Ostrom, E. 1985. "Issues of Definition and Theory: Some Conclusions and Hypothesis." In *Proceedings of the Conference on Common Property Resource Management*. National Research Council. Washington, D.C.: Office of International Affairs.

Overseas Development Administration (ODA). 1988. *Karnataka Social Forestry Project: Report of the ODA/World Bank Monitoring Mission Visit*. London: ODA.

Rice, L. 1897. *Mysore: A Gazetteer Compiled for the Government*. Revised edition. Vol. I. London: Archibald Constable and Co.

Samaja Parivartana Samudaya. 1988. *Whither Common Lands? Rural Poor or Industry? Who Should Benefit from Common Lands' Forestry?* Dharwad: Samaja Parivartana.

Shiva, Vandana, H. C. Sharatchandra, and J. Bandyopadhyay. 1981. *Social, Economic and Ecological Impact of Social Forestry in Kolar*. Bangalore: Indian Institute of Management.

Shyam Sunder, S., and S. Parameshwarappa. 1987. "Social Forestry in Karnataka." *Economic and Political Weekly* 22(46): 2021–26.

Uphoff, Norman T. 1986. *Local Institutional Development: An Analytical Sourcebook with Cases*. West Hartford, Conn.: Kumarian Press.

Venugopal, S. 1989. *Forest Plantations: A Boon to the Rural Economy*. Bangalore: Government of Karnataka.

West, Patrick. 1983. "Collective Adoption of Natural Resource Practices in Developing Nations." *Rural Sociology* 48(1): 44–59.

World Bank. 1983. *The Karnataka Social Forestry Project: Staff Appraisal Report*. Washington, D.C.: World Bank.

INDEX

The United Nations Research Institute for Social Development

The United Nations Research Institute for Social Development (UNRISD) is an autonomous research organization that focuses on the most pressing social problems of development. The Institute emphasizes a holistic, multidisciplinary and political economy approach in its work. While programs are designed by a small staff in Geneva and external coordinators, they are carried out in collaboration with national research teams drawn from local universities and research institutes, mainly in developing countries.

Current research themes include: Environment, Sustainable Development and Social Change; Crisis, Adjustment and Social Change; Participation and Changes in Property Relations in Communist and Post-Communist Societies; Ethnic Conflict and Development; Political Violence and Social Movements; Refugees, Returnees and Local Society; Socio-Economic and Political Impact of Production, Trade and Use of Illicit Narcotic Drugs; and Patterns of Consumption: Qualitative Indicators of Development.

Research results are disseminated through discussion papers, monographs, books and UNRISD News, as well as conferences and the specialized media.